Practical Network Security with OpenSSL

Master Cryptography and OpenSSL Techniques for Secure Communications, PKI, and Hardware Integration in Real-World Applications

Rohan Subhash Patil

www.orangeava.com

First Published: April 2025

Published By: Orange Education Pvt Ltd, AVA®

Address: 9, Daryaganj, Delhi, 110002, India

275 New North Road Islington Suite 1314 London,
N1 7AA, United Kingdom

ISBN (PBK): 978-93-48107-42-8
ISBN (E-BOOK): 978-93-48107-44-2

Scan the QR code to explore our entire catalogue

www.orangeava.com

Dedicated To

My Beloved Parents and In-Laws,

To My Wife Pooja and My Son Swar,

Whose Support and Motivation Mean Everything to Me

About the Author

Rohan Subhash Patil is a Staff Software Engineer at Tarana Wireless, specializing in software development and security implementations. With over twenty years of experience in embedded systems, networking, and security, he has contributed to building robust and secure communication systems across various industries.

Academically, he holds an MTech in Software Systems from BITS Pilani (WILP) and a BE in Electronics from SGGS Nanded. His areas of expertise include network protocol development, cryptographic security implementations, and system optimization.

At Tarana Wireless, Rohan led security and network software development for next-gen products, working on PKI certificate management, TPM integration using OpenSSL, 802.1x, and AAA protocols for Tarana G1 devices. Previously, at Cisco Systems, he tackled L2/L3 protocol challenges for UCS products. At QLogic India, he ensured Converged Network Adapters met RFC standards and optimized performance. He also has experience in embedded software development across various processors and microcontrollers.

Skilled in C and C++, Rohan has authored design documents and developer guides, led technical sessions, and provided mentorship to engineers. He has also spearheaded technical interviews, leveraging his expertise to guide emerging talent.

Outside of work, Rohan enjoys folk music and plays percussion instruments such as the cajón, daphali, and dimdi. He is also passionate about birdwatching and exploring nature with his son.

Driven by a passion for cybersecurity, Rohan continuously pushes the boundaries of innovation in secure, high-performance systems.

About the Technical Reviewer

Naveen Kumar Chandrasekar has five years of experience in the Banking, Financial Services, and Insurance (BFSI) domain, specializing in optimizing business processes through strategic technological solutions. With expertise in Unix/Linux and Windows environments, Naveen is skilled at implementing robust security measures and managing diverse systems. He excels in database operations, API testing, and middleware technologies, ensuring seamless integration and reliable communication across platforms.

Currently, Naveen works as a Senior Engineer in WSO2, where he contributes to enhancing system performance and security. He is passionate about leveraging his technical expertise to drive business value and is eager to take on new challenges in reputable organizations.

Acknowledgements

Writing this book has been a journey filled with learning and growth, and I am deeply grateful to those who have supported me along the way.

I want to express my heartfelt gratitude to my parents and in-laws for their blessings, which have been my source of self-belief and strength.

A special thanks to my wife, Pooja, for her patience and unwavering support and to my son, Swar, who inspires me daily.

I am deeply grateful to my company for providing the time and support needed to complete this book. A special thanks to my previous organizations for the opportunities to learn and grow in network security, cryptography, and OpenSSL, which laid the foundation for this book. A sincere appreciation to the team at Orange Education Pvt Ltd for their seamless collaboration and guidance in reviewing and refining the content.

This book is just the beginning, and I look forward to sharing more in the future.

Preface

This book covers the varied aspects of cryptography and OpenSSL, the importance of security in modern systems, and practical implementations. This book also introduces the fundamental concepts of cryptography in information security. It shows how cryptography is important for industries across sectors. Additionally, this book addresses the basic understanding of cryptography and OpenSSL usage in security. It also gives examples of C-language APIs for OpenSSL library usage. This book provides information about the usefulness of OpenSSL in both standalone applications and when integrated with security hardware as well.

This book takes a practical approach for security professionals and developers and covers a few real-time industry examples as well. It covers information such as OpenSSL, which is basically used for security, PKI, and cryptographic operations. It can be used for securing communications and implementing authentication frameworks. Additionally, it is used in different domains for security purposes. You can design security frameworks for end-to-end secure communications in different domains such as finance, IoT, and so on.

This book is divided into nine chapters. They focus on cryptography basics, basics and advanced OpenSSL, why OpenSSL is better for security implementations, and real-time examples of security implementations. The content is designed to engage learners and pique their interest in security and cryptography tools effectively. The details are listed as follows:

Chapter 1. Cryptography Basics and Network Security: This chapter introduces cryptography, covering fundamental concepts such as the CIA triad, security threats, and mechanisms. Symmetric and asymmetric cryptography, along with hashing, digital signatures, and the public key infrastructure, will be covered. The future trends in cryptography are also explored.

Chapter 2. Getting started with OpenSSL: The chapter explores OpenSSL, beginning with its history and evolution. It then discusses installation across different platforms, an overview of the OpenSSL configuration file, and insights into its library architecture.

Chapter 3. OpenSSL Command Line Interface: This chapter focuses on the OpenSSL command line interface and cryptographic operations. It explains various commands for key and certificate management, PKI implementation, and TLS connection testing, as well as advanced and utility commands.

Chapter 4. OpenSSL C library APIs: This chapter provides an in-depth look at OpenSSL's C library APIs, their organization, and usage. Topics include library initialization, core libcrypto functions, SSL/TLS communication, the Engine and Providers framework, utility functions, and other essential APIs.

Chapter 5. Public Key Infrastructure with OpenSSL: This chapter explores PKI with OpenSSL through command-line and C library APIs. It covers setting up a Certificate Authority, generating certificate signing requests, and managing certificates, as well as certificate validation, revocation mechanisms, and securing web applications or network services.

Chapter 6. Symmetric Key Cryptography with OpenSSL: This chapter examines symmetric key cryptography with OpenSSL, including setup, cipher usage, and key management. It also discusses file encryption/decryption and authenticated encryption techniques.

Chapter 7. OpenSSL Engine for Security Hardware: This chapter introduces the OpenSSL Engine for security hardware integration. It explains the role of hardware security modules and chips, configuring OpenSSL for security hardware interaction, key management, and accelerating cryptographic operations in real-world applications.

Chapter 8. OpenSSL in IoT Security: This chapter highlights OpenSSL's role in IoT security applications. It examines the importance of cryptography in IoT, challenges due to resource constraints, and lightweight cryptography approaches, as well as IoT security implementations using x509 certificates.

Chapter 9. Best Practices, Tips, and Tricks: This chapter presents best practices and tips for using OpenSSL effectively. It shares security best practices, code optimization techniques, and certificate conversion tips, along with common mistakes to avoid and comparisons with OpenSSL alternatives.

Get a Free eBook

We hope you are enjoying your recently purchased book! Your feedback is incredibly valuable to us, and to all other readers looking for great books.

If you found this book helpful or enjoyable, we would truly appreciate it, if you could take a moment to leave a short review with a 5 star rating on Amazon. It helps us grow, and lets other readers discover our books.

As a thank you, we would love to send you a free digital copy of this book, and a **30%** discount code on your next cart value on our official websites:

www.orangeava.com

www.orangeava.in (For Indian Subcontinent)

☑ **Here's how:**

Leave a review for the book on Amazon.

Take a screenshot of your review, and send an email to **info@orangeava.com** (it can be just the confirmation screen).

Once, we receive your screenshot, we will send you the digital file, within 24 hours.

Thank you so much for your support – it means a lot to us!

Downloading the code bundles and colored images

Please follow the links or scan the QR codes to download the
Code Bundles and Images of the book:

https://github.com/ava-orange-education/Practical-Network-Security-with-OpenSSL

The code bundles and images of the book are also hosted on
https://rebrand.ly/07a64d

In case there's an update to the code, it will be updated on the existing GitHub repository.

Errata

We take immense pride in our work at **Orange Education Pvt Ltd,** and follow best practices to ensure the accuracy of our content to provide an indulging reading experience to our subscribers. Our readers are our mirrors, and we use their inputs to reflect and improve upon human errors, if any, that may have occurred during the publishing processes involved. To let us maintain the quality and help us reach out to any readers who might be having difficulties due to any unforeseen errors, please write to us at :

errata@orangeava.com

Your support, suggestions, and feedback are highly appreciated.

DID YOU KNOW

Did you know that Orange Education Pvt Ltd offers eBook versions of every book published, with PDF and ePub files available? You can upgrade to the eBook version at **www.orangeava.com** and as a print book customer, you are entitled to a discount on the eBook copy. Get in touch with us at: **info@orangeava.com** for more details.

At **www.orangeava.com**, you can also read a collection of free technical articles, sign up for a range of free newsletters, and receive exclusive discounts and offers on Print Books and eBooks.

PIRACY

If you come across any illegal copies of our works in any form on the internet, we would be grateful if you would provide us with the location address or website name. Please contact us at **info@orangeava.com** with a link to the material.

ARE YOU INTERESTED IN AUTHORING WITH US?

If there is a topic that you have expertise in, and you are interested in either writing or contributing to a book, please write to us at **business@orangeava.com**. We are on a journey to help developers and tech professionals to gain insights on the present technological advancements and innovations happening across the globe and build a community that believes Knowledge is best acquired by sharing and learning with others. Please reach out to us to learn what our audience demands and how you can be part of this educational reform. We also welcome ideas from tech experts and help them build learning and development content for their domains.

REVIEWS

Please leave a review. Once you have read and used this book, why not leave a review on the site that you purchased it from? Potential readers can then see and use your unbiased opinion to make purchase decisions. We at Orange Education would love to know what you think about our products, and our authors can learn from your feedback. Thank you!

For more information about Orange Education, please visit **www.orangeava.com**.

Table of Contents

Chapter 1

Cryptography Basics and Network Security

Introduction

In today's digital landscape, securing communication and protecting sensitive data are essential aspects of any software system. This chapter aims to provide readers with a foundational understanding of key cryptographic principles and how they apply to modern network security.

Before moving to the OpenSSL aspect of the book, it will be really helpful to understand the information security basics. Hence, this chapter covers the building blocks of cryptography, common algorithms, and practical security mechanisms, offering insights into how these concepts are implemented and leveraged to secure data in transit and at rest. Whether you are developing secure applications or an infrastructure professional tasked with safeguarding systems managing infrastructure, mastering these principles is crucial to building robust and secure systems.

Structure

In this chapter, we will discuss the following topics:

- Confidentiality, Integrity, Availability (CIA) Triad
- Security Threats and Security Mechanisms
- Symmetric Key Cryptography
- Asymmetric Key Cryptography
- Hashing and Digital Signatures
- Public Key Infrastructure
- Future Trends in Cryptography

Confidentiality, Integrity, Availability (CIA) Triad

Let us identify the key elements of the information that needs to be protected using the CIA triad.

***Figure 1.1**: CIA triad*

Confidentiality, Integrity, and Availability serve as a foundational model to understand these security requirements.

Confidentiality: Ensuring that sensitive information is only accessible to authorized individuals, such as personal information, bank account details, and so on. In the context of software, this means securing data both at rest (for example, in databases) and in transit (for example, over networks) using encryption and access control mechanisms. Breaches in confidentiality can lead to unauthorized data exposure, such as leaking customer details or intellectual property.

Let us use the **banking system** as a consistent analogy for all three principles of the **Confidentiality, Integrity, Availability (CIA) triad:**

You access your bank account online using a username and password. The bank also requires two-factor authentication (OTP) to ensure that only you can log in.

Maintained: Your bank encrypts your data and does not allow unauthorized users to access your account.

Violated: If a hacker steals your credentials and logs in, or if a bank employee leaks your account details, confidentiality is broken.

Integrity: Guaranteeing that data remains accurate and unaltered during storage or transmission. This is essential in protecting data from unauthorized modifications, either by malicious actors or accidental errors. Mechanisms such as cryptographic hashes, digital signatures, and version control ensure the integrity of data. In software development, protecting the integrity of code, configuration files, and databases is critical.

Integrity is crucial for ensuring trust, security, and compliance in any system. It builds confidence between users and systems by guaranteeing data reliability and accuracy. Without integrity, attackers could manipulate or inject malicious data, leading to security breaches, fraud, and unauthorized access. Additionally, regulatory frameworks such as GDPR and HIPAA mandate data integrity to safeguard user privacy and confidentiality, making it a fundamental aspect of cybersecurity and compliance.

We will go through a banking system analogy again.

You transfer $50 to a friend. The bank's system ensures that the transaction is correctly recorded, and your balance updates accurately.

Maintained: The bank uses cryptographic signatures and transaction logs to ensure that no one can alter transaction data.

Violated: If a hacker modifies the transaction so that your friend receives $500 instead of $50, or if a system error corrupts your account balance, integrity is compromised.

Availability: Ensuring that systems, services, and data are accessible and operational when needed by authorized users. Downtime or unavailability of critical systems can disrupt business operations, leading to loss of productivity and financial damage. Availability is maintained through backup systems, load balancing, redundant hardware and infrastructure, redundancy, failover mechanisms, and protection against attacks such as Distributed Denial of Service (DDoS) and monitoring alerts for performance to ensure system health.

We will be continuing the same analogy for example.

You need to withdraw cash from an ATM or access your bank's website to check your balance.

Maintained: The bank has backup servers, DDoS protection, and disaster recovery plans to ensure its services are always available.

Violated: If the bank's servers crash due to a cyberattack (DDoS attack), a power failure, or maintenance downtime, you cannot access your money when needed–availability is compromised.

Security Threats

An organizations' network infrastructure needs to defend against different types of threats. Attacks can happen on all three elements of the CIA triad.

The following table shows types of attacks on these three elements:

Attacking Confidentiality	Snooping	Data is intercepted by an unauthorized person. E.g. Tapping
	Traffic Analysis	May be the data is masked, so no information can be extracted but some patterns like - sender, receiver, message length, time of the message etc. can be extracted to make intelligent guesses.
Attacking Integrity	Modification	Some portion of a legitimate message is altered or the message is delayed.
	Masquerading	One entity pretends to be a different entity. E.g. Hoax bank sites.
	Replaying	Subsequent retransmission of a captured message to produce an unauthorized effect. E.g. Bill payment fake reminders with fake links.
	Repudiation	Sender denies that it sent the message or the receiver denies that it received the message.
Attacking Availability	Denial of Service (DoS)	Slowing down or totally interrupt the service of the system. E.g. multiple requests to bring an exam result server down.

***Figure 1.2**: Security threats on CIA*

Security Mechanisms

Encipherment, also known as encryption, is a security mechanism used to protect the confidentiality and integrity of data by converting it from a readable format (plaintext) into an unreadable format (ciphertext). Only authorized users or systems, who possess the correct decryption key, can revert the ciphertext back into its original form (plaintext). This mechanism is widely used in various security protocols and technologies to secure communications, stored data, and user authentication processes.

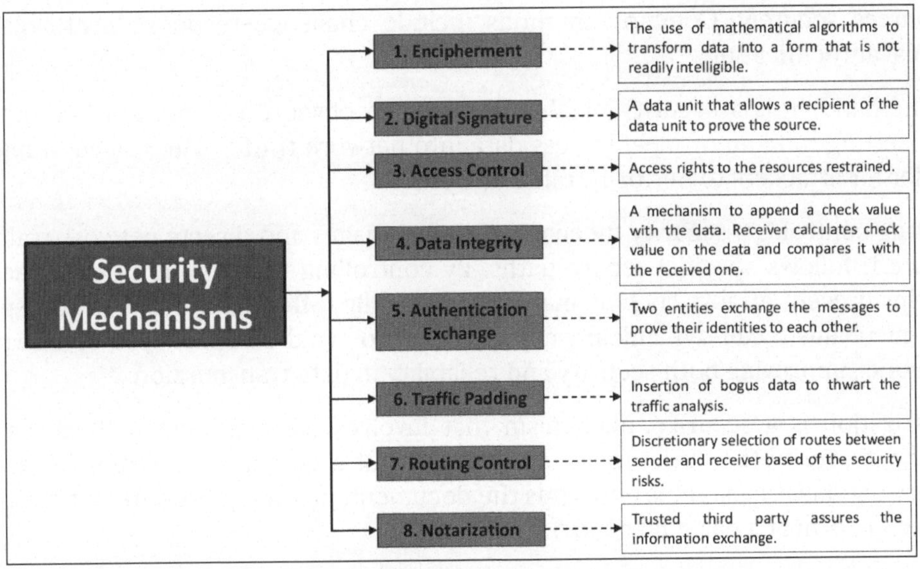

***Figure 1.3**: Security mechanisms*

A digital signature is a cryptographic security mechanism used to verify the authenticity and integrity of digital messages, documents, or transactions. It works by applying the sender's private key to generate a unique signature for a message. The recipient uses the sender's public key to verify the signature, ensuring that the message has not been tampered with and confirming the sender's identity. This provides non-repudiation (the sender cannot deny having sent the message) and assures data integrity. Digital signatures are widely used in secure communications, software distribution, and legal documents.

Access control is a security mechanism that regulates who or what can view or use resources in a computing environment. It ensures that only authorized users have access to specific data or systems by enforcing policies and permissions. Access control methods include Role-Based Access Control (RBAC), where access is granted based on a user's role, and Mandatory Access Control (MAC), where strict rules govern access. This mechanism is critical for protecting sensitive information and preventing unauthorized access to systems or data.

Data integrity ensures that information remains accurate, consistent, and unaltered during storage or transmission. Mechanisms such as hashing, checksums, and digital signatures are used to detect unauthorized changes or corruption in data. These tools verify that data has not been tampered with, ensuring its reliability and trustworthiness.

An authentication exchange is a security mechanism where two entities (for example, a user and a server) verify each other's identities before granting access. This process typically involves the exchange of credentials, such as passwords, cryptographic keys, or tokens, ensuring that only authorized users or systems can communicate or access resources securely. Common methods include challenge-response protocols and mutual authentication.

Traffic padding is a security mechanism used to obscure communication patterns by inserting random or meaningless data into network traffic. The goal is to make it harder for attackers to perform traffic analysis.

Routing control is a security mechanism that manages and directs network traffic to ensure it follows specific, secure paths. By controlling the routing of data packets, it helps prevent attacks such as man-in-the-middle (MITM) and traffic interception. This mechanism can dynamically adjust routes to avoid compromised or untrusted networks, improving both security and reliability in data transmission.

Notarization is a security mechanism that involves using a trusted third party (a notary) to verify the authenticity and integrity of a document or transaction. The notary digitally timestamps and signs the document, providing proof that it existed in a specific form at a particular time.

If you check these security mechanisms carefully, you will find that cryptography is an important aspect of them. Cryptography is a huge topic of study/research, and there are many books and articles written on it. Considering the overall topic of the books is Network security with OpenSSL, we need to cover the basics of cryptography for a quick reference, or you can say just for a refresh of your existing knowledge on the topic.

Cryptography

As mentioned earlier, cryptography is a deep topic, and we will cover the basics here just to stick with the main topic of the book.

Let us start with the brief history of cryptography.

Cryptography, the science of securing communication, has a long history rooted in the need for confidentiality in military and diplomatic affairs. One of the earliest known cryptographic methods was used by Julius Caesar in ancient Rome, where he employed the Caesar Cipher, a substitution technique that shifted letters in the alphabet to encode messages.

During the Renaissance, the development of more sophisticated encryption methods emerged, such as the polyalphabetic Vigenère cipher, which remained one of the strongest encryption techniques for centuries. The 19th century brought the mechanization of cryptography, exemplified by devices such as the German Enigma machine, used during World War II. The breaking of the Enigma code by Allied cryptanalysts, including those at Bletchley Park, had a profound impact on the war and the field of cryptography.

In the 20th century, the field of cryptography advanced significantly with the introduction of computers. The invention of public-key cryptography in the 1970s, particularly the RSA algorithm, revolutionized secure communication by enabling parties to exchange encrypted information without sharing a secret key beforehand. Today, cryptography forms the backbone of digital security, safeguarding online transactions, communications, and sensitive data across the Internet.

Let us have fun with the Caesar Cipher example.

In this cipher, each letter in the plaintext is shifted by a fixed number of positions down the alphabet. Caesar is said to have used a shift of three, meaning each letter in his messages was replaced by the letter three positions later in the alphabet.

For example, in the Caesar cipher with a shift of three, the alphabet is mapped as follows:

Plaintext (p):

a b c d e f g h i j k l m n o p q r s t u v w x y z

Ciphertext (C):

d e f g h i j k l m n o p q r s t u v w x y z a b c

Mathematically, this process can be represented as shifting the numeric position of each letter. For instance, the letter "a" is in the 0th position, and after shifting by 3, its corresponding ciphertext becomes "D." Using modular arithmetic, this can be expressed as:

- Ciphertext of "a" = (0 + 3) mod 26 = 3 = "d"
- Decryption of "E" = (4 - 3) mod 26 = 1 = "b"

Thus, if the phrase **"*orange is my favorite fruit*"** is encrypted using the Caesar cipher with a shift of 3, the ciphertext would be:

rudqjh lv pb idyrulwh iuxlw

For letters near the end of the alphabet, such as "x", "y", and "z" the Caesar cipher wraps around to the beginning. For example:

"x" corresponds to 23, so (23 + 3) mod 26 = 0, which becomes "a"

In general, the encryption function E(p,k)E(p, k)E(p,k) with a shift of k can be written as:

```
C=E(p,k)=(p+k)mod 26
```

For decryption, the function **`D(C,k)`** works as follows:

```
p=D(C,k)=(C-k)mod26
```

By adjusting the shift k, the Caesar cipher can be generalized to any number of positions, not just the original shift of 3.

Let us move from the history of cryptography to modern-day cryptography.

By understanding the basic principles and mechanisms, we can appreciate how cryptography shields data from prying eyes, ensuring confidentiality, integrity, and authenticity in our everyday digital interactions.

Symmetric Key Cryptography

Imagine that you and a friend are in a crowded room and want to share secret messages with each other without anyone else understanding. You both agree beforehand on a specific code language that only the two of you know. Every time you want to communicate, you both use this same code to write messages and then decode them. As long as no one else knows this secret code, your messages are secure.

In symmetric key cryptography, this "*secret code*" is like a shared key. Both the sender and receiver use the same key to encrypt and decrypt messages. If anyone else discovers the key, they can understand all the messages. So, just as in our analogy, the key must be kept secret to ensure the security of communication.

A real-life example of this is a locker with a combination lock shared by two people – both people need the same combination (key) to lock and unlock it.

Figure 1.4 shows how the shared secret key is used by the sender and recipient.

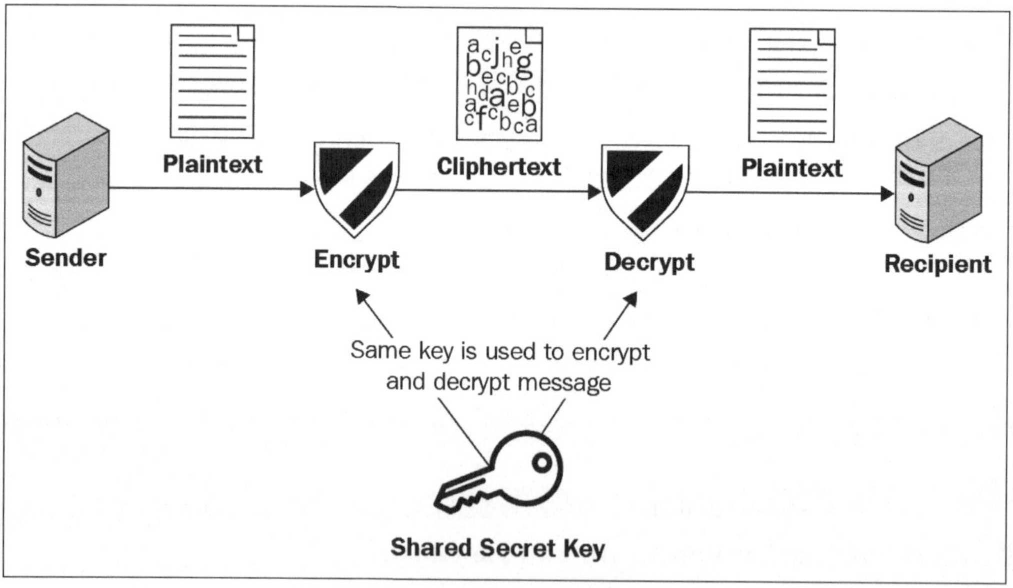

Figure 1.4: *Symmetric key cryptography*

Just for better understanding of this you can check the following encryption-decryption flow:

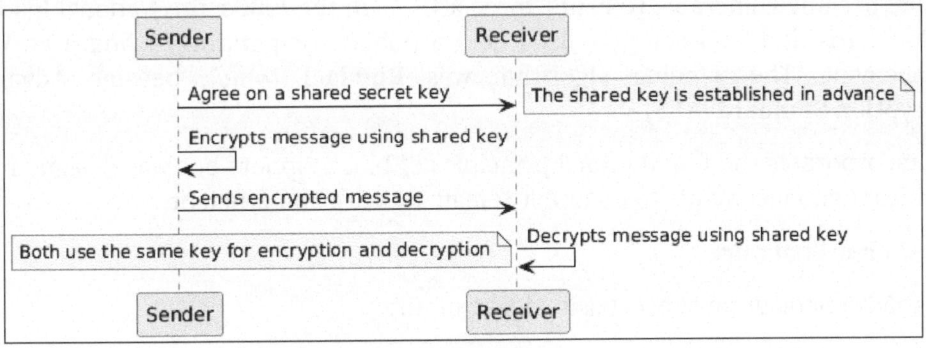

***Figure 1.5**: Encryption decryption flow*

Before moving towards advanced asymmetric key algorithms, let us understand the basics of the block cipher technique, which is the base of advanced techniques such as AES.

Block Ciphers

A block cipher is a type of symmetric encryption algorithm that encrypts data in fixed-size chunks or "*blocks*." For each block, it uses a specific key to perform transformations that convert plaintext (original data) into ciphertext (encrypted data) in a way that is reversible only with the same key.

- **Block Size**: The data is divided into blocks of a fixed size (for example, 64 bits for DES, 128 bits for AES).
- **Key**: Both the sender and receiver share the same secret key, which determines how the data is transformed during encryption and decryption.
- **Transformation Rounds**: Block ciphers use multiple rounds of transformations to ensure security. Each round typically includes operations such as substitution (replacing parts of the data) and permutation (reordering data).
- **Modes of Operation**: Block ciphers generally operate on blocks of data, but we can use modes of operation (such as ECB, CBC, or GCM) to handle larger messages securely.

A classic example of a block cipher is the Data Encryption Standard (DES), which uses 16 rounds of transformations on 64-bit blocks, though it is no longer secure for modern use due to its short 56-bit key size. We will not discuss DES anywhere in this book as it is considered to be insecure considering modern brute force techniques. We will only cover AES, which is more advanced and still considered to be a stronger security mechanism.

Advanced Encryption Standard (AES)

As DES became vulnerable to brute-force attacks in the 1990s, the National Institute of Standards and Technology (NIST) held a public competition to find a stronger replacement. The winning algorithm was **Rijndael**, which became **Advanced Encryption Standard (AES).**

AES incorporates the foundational principles of block ciphers but was designed with significant enhancements to ensure it remains secure and efficient.

AES Cipher Structure

The following diagram shows basic AES structure:

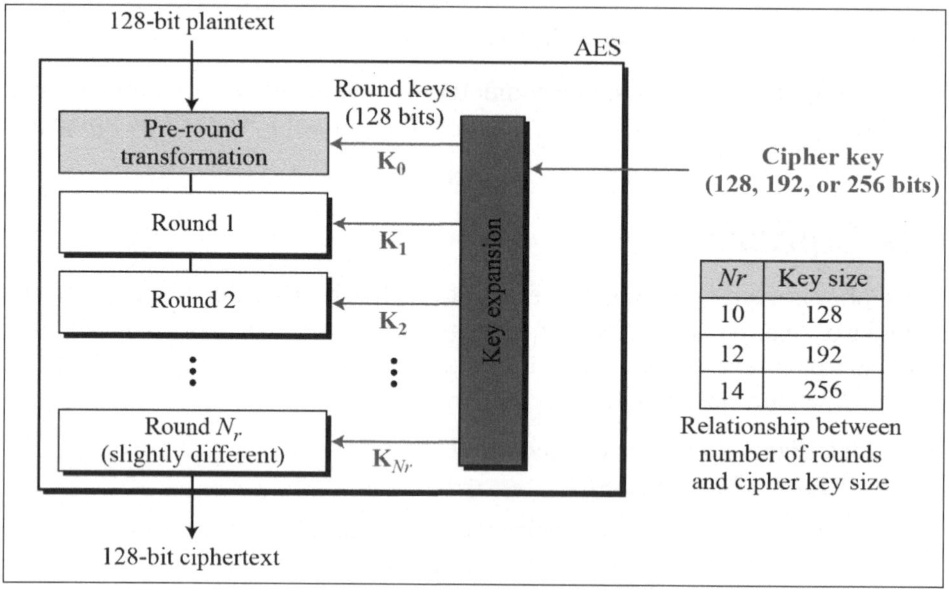

***Figure 1.6**: AES Cipher structure*

In *Figure* 1.7, round structure for *Figure* 1.6 is expanded:

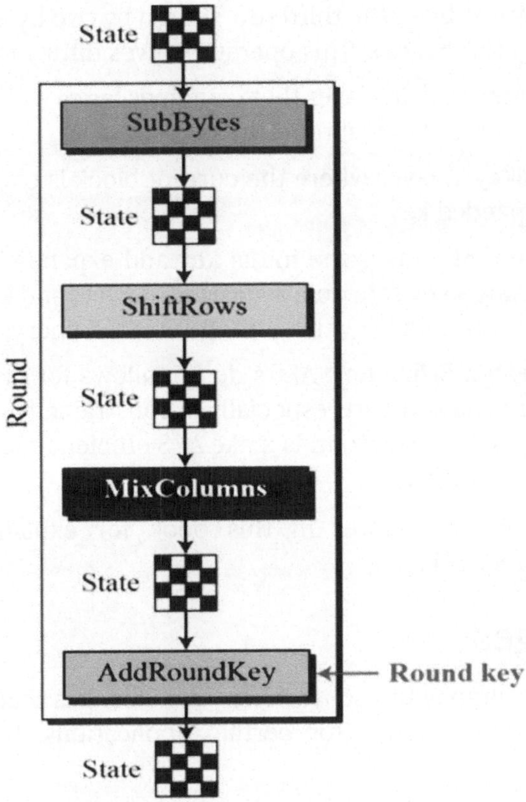

***Figure 1.7**: Rounds structure in AES*

- **Fixed Block Size:** AES operates on fixed 128-bit blocks, ensuring it can handle large data volumes securely and efficiently.
- **Flexible Key Sizes**: AES allows for 128-bit, 192-bit, or 256-bit keys. The key size determines the number of rounds in the encryption process:
  - 128-bit key = 10 rounds
  - 192-bit key = 12 rounds
  - 256-bit key = 14 rounds
- **Substitution-Permutation Network (SPN):** Unlike DES, AES is built on an SPN structure instead of a Feistel network. This design uses layers of substitutions and permutations for each round, which enhances security. Each round consists of:
  - **`SubBytes`**: Each byte of the block is replaced with a corresponding byte from a fixed 16×16 substitution table called the S-Box. This provides nonlinearity to the encryption process.
  - **`ShiftRows`**: The rows of the state (the current block of data) are shifted cyclically to the left. The first row remains the same, the second row

shifted by one byte, the third row shifted by two bytes, and the fourth row shifted by three bytes. This operation gives diffusion.

  - `MixColumns`: A mixing layer that combines bytes within each column of the state (except in the final round).
  - `AddRoundKey`: A layer where the current block is combined with a portion of the expanded key.

- **Key Expansion:** AES takes the initial key and expands it into a longer set of round keys using a key schedule algorithm. Each round key is derived from the original key but is unique, which strengthens the encryption.
- **Rijndael's Design Efficiency:** AES's design allows for fast implementation on both hardware and software, especially in constrained environments. Its block structure and SPN-based rounds make AES efficient and resistant to common cryptographic attacks.

We will have a separate chapter in this book for explaining symmetric key cryptography with OpenSSL.

Key Challenges

Symmetric key cryptography has some inherent challenges that lead to the adoption of asymmetric key cryptography for certain applications. Here are the primary challenges:

- **Key Distribution Problem**
  - In symmetric cryptography, both parties need the same key for encryption and decryption, so the key must be shared securely before any communication.
  - For secure communication across large networks (such as the internet), securely distributing a unique key to each pair of users is impractical and risky.
  - For example, if two people want to communicate securely, they have to meet in person or rely on a secure channel to exchange the key. This process becomes extremely difficult at scale.
- **Scalability Issues**
  - With symmetric key cryptography, a separate key is required for each pair of users. In a large network, the number of keys grows exponentially.
  - For example, in a network of 10 users, 45 unique keys are required for each pair to communicate securely. For 1000 users, almost half a million keys are needed, making management complex and unscalable.

- **Lack of Digital Signatures and Authentication**
  - Symmetric cryptography does not inherently support digital signatures, making it difficult to verify the origin and authenticity of a message.
  - Since both parties use the same key, any party could have created a message. This leads to problems in verifying who sent the message or if it was altered.
- **Single Point of Failure**
  - If the symmetric key is compromised, the security of all communication between the two parties is at risk, as both encryption and decryption rely on the same key.
  - This is particularly dangerous in large networks because compromising one key can expose a large volume of data.

Symmetric Key Distribution

As discussed, key distribution is a major challenge in asymmetric key cryptography. To address the key distribution challenge in symmetric key cryptography, several practical methods are commonly used, often combining both symmetric and asymmetric techniques. Here are some key approaches:

- **Hybrid Cryptography with Asymmetric Key Exchange**
  - **How It Works**: In hybrid cryptography, asymmetric encryption (for example, RSA, Diffie-Hellman) is used to securely exchange a temporary symmetric key. Once the symmetric key is shared, it is used for fast, efficient encryption of the actual data.
  - **Example**: Transport Layer Security (TLS), used in HTTPS, is a hybrid protocol. The client and server first use asymmetric cryptography to securely negotiate a symmetric session key. This session key is then used for the rest of the encrypted communication, improving performance while ensuring security.
  - **Benefits**: Provides strong security by leveraging the strengths of both symmetric and asymmetric encryption, ensuring the symmetric key is exchanged securely.
- **Pre-Shared Keys (PSKs)**
  - **How It Works**: In environments where secure key exchange is not feasible (for example, IoT devices or closed networks), a shared key may be manually distributed and pre-installed on devices or systems.
  - **Example**: Wi-Fi networks often use a pre-shared key (PSK) for access (for example, WPA2-PSK).
  - **Benefits**: Simple to implement for smaller networks but less secure

and scalable, as the shared key must be updated manually and can be compromised if not kept secure.

- **Key Distribution Centers (KDCs)**
  - **How It Works**: A KDC is a trusted server that securely manages and distributes keys to authorized users. Each user has a long-term symmetric key shared only with the KDC. When two users want to communicate, the KDC generates a temporary session key and sends it encrypted to each user using their respective long-term keys.
  - **Example**: Kerberos, a widely used network authentication protocol, relies on a KDC to distribute symmetric keys for secure communication.
  - **Benefits**: Reduces the need for individual key exchanges between every pair of users and improves scalability by using a central authority. However, the KDC itself becomes a single point of failure and must be kept secure.
- **Diffie-Hellman Key Exchange (DHKE) with Symmetric Ciphers**
  - **How It Works**: The Diffie-Hellman protocol enables two parties to generate a shared secret key over an insecure channel without ever transmitting the key itself. This shared secret can then be used as the symmetric encryption key for their communication.
  - **Example**: Often used in VPNs and TLS protocols as a means to securely establish session keys without pre-shared keys.
  - **Benefits**: Avoids key distribution entirely by allowing two parties to independently compute a shared key. However, DHKE is vulnerable to man-in-the-middle attacks without prior authentication.

Note: *We will discuss this method in more detail along with a mathematical explanation after RSA because it utilizes the concepts of prime numbers and primitive roots, which in general are used in asymmetric key cryptography.*

- **Public Key Infrastructure (PKI) for Key Exchange and Authentication**
  - **How It Works**: In PKI, digital certificates (issued by trusted Certificate Authorities, or CAs) authenticate public keys, which can then be used to exchange symmetric keys securely.
  - **Example**: PKI is widely used in email encryption (for example, S/MIME) and secure web communications (HTTPS). A client encrypts a symmetric key with the server's public key, and the server uses its private key to decrypt it.
  - **Benefits**: Enables secure and scalable key distribution on a large scale by using a hierarchical trust model, ensuring that symmetric keys are exchanged only with authenticated entities. PKI infrastructure, however, can be complex and expensive to maintain.

Asymmetric Key Cryptography

Asymmetric cryptography, also known as public-key cryptography, solves challenges posed by symmetric key cryptography by using two keys: a public key (shared with anyone) and a private key (kept secret).

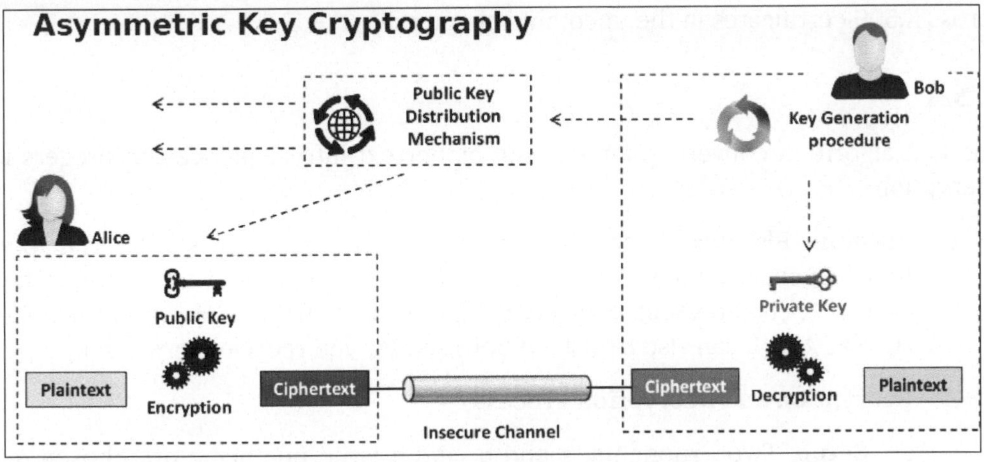

***Figure 1.8**: Asymmetric key cryptography*

Here is how it addresses the main issues:

- **Simplified Key Distribution**: Since only the public key needs to be shared openly, there is no need for a secure channel to distribute keys. Users can encrypt messages with the receiver's public key, which only the receiver's private key can decrypt.
- **Scalability**: Each user only needs a single public-private key pair, reducing the complexity of key management across networks. This means the key distribution grows linearly rather than exponentially, allowing large-scale secure communication.
- **Digital Signatures and Authentication**: Asymmetric cryptography allows digital signatures, enabling users to verify the sender's identity and the integrity of the message. This is done by signing the message with the sender's private key, which anyone can verify using the sender's public key.
- **Increased Security**: Since the private key is never shared, it remains secure as long as the user protects it. Even if someone intercepts the public key, it cannot be used to decrypt messages or forge signatures.

By solving these issues, asymmetric cryptography has become essential for applications requiring secure communication over untrusted networks, such as secure web browsing (HTTPS), email encryption, and digital signatures. However, symmetric key cryptography is still widely used for bulk data encryption because it is faster and more efficient, especially when combined with asymmetric cryptography for secure key exchange.

To understand these concepts better, we can consider one of the popular algorithms, RSA, with its mathematical formulation. We do not need to go into much details, but we need to understand some basics as this part comes into the picture when we come across X.509 certificates in the upcoming chapters.

RSA

The RSA algorithm converts plaintext and ciphertext into sequences of integers for encryption.

1. **Encoding Plaintext**: Each character in the plaintext, such as "ABC," is mapped to a sequence of numbers. For example, "ABC" might become 000102, where each letter is represented by a two-digit code from 00 to 25. Other mappings, such as ASCII, can also be used if both sender and receiver agree on it.
2. **Encryption and Decryption Process**:
    a. **Setup**: Two exponents, `e` and `d`, and a large number n are chosen. `n` is selected to be large enough to represent each character as an integer less than `n`.

    b. **Encryption Formula**: The ciphertext `C` for a plaintext character `P` is calculated using:

    ```
    C = P^e mod n
    ```

    c. **Decryption Formula**: To recover the plaintext P from the ciphertext C, the receiver uses:

    ```
    P = C^d mod n
    ```

    d. When combined, these formulas ensure P can be recovered because:

    ```
    P = (P^e mod n)^d mod n = P^ed mod n
    ```

    Key Roles: Both parties know n (the modulus). The sender uses e (public exponent) to encrypt, while only the receiver has d (private exponent) to decrypt.

RSA is an asymmetric encryption method, where:

- Public key (used for encryption) is `PU = {e, n}`
- Private key (used for decryption) is `PR = {d, n}`

Mathematics for Diffie-Hellman Key Exchange (DHKE)

As discussed earlier, it utilizes the concepts of prime numbers and primitive roots similar to what we discussed previously in RSA. Hence, we will cover it in this section.

In 1976, Stanford University professors Whitfield Diffie and Martin Hellman introduced the Diffie-Hellman Key Exchange (DHKE) protocol. This groundbreaking method allows two parties to establish a shared secret key over an insecure communication channel, making it a foundational technique in cryptography and still widely used today.

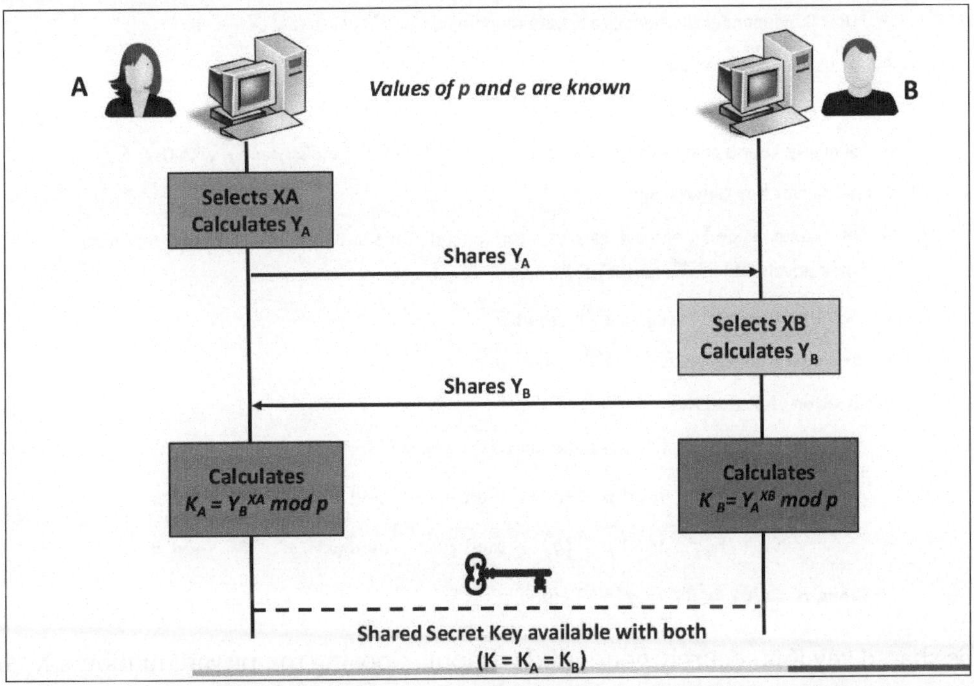

***Figure 1.9**: Diffie-Hellman Key Exchange (DHKE)*

Mathematical formulation:

Mathematical Formulation

The protocol relies on two public values known to both users:

1. A prime number p
2. A primitive root g of p

Let's walk through the process by which two users, A and B, establish a shared secret key:

1. **Random Number Selection:**
   - User A chooses a private random number X_A such that $X_A < p$.
   - User B independently chooses a private random number X_B such that $X_B < p$.
2. **Public Value Computation:**
   - User A computes a public value $Y_A = g^{X_A} \mod p$ and shares Y_A with User B.
   - Similarly, User B computes a public value $Y_B = g^{X_B} \mod p$ and shares Y_B with User A.
3. **Shared Secret Key Generation:**
   - After exchanging Y_A and Y_B, each user can compute the shared secret key without revealing their private values X_A and X_B:
     - User A calculates $K_A = Y_B^{X_A} \mod p$.
     - User B calculates $K_B = Y_A^{X_B} \mod p$.
4. **Verification of Shared Key:**
   - These calculations result in the same shared secret key K for both users:

$$K_A = Y_B^{X_A} \mod p = (g^{X_B} \mod p)^{X_A} \mod p = g^{X_A \cdot X_B} \mod p$$

$$K_B = Y_A^{X_B} \mod p = (g^{X_A} \mod p)^{X_B} \mod p = g^{X_A \cdot X_B} \mod p$$

Thus, $K = K_A = K_B = g^{X_A \cdot X_B} \mod p$.

This shared key K is securely generated without exposing the private numbers X_A and X_B, ensuring that even if an eavesdropper intercepts Y_A and Y_B, they cannot compute K without knowing the private exponents. The established shared key can now be used as a symmetric encryption key for secure communication.

Example

Let us choose the following values:

- Prime number p: 23
- Primitive root g: 5

Two users, Alice and Bob, want to establish a shared secret key.

Step-by-Step DHKE Example

1. **Private Key Selection:**
   - Alice picks a private random number $X_A = 6$.
   - Bob picks a private random number $X_B = 15$.
2. **Compute Public Values:**
   - Alice calculates her public value $Y_A = g^{X_A} \mod p$:

     $$Y_A = 5^6 \mod 23 = 15625 \mod 23 = 8$$

     Alice shares $Y_A = 8$ with Bob.
   - Bob calculates his public value $Y_B = g^{X_B} \mod p$:

     $$Y_B = 5^{15} \mod 23 = 30517578125 \mod 23 = 19$$

     Bob shares $Y_B = 19$ with Alice.
3. **Compute Shared Secret Key:**
   - Using Bob's public value Y_B, Alice calculates the shared key $K_A = Y_B^{X_A} \mod p$:

     $$K_A = 19^6 \mod 23 = 47045881 \mod 23 = 2$$
   - Using Alice's public value Y_A, Bob calculates the shared key $K_B = Y_A^{X_B} \mod p$:

     $$K_B = 8^{15} \mod 23 = 35184372088832 \mod 23 = 2$$
4. **Result:**
   - Both Alice and Bob arrive at the same shared secret key $K = 2$.
   - This shared key $K = 2$ can now be used as a symmetric encryption key for secure communication between Alice and Bob.

This example shows how the DHKE process generates a shared key K using a public channel without revealing the private numbers X_A or X_B.

Hashing

In cryptography, Hashing is a process of converting data of any size (for example, file, password, message) into a fixed-size string of characters, usually a hexadecimal value, using a mathematical function known as a hash function. A hash function (H) takes a message of any length (M) and produces a fixed-size hash value (h). This can be written as h = H(M), where h is also known as the hash code or digest.

A good hash function should create hash codes that are random and evenly distributed but always the same size. This is important for network security because:

- Regardless of the input message's length, the hash code length remains constant, allowing for predictable storage and transmission needs.
- Even a slight change in the message will result in a completely different hash code. This helps detect any modifications to the message, making it effective against tampering attacks.

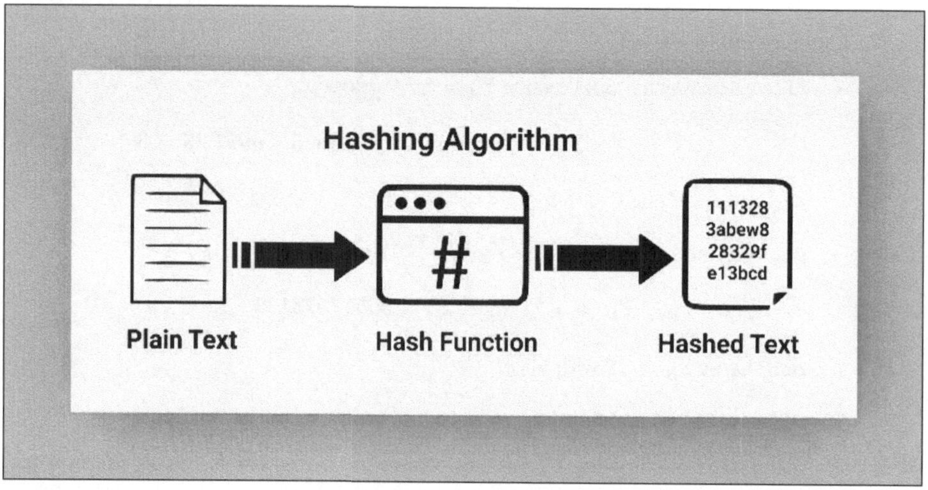

***Figure 1.10**: Hashing*

Secure Hashing Algorithm (SHA and SHA-512 Explained)

Secure Hash Algorithm (SHA) refers to a group of cryptographic hash functions that ensure data integrity by transforming an input (message) into a fixed-size hash, or "*digest*," that uniquely represents the input. Different versions of SHA, including SHA-1, SHA-256, and SHA-512, vary in security and efficiency.

Understanding SHA-512

SHA-512, part of the SHA-2 family, generates a 512-bit (64-byte) hash. Its large hash size offers strong resistance to cryptographic attacks, such as collisions (two different inputs producing the same hash) and pre-image attacks (reconstructing the original message from the hash).

Key characteristics of SHA-512:

- **Fixed-Length Output**: Regardless of input size, SHA-512 always produces a 512-bit (64-byte or 128-character in result) hash.
- **Consistency**: The same input always generates the same hash value.
- **Collision Resistance**: With 2^512 possible values, it is practically impossible for two distinct inputs to have the same hash.

- **Avalanche Effect**: Small changes to the input lead to entirely different hash outputs.
- **Pre-Image Resistance**: Given a hash, it is computationally infeasible to recover the original message.

How SHA-512 Operates

SHA-512 processes data in 1024-bit (128-byte) blocks, using a series of complex bitwise operations, shifts, and modular additions across multiple rounds. Here is an overview of the key stages:

1. **Padding**: The message is padded so its length is a multiple of 1024 bits. Padding consists of a single '1' bit, followed by zeros, and ends with a 128-bit block representing the original message length.
2. **Message Schedule**: The padded message is divided into 1024-bit blocks, which are split further into 16 64-bit words. An 80-word schedule is derived for each round of processing.
3. **Initialization Vectors**: SHA-512 starts with eight preset 64-bit values, which are continually updated with each message block.
4. **Processing**: Each block goes through 80 rounds, where intermediate values are mixed with message parts and predefined constants.
5. **Final Output**: After all blocks are processed, the eight 64-bit values are combined to produce the final 512-bit hash.

Example of padding

Suppose the input message is:

```
"AvaOrange"
```

Original Message: "*AvaOrange*" consists of 9 characters, which is 72 bits (since each character is 8 bits).

In binary, "*AvaOrange*" is:

01000001 01110110 01100001 01001111 01110010 01100001 01101110 01100111 01100101

Padding Step 1: Append a single '1' bit to the binary message.

After appending '1', we have:

01000001 01110110 01100001 01001111 01110010 01100001 01101110 01100111 01100101 1

Padding Step 2: Add '0' bits until the total length is 896 bits (since SHA-512 reserves the last 128 bits for the message length). Currently, we have 73 bits (72 bits + 1 bit). So, we need to add 823 more '0' bits to reach 896 bits.

After adding '0's, the padded message becomes:

01000001 01110110 01100001 01001111 01110010 01100001 01101110 01100111 01100101 1 followed by 823 zeros

Padding Step 3: Append the original message length in bits (72) as a 128-bit binary number.

In binary, 72 is:

00000000 00000000 00000000 00000000 00000000 00000000 00000000 00000000 00000000 00000000 00000000 00000000 00000000 00000000 01001000

Final Padded Message: The complete padded message now consists of 1024 bits and is ready for SHA-512 processing.

This padded message ensures the original input length is securely encoded, allowing SHA-512 to maintain data integrity and follow a standardized structure for any message input.

Due to its strong collision resistance, SHA-512 is widely used in SSL/TLS security, digital signatures, and secure password hashing.

Digital Signatures

A digital signature is a mathematical scheme that uses cryptographic techniques to validate the origin and integrity of a digital message or document. Unlike handwritten signatures, digital signatures are unique to each document and rely on a pair of cryptographic keys–a private key for signing and a public key for verification.

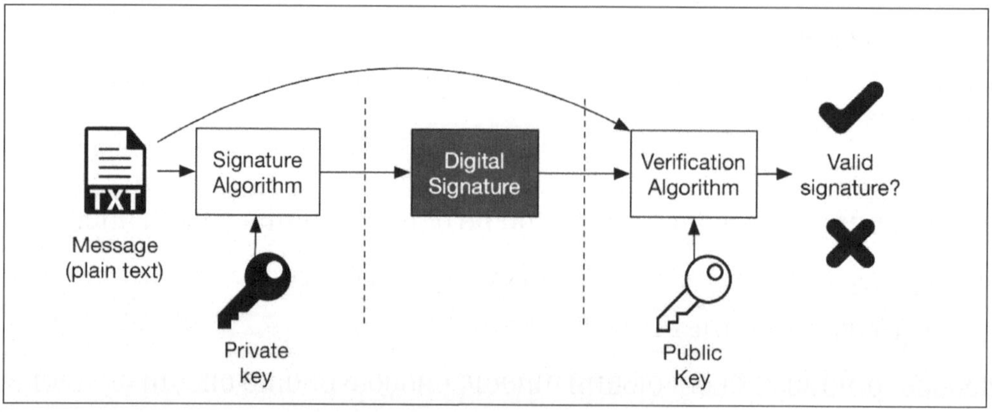

Figure 1.11: *Digital signature mechanism*

Digital signatures rely on asymmetric cryptography and hash functions. The process can be divided into two key operations:

1. **Signing the Message**:
   a. The sender creates a cryptographic hash of the message using a secure hash algorithm (for example, SHA-256).
   b. This hash value is then encrypted with the sender's private key, creating the digital signature.
   c. The digital signature, along with the original message, is sent to the recipient.
2. **Verifying the Signature**:
   a. The recipient uses the sender's public key to decrypt the digital signature, obtaining the hash value.
   b. The recipient independently computes the hash of the received message using the same hash algorithm.
   c. If the computed hash matches the decrypted hash, the signature is valid, ensuring the message's integrity and authenticity.

Public Key Infrastructure (PKI)

Public Key Infrastructure (PKI) is a comprehensive framework used for managing digital certificates and public-key encryption, crucial for securing online communications, digital transactions, and identity verification. PKI provides the tools and protocols necessary for generating, managing, distributing, and revoking digital certificates, which authenticate entities and establish trust in a networked environment.

Understanding a Certificate (X.509)

PKI certificates, often in the X.509 format, are digital credentials issued by a Certificate Authority (CA) to authenticate entities and secure communications. Each certificate includes fields such as the entity's public key, issuer details, and validity period, and is digitally signed by the CA. This signature enables recipients to verify the certificate's authenticity and trustworthiness using the CA's public key.

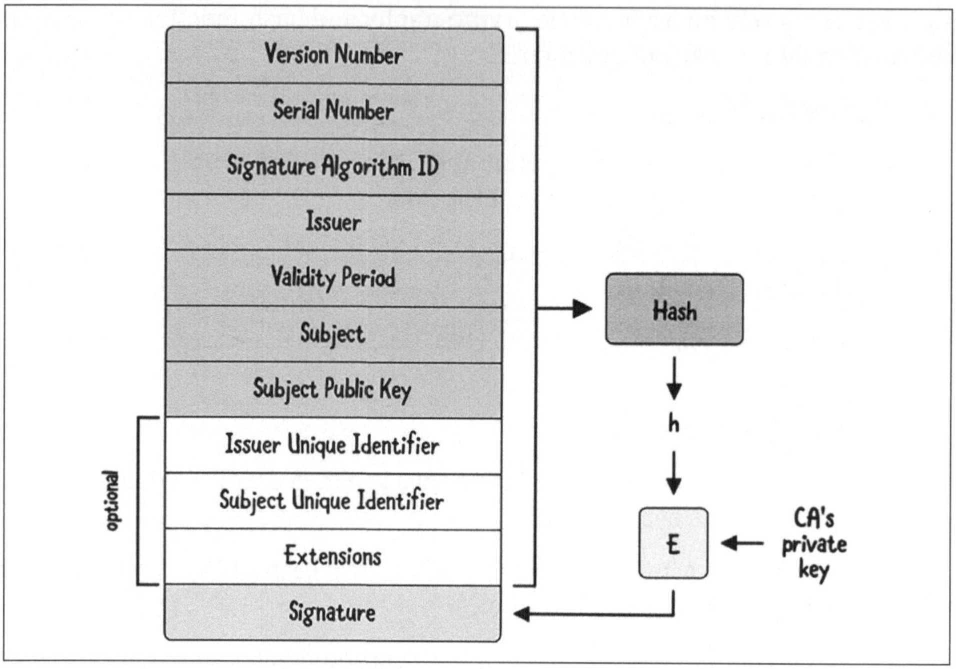

Figure 1.12: X.509 *certificate structure*

The fields of an X.509 certificate include:

- **Version Number**: Specifies the version of the X.509 standard to which the certificate conforms.
- **Serial Number**: A unique identifier assigned to the certificate by the Certificate Authority (CA) for tracking purposes.
- **Signature Algorithm ID**: Indicates the digital signature algorithm (for example, RSA or DSA) used by the CA to sign the certificate.
- **Issuer**: Contains the name of the CA that issued the certificate.
- **Validity Period**: Defines the time frame during which the certificate is valid, specified with start and end dates.
- **Subject**: Identifies the entity (individual or organization) to whom the certificate is issued.
- **Subject Public Key**: Holds the public key associated with the subject, along with the algorithm used to generate the key.
- **Issuer Unique Identifier (Optional)**: Allows a CA to distinguish itself uniquely, useful if multiple CAs work as a single logical entity.
- **Subject Unique Identifier (Optional)**: Enables multiple certificate holders to be represented as a single logical entity.

- **Extensions (Only in v3)**: Provides additional information to support features such as certificate revocation lists and hierarchical certification.
- **Signature**: The CA's digital signature over the certificate's contents. This signature is created by hashing the certificate fields and encrypting the result with the CA's private key.

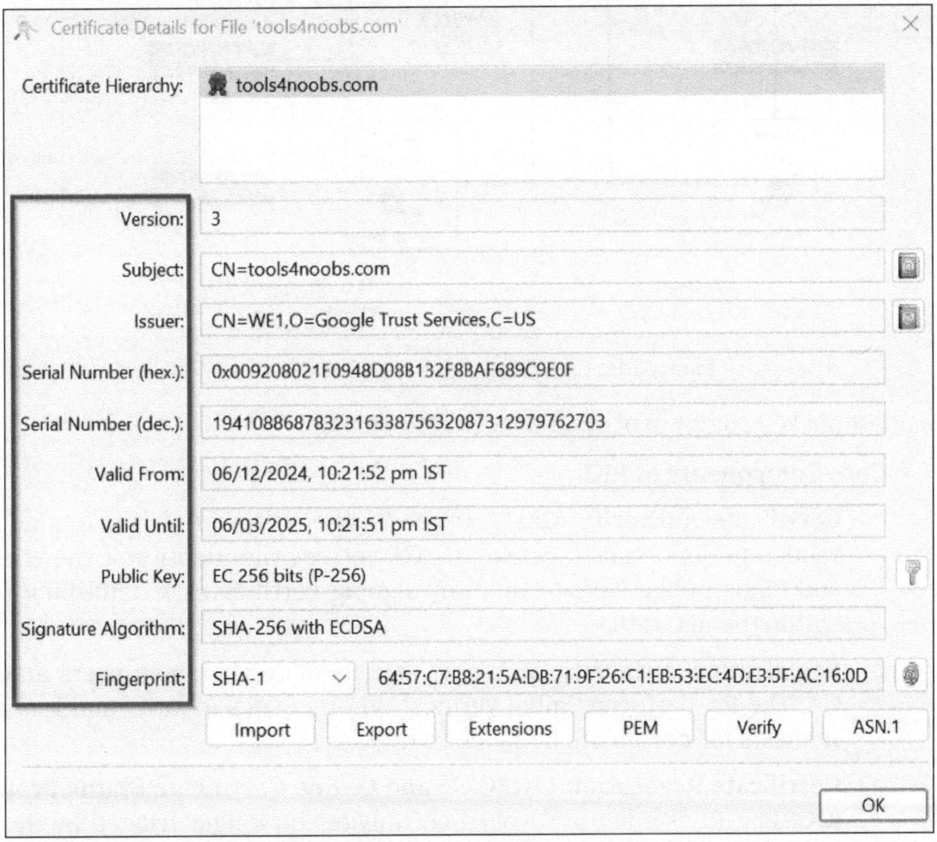

Figure 1.13: X.509 *Certificate example*

To verify a certificate's authenticity, the recipient can use the CA's public key to decrypt the signature and compare the resulting hash with a newly computed hash of the certificate fields. If they match, the certificate is confirmed as authentic.

Figure 1.14 shows how the certificate shown in the preceding structure is signed and verified by the CA.

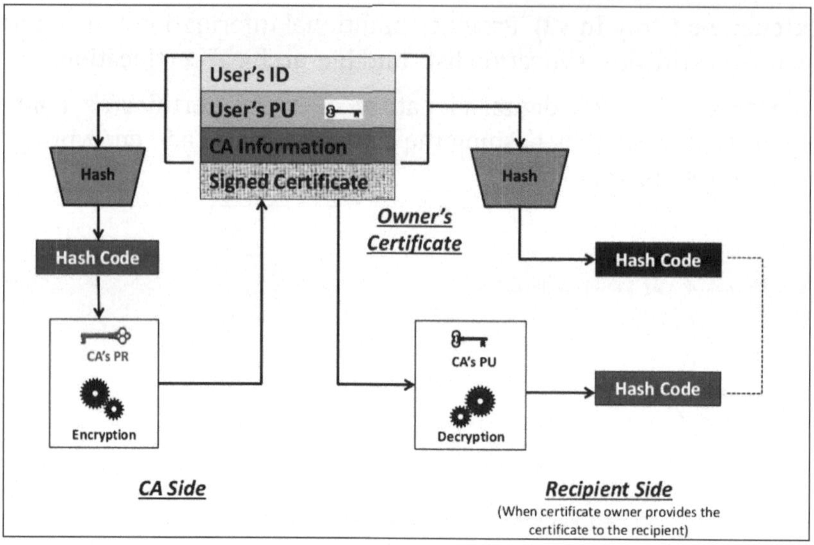

***Figure 1.14**: Certificate signing and verification*

Here are some key components and concepts to include:

- **Core Components of PKI**
    - **Certificate Authority (CA)**: A trusted entity responsible for issuing and validating digital certificates. The CA verifies the identity of the entities and binds public keys to them by signing certificates, establishing trust within the network.
    - **Registration Authority (RA)**: Acts as a mediator between users and the CA. The RA performs initial verification of a user's identity and forwards requests for certificate issuance to the CA.
    - **Certificate Revocation List (CRL) and Online Certificate Status Protocol (OCSP)**: CRL is a list of revoked certificates no longer trusted by the CA, while OCSP provides real-time certificate status, allowing entities to verify certificate validity promptly.
    - **Digital Certificates**: Standardized formats (for example, X.509) for representing public keys and associated identity data, such as the owner's name, the certificate issuer, expiration dates, and the signature of the issuing CA.
- **PKI Process Workflow**
    - **Key Generation**: The creation of a key pair (public and private keys). The private key is kept secure by the owner, while the public key is distributed via a digital certificate.
    - **Certificate Issuance**: Following identity verification, the CA signs the certificate, binding the identity to the public key, and issues it to the entity.

   - **Certificate Storage**: Certificates are stored in a directory accessible by entities within the network to enable trusted interactions.
   - **Authentication and Encryption**: Using the certificate, entities can verify each other's identity, establish encrypted communication channels, and securely sign data.
   - **Certificate Revocation**: When a certificate is no longer trustworthy, the CA revokes it and updates the CRL or OCSP for continuous trust management.
- **Cryptographic Operations in PKI**
   - **Encryption and Decryption**: PKI relies on asymmetric encryption, where data encrypted with a recipient's public key can only be decrypted by their private key, ensuring confidentiality.
   - **Digital Signatures**: Provide data integrity and authenticity. A sender signs data with their private key, and the receiver verifies it using the sender's public key.

Certificate Chain

A certificate chain establishes a path of trust from a peer certificate to the root CA, with each certificate signed by the one above it in the hierarchy. It generally includes:

- **Peer Certificate**: The site or server certificate, often issued by an intermediate CA, is presented during TLS connections.
- **Intermediate Certificates**: Optional CA certificates that link the peer certificate to the root, bridging the trust gap.
- **Root Certificate**: A self-signed certificate from the root CA, anchoring trust.

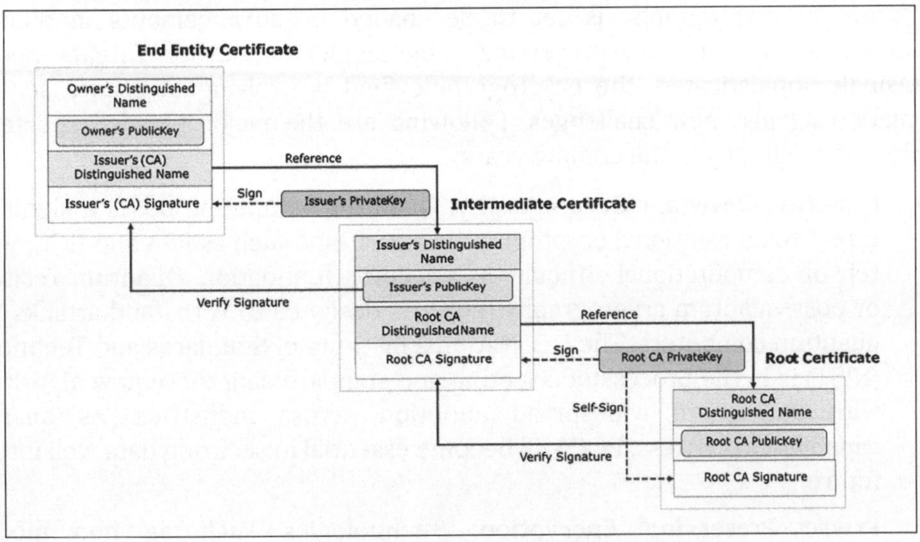

Figure 1.15: *Certificate chain*

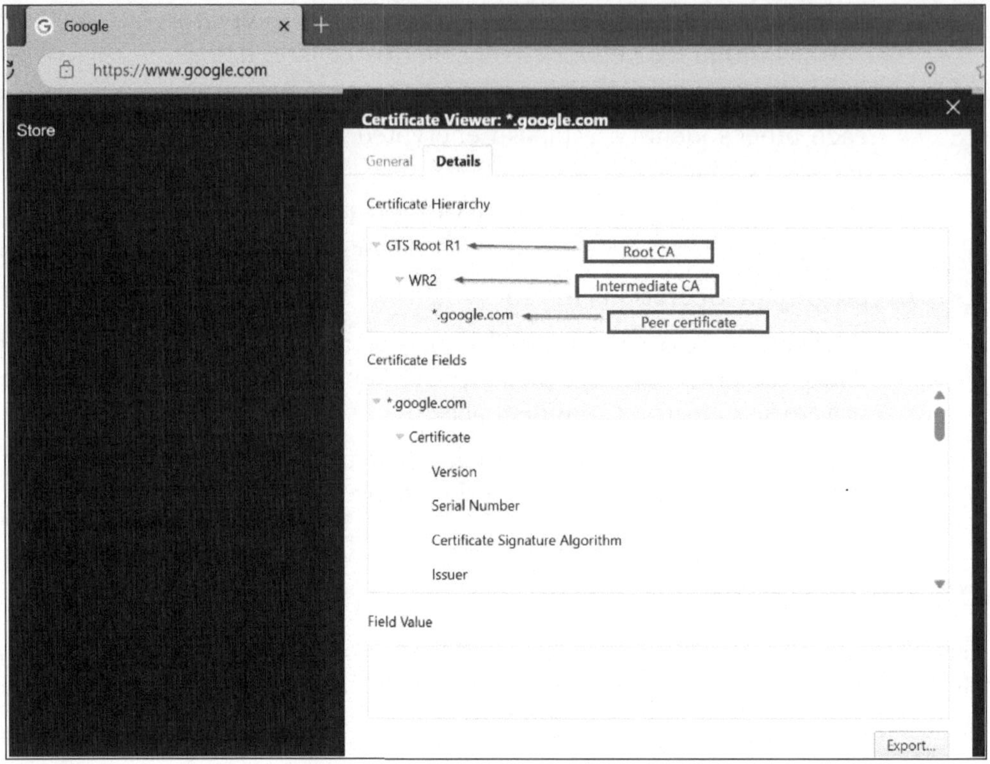

Figure 1.16: *Certificate Chain example*

Future Trends in Cryptography

The future of cryptography is set to be shaped by advancements in quantum computing, AI, and privacy-preserving technologies. As cyber threats become increasingly sophisticated, the cryptographic field is evolving to secure sensitive information against new challenges. Following are the major trends expected to redefine cryptography in the coming years:

- **Quantum-Resistant Cryptography**: Quantum computing poses a significant threat to conventional cryptographic algorithms such as RSA and ECC, which rely on computational difficulty as a security foundation. Quantum-resistant, or post-quantum cryptography (PQC), is designed to withstand attacks from quantum computers. The U.S. National Institute of Standards and Technology (NIST) is in the process of selecting and standardizing these new algorithms, with anticipated widespread adoption across industries. As quantum capabilities progress, PQC will become essential in securing data well into the future.
- **Privacy-Preserving Encryption**: Technologies such as homomorphic encryption (HE), zero-knowledge proofs (ZKP), and secure multi-party

computation (SMPC) are enabling computation on encrypted data without decryption, which preserves data privacy while performing necessary analyses. Homomorphic encryption, for example, allows data to be processed in its encrypted form, preventing unauthorized access during computations. These privacy-preserving cryptographic techniques will be increasingly vital for sectors such as healthcare, finance, and public safety, where sensitive data often needs secure, privacy-conscious processing.

- **Decentralized Cryptography and Blockchain Security**: Blockchain's cryptographic foundations offer secure, immutable ledgers ideal for verifying transactions and ensuring data integrity without central control. Future cryptographic advances will likely focus on developing more efficient consensus algorithms, reducing energy consumption, and integrating quantum-resistant features. Additionally, decentralized identity systems using blockchain are expected to transform how personal information is protected and verified, reducing reliance on traditional, vulnerable forms of identity management.
- **Lightweight Cryptography for IoT**: The proliferation of Internet of Things (IoT) devices presents unique challenges due to limited processing power, memory, and energy capacity. Lightweight cryptography, which minimizes computational requirements while maintaining strong security, is being developed to protect IoT networks. The advancement of these streamlined algorithms will help secure communication among billions of interconnected devices in environments ranging from industrial automation to healthcare.
- **Automated Cryptographic Protocols with AI**: AI and machine learning are beginning to influence cryptography, particularly in designing and verifying cryptographic protocols. Automated tools driven by AI can assess the strength of algorithms, detect weaknesses, and ensure proper protocol implementation. This trend will improve cryptographic accuracy, efficiency, and resilience against vulnerabilities, creating more robust systems that can better resist sophisticated attacks.

Cryptography's future will be defined by its adaptability to new computing paradigms and its ability to address privacy and security challenges in a data-driven world. As these technologies advance, cryptography will continue to be a crucial pillar of secure digital infrastructure, enabling trust and privacy in an increasingly interconnected society.

Conclusion

As we have seen, cryptography is at the heart of secure communication, enabling the confidentiality, integrity, and authenticity of data across various applications. From classical ciphers to modern encryption techniques, cryptographic methods are constantly evolving to meet the demands of a digital world that is increasingly connected and, consequently, vulnerable to threats.

In the upcoming chapters, we will explore how cryptographic techniques are implemented in practice through OpenSSL, a widely used open-source toolkit for secure communication. OpenSSL provides robust libraries for encryption, digital signatures, and certificate management, equipping developers with the tools to protect data in real-world applications. By diving into OpenSSL, we can see how the cryptographic principles covered here come to life, enabling secure, reliable interactions in applications ranging from secure web browsing to email encryption and beyond.

CHAPTER 2
Getting Started with OpenSSL

Introduction

OpenSSL is the most widely used open-source toolkit for cryptography and secure communications. This project is managed by the OpenSSL Technical Committee (responsible for decision-making) and the OpenSSL Management Committee (overseeing governance). These committees ensure that OpenSSL adheres to high standards of security and functionality, guiding its development and maintenance.

OpenSSL implements most of the cryptographic algorithms discussed in the previous chapter and is continually updated with the latest developments in these algorithms. This ensures that it remains at the forefront of cryptographic technology, providing robust security solutions. It contains Transport Layer Security (TLS) and Public Key Infrastructure (PKI) stacks, which can be used both as APIs and from the command line, making it versatile for various applications. A significant portion of the computer network infrastructure relies on it, underscoring its importance in securing communications worldwide.

A dedicated global team is involved in the development and maintenance of OpenSSL, reflecting its vibrant open-source community. This community-driven approach allows for continuous improvements and innovations, ensuring that OpenSSL evolves to meet the changing demands of cybersecurity.

OpenSSL is licensed under an Apache-style license, allowing use in both commercial and non-commercial projects, provided the simple license conditions are followed. This licensing flexibility has contributed to its widespread adoption across different industries.

The OpenSSL library is written in the C programming language and is available for most Unix-like operating systems, Microsoft Windows, and VMS. This broad compatibility ensures that OpenSSL can be used in a wide range of environments, from servers to personal computers.

Structure

In this chapter, we will discuss the following topics:

- History and Evolution of OpenSSL
- OpensSSL Installation on Different Platforms (Linux, Windows, OpenVMS, and macOS)
- OpenSSL Configuration File (`openssl.cnf`)
- OpenSSL Library Architecture

History and Evolution of OpenSSL

The OpenSSL project started in the late 1990s with the sole purpose of providing free tools for computer security, specifically encryption and decryption. Its goal was to make strong cryptographic tools accessible to everyone, fostering a more secure digital world. Over the years, OpenSSL has grown to become a cornerstone of secure communications, trusted by millions of users and organizations globally.

The First Version

Version 1.0, which was released in 2010, was a significant milestone in OpenSSL's history. This included TLS protocol support and enhanced several cryptographic algorithms. Most importantly, it made OpenSSL the go-to choice for setting up secure ways to communicate over the internet.

One of the defining characteristics of OpenSSL is its vibrant open-source community. Contributors from around the world continuously work to enhance the library's functionality, security, and performance. The collaborative nature of open-source development has been instrumental in driving OpenSSL forward, ensuring its relevance in an ever-changing digital landscape.

Significant Version-to-Version Changes

In this section, we will cover how OpenSSL evolved from version to version. This is important to understand what it takes to consider for a version change. In your development environment also, you need to upgrade to newer versions from time to time based on what features you are getting and what efforts are involved in upgrading.

OpenSSL 0.9.x Series

- **Initial Release**: Marked the beginning of OpenSSL's journey as an open-source implementation of SSL/TLS protocols. This release set the foundation for secure communications by providing a free and open-source toolkit that was accessible to developers worldwide.

- **SSL/TLS Support:** Introduced support for SSL and early versions of TLS protocols, enabling secure communication over networks. These protocols were essential for establishing encrypted connections, protecting data in transit, and ensuring privacy and data integrity.

  SSL and TLS are different protocols, with TLS being the more secure and modern successor to SSL. In conclusion, while TLS evolved from SSL, they are not the same, and the use of SSL is no longer recommended due to security concerns.

  While many people still colloquially refer to secure connection as "SSL," the correct term for current secure communications is TLS. Hence, we can use the TLS word in this section.

- **Cryptographic Algorithms:** Provided implementations of cryptographic algorithms such as RSA, DSA, and DES for encryption and digital signatures. These algorithms are fundamental for securing data and verifying the authenticity of digital communications.
- **Basic Functionality:** Included basic functionality for creating TLS connections, certificate management, and cryptographic operations. This initial functionality allowed developers to start integrating encryption into their applications and manage digital certificates efficiently.

OpenSSL 1.0.x Series

- **TLS Protocol Support:** Expanded TLS protocol support, including newer versions such as TLS 1.1 and TLS 1.2, enhancing security and compatibility. These updates were crucial for addressing vulnerabilities in earlier versions and providing stronger encryption methods.
- **Security Enhancements:** Improved security features, such as enhanced cipher suites, to mitigate vulnerabilities and address emerging threats. This series introduced more robust cryptographic practices to protect against evolving cyber threats.
- **Performance Optimizations**: Introduced optimizations to improve performance, reducing computational overhead and latency in SSL/TLS handshakes. These improvements ensured that secure communications could be established more quickly, enhancing user experience.
- **Stability and Reliability**: Enhanced stability and reliability through bug fixes, error handling improvements, and stricter adherence to protocol specifications. These changes made OpenSSL more reliable for production use in various applications.

OpenSSL 1.1.x Series

- **Security Improvements:** Implemented rigorous security measures, including enhanced cryptographic algorithms, random number generation, and vulnerability fixes. These measures strengthened the overall security framework of OpenSSL, making it more resistant to attacks.
- **API Enhancements:** Introduced improvements to the OpenSSL API, making it more intuitive and developer-friendly while maintaining backward compatibility. These enhancements made it easier for developers to implement secure communications in their applications.
- **Platform Support:** Expanded platform support to include newer operating systems and architectures, ensuring compatibility with evolving technology stacks. This ensured that OpenSSL could be used in a wider range of environments, from desktops to mobile devices and servers.
- **Deprecated Features:** Deprecated outdated cryptographic algorithms and insecure practices to promote best security practices and maintain code integrity. This encouraged developers to transition to more secure algorithms and methods.

OpenSSL 3.0.x Series

- **Modular Architecture:** Introduced a modular architecture, enabling better code organization, maintainability, and ease of integration with external projects. This modularity made it easier to extend and customize OpenSSL for specific use cases.
- **FIPS Compliance:** Achieved Federal Information Processing Standards (FIPS) 140-2 compliance for cryptographic modules, ensuring adherence to government security standards. This compliance is critical for applications that require a high level of security assurance.
- **LibreSSL Compatibility:** Enhanced compatibility with LibreSSL, a fork of OpenSSL, to facilitate code sharing and interoperability between the two projects. This compatibility allowed for a more collaborative development environment and shared advancements.
- **Deprecated Functionality:** Continued to deprecate legacy features and insecure practices, encouraging migration to modern cryptographic algorithms and protocols.

Version Skip

To avoid confusion with one of the OpenSSL modules, the version number 2 got skipped, and it went from 1.1.1 to 3.0 in 2018.

Latest Versions: As per the OpenSSL official page, this is the latest development update.

Date	Item
22-Oct-2024	Final version is 3.4.0 is available with new features and removed unsupported ciphers and algorithms.
09-Apr-2024	Deprecation and Replacement function.
08-Apr-2024	Security Advisory (https://www.openssl.org/news/secadv/20240408.txt): one low severity fix.
29-Mar-2024	Beta 1 of OpenSSL 3.3 is now available: please download and test it.
20-Mar-2024	Alpha 1 of OpenSSL 3.3 is now available: please download and test it.
30-Jan-2024	OpenSSL 3.2.1 is now available, including bug and security fixes.

Table 2.1: *Latest Versions*

Challenges and Actions

The widespread adoption of OpenSSL also brought attention to its security vulnerabilities. High-profile incidents, such as the Heartbleed bug in 2014, underscored the importance of robust security practices in open-source projects. In response, the OpenSSL development team implemented rigorous code review processes, enhanced testing procedures, and established proactive security measures to mitigate future risks.

Further collaborations with security researchers and industry experts helped to identify the vulnerability promptly.

Feature Enhancements and Adoption of New Algorithms

Subsequent versions of OpenSSL have focused on modernization and feature enhancements to address the evolving needs of users and applications. Support for newer cryptographic algorithms, such as Elliptic Curve Cryptography (ECC), and advancements in key exchange protocols have further strengthened OpenSSL's security posture.

Additionally, efforts to optimize performance and compatibility with emerging technologies, such as Internet of Things (IoT) devices and cloud-based architectures, have expanded OpenSSL's utility across diverse computing environments. The project's flexibility and adaptability have ensured its relevance in an increasingly interconnected world.

OpenSSL Installation

As mentioned earlier, OpenSSL is available on various operating systems such as Linux, macOS, BSD, Windows, and so on. We will cover installation on Linux, Windows, and OpenVMS in this book.

Prerequisites for OpenSSL installation from source code across all platforms:

- A "*make*" utility for building OpenSSL from the source.
- Perl 5 with core modules (Needed for configuration scripts).
- Compatible compiler installed and configured where the version meets the requirements specified by the OpenSSL documentation.
- A development environment in the form of development libraries and C header files.
- Obviously, your operating system should support OpenSSL.

Source Download:

```
git clone https://github.com/openssl/openssl.git
```

All the instructions are available in **`INSTALL.md`**, but we will elaborate here more on what problem you may face during installation and how to resolve those.

Installing on Linux

In this section, we will cover the installation process on Linux distributions. There are slight differences in commands for different distributions but the process is almost the same.

Installation Using package Managers

Debian

1. Update the package list:

   ```
   sudo apt update
   ```

2. Install OpenSSL:

   ```
   sudo apt-get install openssl
   ```

CentOS/Red Hat

1. Update the package list:

   ```
   sudo yum update
   ```

2. Install OpenSSL:

   ```
   sudo yum install openssl
   ```

Fedora

1. `sudo dnf update`
2. Install OpenSSL:

   ```
   sudo dnf install openssl
   ```

Arch Linux

1. Update the package list:

   ```
   sudo pacman -Syu
   ```

2. Install OpenSSL:

   ```
   sudo pacman -S openssl
   ```

Linux Installation from Source Code

Clone the repo as mentioned earlier from git clone:

1. Configure:

   ```
   ./configure
   ```

2. Build:

   ```
   make
   ```

3. Build test (Optional but recommended to build test):

   ```
   make test
   ```

4. Install:

   ```
   make install
   ```

5. Check if **`openssl version`** matches with the installed version:

   ```
   openssl version
   ```

Issues Usually Seen on Installation from Source Code:

1. **`openssl`**: error while loading shared libraries:

   `libssl.so.3: cannot open shared object file: No such file or directory.`

   This is because shared library path is not added to linker.

   Solution:

   ```
   sudo ldconfig /usr/local/lib64/
   ```

2. Missing dependency for development library **zlib**

   `zlib not found`

   Solution:

   `Install zlib development library`

   Debian

   `Sudo apt-get install zlib1g-dev`

   Redhat

   `sudo yum install zlib-devel`

   Arch Linux

   `sudo pacman -S zlib`

   Fedora

   `sudo dnf install zlib-devel`

3. Issue while **./Configure**

   Cannot locate **configdata.pm**

   This issue is because of **perl** interpreter is not installed.

   Solution:

   `Install perl`

   Debian

   `sudo apt install perl`

   Red Hat

   `sudo yum install perl`

   Fedora

   `sudo dnf install perl`

   Arch Linux

   `sudo pacman -S perl`

4. Unable to locate openssl

   Error:

   openssl: command not found

   This usually happens because of environmental variable or path is not set.

   Solution:

   ```
   echo 'export PATH="/usr/local/bin:$PATH"' >> ~/.bashrc
   source ~/.bashrc
   ```

Check that the symbolic link is correctly set:

```
sudo ln -sf /usr/local/bin/openssl /usr/bin/openssl
```

Installing on Windows

In this section, we will cover installation of OpenSSL on the Windows platform. Please make sure you are taking care of the prerequisites mentioned in this section.

Installation from Source Code

Prerequisites:

1. **Git**: Make sure Git is installed on your system and added correctly to the path.

   This is required for resource code download.

2. **NASM**: Install NASM from https://www.nasm.us/.

   This is required for compiling assembly source files. You can skip NASM, but this will impact performance optimization.

3. **Perl**: Download and install Strawberry Perl from Strawberry Perl.

   This is necessary for running the OpenSSL configuration scripts.

4. **Visual Studio**: Install Visual Studio from the Microsoft page. During the installation, select the "**`Desktop development with C++`**" workload.

Download source:

```
git clone https://github.com/openssl/openssl.git
cd openssl
```

Configure:

For 64-bit systems:

```
perl Configure VC-WIN64A
```

For 32-bit systems:

```
perl Configure VC-WIN32
```

Build

```
nmake
nmake test
```

Install

```
nmake install
```

Verify installation

```
openssl version
```

Common Issues During Installation

During the installation, you may come across the following issues:

1. **Error**:

   ```
   'perl' is not recognized as an internal or external command
   'nasm' is not recognized as an internal or external command
   ```

   Most installation errors occur because the aforementioned prerequisites are not installed properly.

   Solution:

   Make sure the prerequisites are installed correctly.

2. **Error**:

   ```
   Command line error D8021 : invalid numeric argument
   '/Wno-pointer-sign'
   ```

   Solution:

   Make sure **`LIB`**, **`INCLUDE`**, and **`PATH`** variable are set correctly.

Installing on OpenVMS

1. **Download:** For this, we will use an alternate (**`ftp`**) way of downloading the source just to explore this option:

   ```
   FTP ftp.openssl.org
   ftp> cd /source
   ftp> binary
   ftp> get openssl-3.3.0.tar.gz
   ftp> bye
   ```

2. **Unpack**

   ```
   tar -xvzf  openssl-3.3.0.tar.gz
   ```

3. **Configure**

   ```
   @config.com vms
   ```

4. **Build**

   ```
   @build.com
   ```

5. **Install**

   ```
   @install
   ```

Common Issues while Installation

During the installation, you may come across the following issues:

1. **Linking error**:

   ```
   %LINK-W-NUDFSYMBOL, Symbol DECC$SHR referenced in PSECT, but not
   defined.
   ```

   This could be due to library definition problem.

   Solution:

   You may need to specifically define locations, shown as follows:

   ```
   DEFINE LNK$LIBRARY SYS$LIBRARY:VAXCRTL
   DEFINE DECC$SHR SYS$SHARE:DECC$SHR.EXE
   DEFINE DECC$CRTLMAP SYS$SHARE:DECC$CRTLMAP.EXE
   ```

2. **Header file missing**:

   ```
   %CC-F-NOINCLFILE, Cannot find include file "openssl/opensslconf.h".
   ```

   Solution: Set include path correctly

   ```
   SET DEFAULT [openssl unpacked directory]
   @config.com vms
   ```

Installation on macOS

This section covers the installation of OpenSSL on macOS. Similar to other OS platforms discussed earlier, we can install it directly or from the source code.

Direct Installation

1. Update homebrew
2. brew update
3. Install OpenSSL
4. brew install openssl
5. Verify version
6. openssl version

Installing from Source Code

Prerequisites:

- Xcode tools
- Perl installation

1. **Download**

   ```
   curl -O https://www.openssl.org/source/openssl-3.0.0.tar.gz
   ```

2. **Extract**

   ```
   tar -xzvf openssl-3.0.0.tar.gz
   ```

3. **Configure(target platform darwin64-x86_64-cc)**

   ```
   ./Configure darwin64-x86_64-cc --prefix=/usr/local/openssl --opens-
   sldir=/usr/local/openssl
   ```

4. **Build**

   ```
   make
   ```

5. **Install**

   ```
   sudo make install
   ```

6. **Set environment variables**

   ```
   export PATH="/usr/local/openssl/bin:$PATH"
   export LDFLAGS="-L/usr/local/openssl/lib"
   export CPPFLAGS="-I/usr/local/openssl/include"
   export PKG_CONFIG_PATH="/usr/local/openssl/lib/pkgconfig"
   ```

7. **Reload profile**

   ```
   source ~/.zshrc
   ```

8. **Verify installation**

   ```
   openssl version
   ```

Common Issues

Mentioned here are some of the common issues you might encounter:

1. **Configure failed**

   ```
   /Configure: /usr/bin/perl: bad interpreter: No such file or
   directory
   ```

   Solution:

   ```
   Install perl
   ```

2. `make: *** No rule to make target`

   This is because **xcode** is not installed.

   Solution:

   ```
   xcode-select --install
   ```

Openssl Configuration File (openssl.cnf)

The Openssl configuration file helps load configuration without explicitly specifying it on the command line.

Its primary purpose is to define default settings and parameters for OpenSSL commands and operations. Here are some key purposes of the `openssl.cnf` file:

- **Path for Unix-like system**: `/etc/ssl/openssl.cnf`
- **Default Configuration:** It provides a default configuration for OpenSSL commands and utilities. When you run OpenSSL commands without specifying the configuration options, OpenSSL refers to the `openssl.cnf` file to determine default behavior.
- **Customization:** It allows users to customize OpenSSL behavior according to their specific requirements. You can modify settings such as default key sizes, encryption algorithms, certificate extensions, and more to tailor OpenSSL to your needs.
- **Security Configuration:** The `openssl.cnf` file enables users to configure security-related parameters such as cipher suites, protocol versions, key lengths, and certificate revocation settings. This helps in ensuring that OpenSSL operates securely according to best practices and security policies.
- **Certificate Authority (CA) Operations:** For organizations operating their own certificate authority, the `openssl.cnf` file is crucial. It defines settings for generating certificate signing requests (CSRs), issuing certificates, managing certificate revocation lists (CRLs), and configuring CA-specific options.
- **Server and Client Configurations**: OpenSSL can be used to set up SSL/TLS servers and clients. The `openssl.cnf` file allows users to define settings for SSL/TLS server configurations (for example, specifying server certificates, private keys, and supported cipher suites) and client configurations (for example, specifying trusted CA certificates and certificate verification options).
- **Cryptographic Operations:** In addition to SSL/TLS-related operations, OpenSSL supports various cryptographic operations such as key generation, digital signatures, encryption, and decryption. The `openssl.cnf` file provides settings relevant to these cryptographic operations, such as default hash algorithms, random number generator configuration, and more.

The sample file with the required comments is available at OpenSSL's official GitHub repository:

https://github.com/openssl/openssl/blob/master/apps/openssl.cnf

Tips and Tricks

- **Organize Sections:** Group related directives together with comments for clarity. This makes it easier to find and modify settings later.
- **Use Explicit Paths:** Specify full paths for directories and files in the configuration to avoid ambiguity and ensure consistency across systems.

- **Disable Weak Algorithms**:

```
# Disable SSLv2 and SSLv3
ssl_conf = ssl_conf_options = NO_SSLv2 NO_SSLv3

# Disable weak ciphersuites
ssl_conf_options = SSL_OP_NO_SSLv2 SSL_OP_NO_SSLv3 SSL_OP_NO_
TLSv1 SSL_OP_NO_TLSv1_1
```

- **Enable Perfect Forward Secrecy (PFS):**

```
# Enable PFS cipher suites
ssl_conf_options = SSL_OP_SINGLE_DH_USE SSL_OP_SINGLE_ECDH_USE
```

- **Set Default Digest Algorithm**:

```
# Use SHA-256 as the default digest algorithm
default_md = sha256
```

- **Customize Certificate Extensions:**

```
# Customize certificate extensions
[ req ]
req_extensions = v3_req

[ v3_req ]
subjectAltName = @alt_names

[ alt_names ]
DNS.1 = example.com
DNS.2 = www.example.com
```

- **Configure Revocation Checking**:

```
# Enable certificate revocation checking
crl_check = all
Optimizing Performance:

# Adjust session cache settings
ssl_session_cache = shared:SSL:10m
ssl_session_timeout = 1h

# Limit maximum number of sessions
ssl_session_tickets = off
Using Strong Random Number Generator:

# Use /dev/urandom as the random number generator
RANDFILE = /dev/urandom
```

- **Implementing Certificate Pinning:**

  Key rotation

  ```
  # Set certificate and CRL lifetimes
  default_days = 365
  crl_days = 30
  ```

OpenSSL Library Architecture

This section references information and diagrams from www.openssl.org. However, a simplified explanation is provided for better understanding.

OpenSSL architecture evolves with each release. There are two architectures described in OpenSSL documentation, Current Architecture and To Be Architecture. Current architecture is till 3.0.0, and the team is planning to evolve to the To Be architecture till the 4.0 release.

Current Architecture (Till 3.0.0)

Figure 2.1 depicts the diagram of Current Architecture:

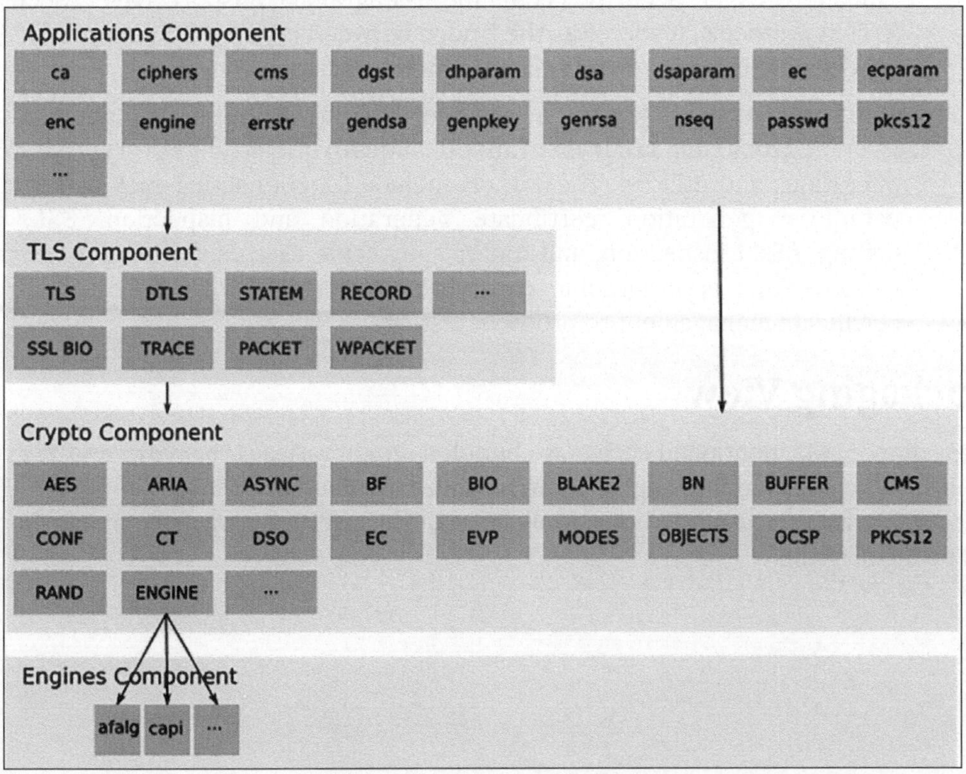

Figure 2.1: *Current Architecture*

OpenSSL architecture is organized into four primary components, each serving a distinct purpose:

- **libcrypto:** At the heart of OpenSSL, **libcrypto** serves as the foundational library, offering implementations for a wide array of cryptographic primitives. Beyond primitives, it furnishes supporting services vital for both **libssl** and **libcrypto**. Additionally, **libcrypto** hosts implementations of crucial protocols such as Cryptographic Message Syntax (CMS) and Online Certificate Status Protocol (OCSP).
- **Engine: libcrypto**'s capabilities can be extended through the Engine API. Engines are typically dynamic modules that augment **libcrypto**'s functionality. These modules register with **libcrypto** and utilize provided hooks to furnish cryptographic algorithm implementations. While many engines offer alternative implementations of algorithms already present in **libcrypto** (for example, for hardware acceleration), some introduce entirely new algorithms absent from the default OpenSSL suite. Notably, the GOST engine introduces the GOST algorithm family. Engines can be included in the OpenSSL distribution or provided separately by third-party sources.
- **libssl: libssl**, relying on **libcrypto**, specializes in implementing the Transport Layer Security (TLS) and Datagram Transport Layer Security (DTLS) protocols. It serves as the bridge between cryptographic functionality provided by **libcrypto** and secure communication channels.
- **Applications:** Comprising a suite of command-line tools, applications leverage **libssl** and **libcrypto** functionalities to offer a range of cryptographic operations and utilities. These tools include functionalities such as key and parameter generation, certificate generation and inspection, SSL/TLS testing, ASN.1 inspection, and more. They serve as a user-friendly interface to OpenSSL's cryptographic capabilities, catering to diverse needs from certificate management to protocol testing.

Packaging View

The components mentioned earlier are bundled into libraries (**libcrypto** and **libssl**) along with corresponding engine interfaces and include an "**openssl**" command line executable for executing various applications. The packaging view is shown in the following diagram:

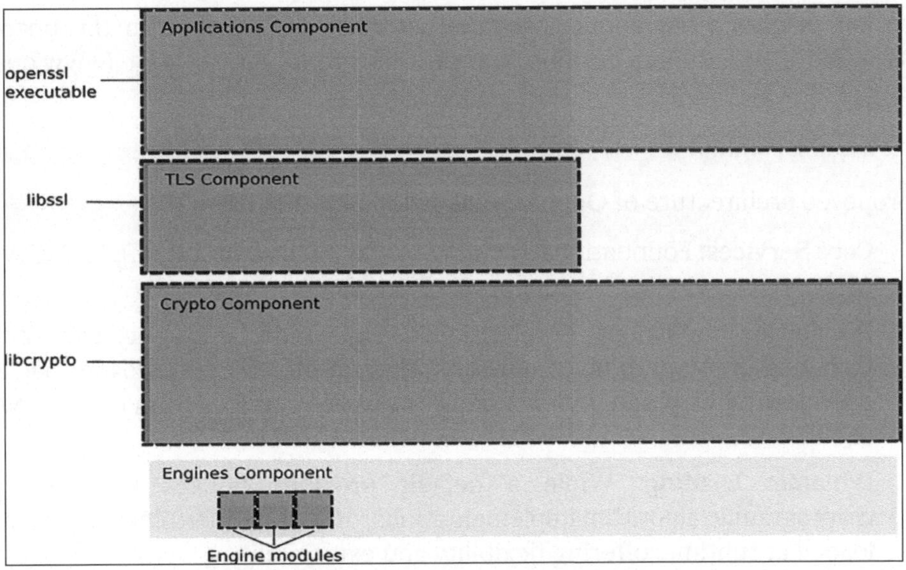

Figure 2.2: *Packaging View*

To Be Architecture

Let us understand To Be Architecture from *Figure* 2.3:

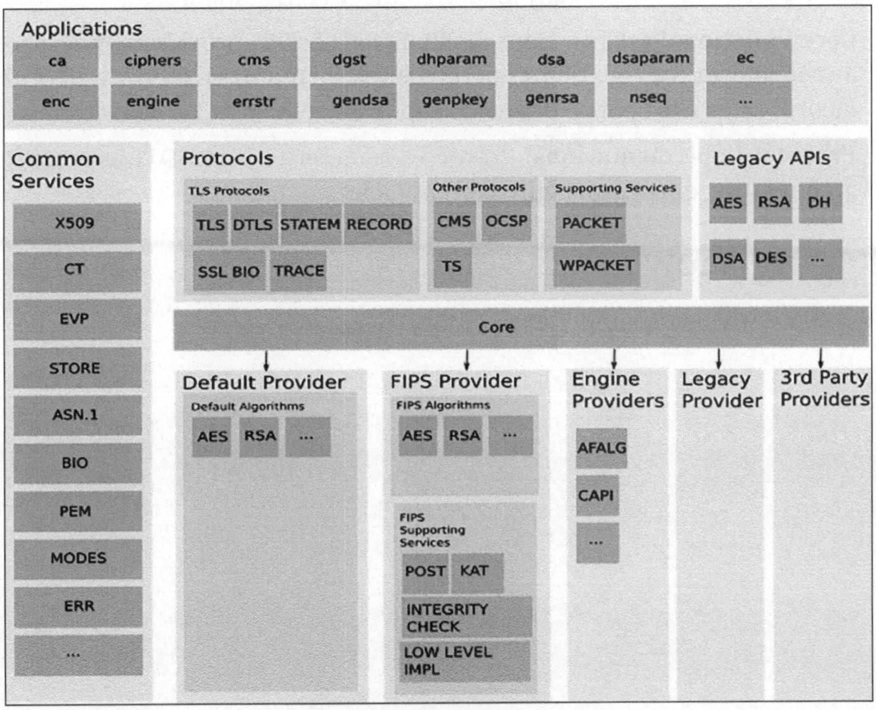

Figure 2.3: To Be Architecture

Let us not discuss more about this here, as these are covered in the upcoming chapters. But if you are still curious, you can refer to its official page (www.openssl.org).

Here is a quick summary:

The proposed architecture of OpenSSL has several key features:

- **Core Services:** Foundational building blocks such as BIO, X509, SECMEM, and ASN1 cater to application and provider needs.
- **Providers:** Implement cryptographic algorithms and ancillary services, including cryptographic primitives, serialization, and store loader backends. Providers may operate independently or utilize services from other providers or the Core.
- **Dynamic Loading:** While a default provider houses OpenSSL's core cryptographic algorithm implementations, other providers can be dynamically loaded at runtime, offering flexibility and extensibility.
- **Legacy Support:** Legacy provider modules ensure support for older algorithms, with a defined policy for transitioning algorithms from the default provider to legacy ones.
- **FIPS Compliance:** A FIPS provider, embodying the OpenSSL FIPS Cryptographic Module, can be dynamically loaded to meet FIPS standards.
- **Core Functionality:** The Core facilitates access to provider services, offering a mechanism for locating concrete implementations such as algorithms. It incorporates a property-based lookup feature for precise algorithm selection.
- **Protocol Implementations:** Protocols such as TLS and DTLS are part of the architecture, ensuring secure communication channels.

Packaging View

Figure 2.4 shows the Packaging View:

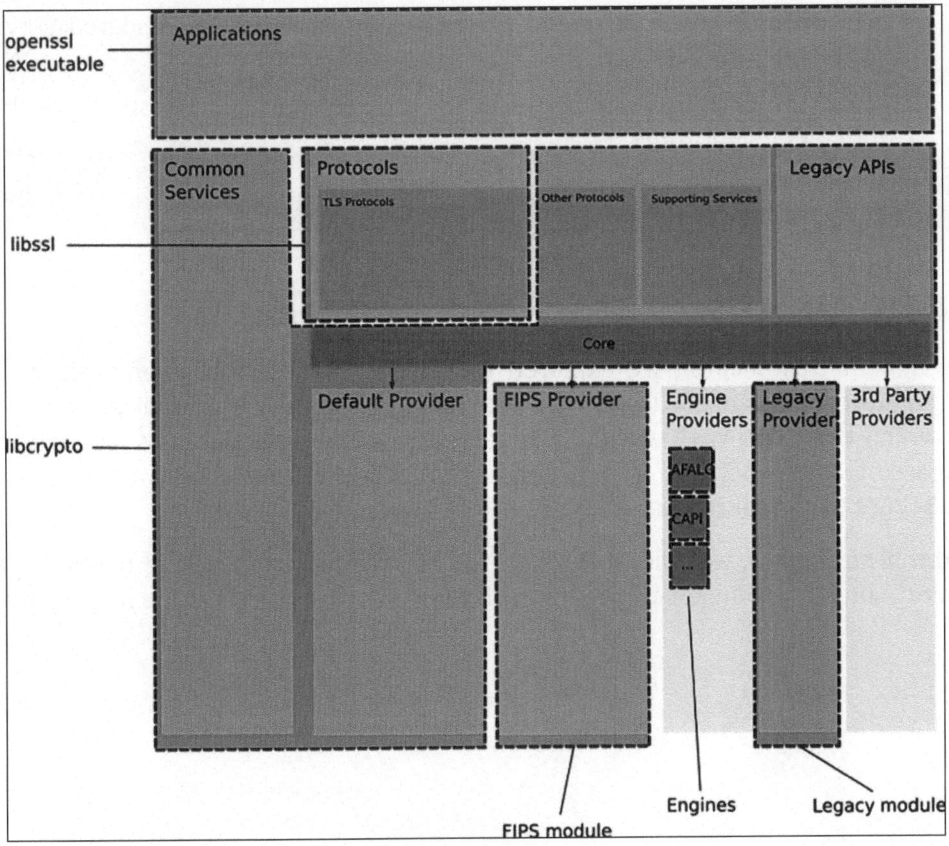

Figure 2.4: *Packaging View*

- **Openssl Executable:** The command-line application for interacting with OpenSSL.
- **`libssl`:** Housing components directly pertinent to TLS and DTLS, with certain supporting services migrated to **`libcrypto`**.
- **`libcrypto`:**

  A comprehensive library encompassing:

  - Core services implementations (for example, X509, ASN1, EVP, and OSSL_STORE).
  - The Core itself.
  - Protocols unrelated to TLS or DTLS.
  - Protocol supporting services (for example, Packet and Wpacket).
  - Default provider with implementations of all default algorithms.
  - Libcrypto-Legacy: Offering legacy "*low-level*" APIs, with algorithm implementations sourced from any provider.

- **FIPS Module:** Hosting the FIPS Provider, ensuring FIPS-validated services registered with the Core.
- **Legacy Module:** Containing the legacy provider for maintaining compatibility with older algorithms.

This packaging strategy facilitates modularization and organization of OpenSSL's components, enhancing maintainability and extensibility.

Conclusion

Throughout this chapter, we explored the history, installation, configuration, and architecture of OpenSSL, laying the groundwork for practical applications in the upcoming chapters. With a solid understanding of its fundamentals, you are now prepared for a deeper dive into leveraging OpenSSL for encryption, authentication, and secure communications.

In the next chapter, we will go through the important commands in detail to get a practical understanding of cryptography basics that we covered in the first chapter.

CHAPTER 3
OpenSSL Command Line Interface

Introduction

The OpenSSL man page provides comprehensive documentation of all available commands. However, to facilitate understanding and practical application, we will categorize these commands based on specific use cases. This approach will help users quickly find the relevant commands for tasks such as key generation, certificate management, encryption, and decryption.

We will thoroughly explain each category with practical examples. This method ensures that users can see how commands are applied in real-world scenarios, enhancing their grasp of OpenSSL's capabilities.

Additionally, we will address common errors encountered while executing these commands. By understanding these errors and their solutions, users can troubleshoot issues more effectively, minimizing downtime and frustration.

While OpenSSL is compatible with multiple platforms, including Windows and macOS, our focus will be on a Linux-based platform. Linux is a natural environment for OpenSSL due to its widespread use in servers and development environments. The commands and examples provided will be tailored to Linux, ensuring that users can follow along and replicate the processes on their own systems.

By structuring our coverage in this manner, we aim to provide a clear, practical guide that not only demonstrates how to use OpenSSL but also equips users with the knowledge to handle and resolve any issues they might encounter.

Structure

In this chapter, we will cover the commands categorized as follows:

- Basic Commands
- Cryptographic Operations

- Key and Certificate Management
- Public Key Infrastructure (PKI)
- TLS Connection Testing
- Advanced Commands
- Miscellaneous Utility Commands

We will also cover some sample scripts for using these commands efficiently.

Basic Commands

These commands provide information on the OpenSSL environment you are working on.

Any logical operations are not performed with these commands. Most likely, these will be your first commands after OpenSSL installation.

`openssl` Version

Knowing the OpenSSL version is crucial before starting OpenSSL-based development because it ensures compatibility with the features and functions required for your project. Different versions of OpenSSL have various capabilities, bug fixes, and security patches, so being aware of the version helps in avoiding deprecated functions and potential security vulnerabilities. Additionally, understanding the version allows developers to utilize the latest enhancements and maintain consistent behavior across different environments. It also helps in troubleshooting issues more effectively by referencing the correct documentation and support resources.

Usually, users prefer these commands to make sure OpenSSL is installed correctly with the expected version.

Version check is also helpful when we are debugging some issue that is reproducible on a specific version.

Sample output:

```
OpenSSL 3.3.0 9 Apr 2024 (Library: OpenSSL 3.3.0 9 Apr 2024)
```

Though this command is normally used without any additional parameters, if needed, we can use the `-a` parameter to get more information.

```
openssl version -a
OpenSSL 3.3.0 9 Apr 2024 (Library: OpenSSL 3.3.0 9 Apr 2024)
built on: Sun May 19 09:52:26 2024 UTC
platform: linux-x86_64
options:  bn(64,64)
compiler: gcc -fPIC -pthread -m64 -Wa,--noexecstack -Wall -O3
-DOPENSSL_USE_NODELETE -DL_ENDIAN -DOPENSSL_PIC -DOPENSSL_BUILD-
```

```
ING_OPENSSL -DNDEBUG
OPENSSLDIR: "/usr/local/ssl"
ENGINESDIR: "/usr/local/lib64/engines-3"
MODULESDIR: "/usr/local/lib64/ossl-modules"
Seeding source: os-specific
CPUINFO: OPENSSL_ia32cap=0x7ffaf3bfffebffff:0x18c05fdef3bfa7eb
```

From the preceding command, you can see what parameters are used during OpenSSL compilation and directory paths.

`openssl` Help

This will list all primary commands available in this version.

We can use **`--help`** for details of specific commands to give related options:

Example:

```
openssl verify -help
```

Figure 3.1 shows the output for the **`--help`** command:

```
Usage: verify [options] cert.pem...
Valid options are:
 -help                  Display this summary
 -verbose               Print extra information about the operations being performed.
 -CApath dir            A directory of trusted certificates
 -CAfile infile         A file of trusted certificates
 -no-CAfile             Do not load the default certificates file
 -no-CApath             Do not load certificates from the default certificates directory
 -untrusted infile      A file of untrusted certificates
 -trusted infile        A file of trusted certificates
 -CRLfile infile        File containing one or more CRL's (in PEM format) to load
 -crl_download          Attempt to download CRL information for this certificate
 -show_chain            Display information about the certificate chain
 -nameopt val           Various certificate name options
 -policy val            adds policy to the acceptable policy set
 -purpose val           certificate chain purpose
 -verify_name val       verification policy name
 -verify_depth int      chain depth limit
 -auth_level int        chain authentication security level
 -attime intmax         verification epoch time
 -verify_hostname val   expected peer hostname
 -verify_email val      expected peer email
 -verify_ip val         expected peer IP address
 -ignore_critical       permit unhandled critical extensions
 -issuer_checks         (deprecated)
 -crl_check             check leaf certificate revocation
 -crl_check_all         check full chain revocation
 -policy_check          perform rfc5280 policy checks
 -explicit_policy       set policy variable require-explicit-policy
 -inhibit_any           set policy variable inhibit-any-policy
 -inhibit_map           set policy variable inhibit-policy-mapping
 -x509_strict           disable certificate compatibility work-arounds
 -extended_crl          enable extended CRL features
 -use_deltas            use delta CRLs
 -policy_print          print policy processing diagnostics
 -check_ss_sig          check root CA self-signatures
 -trusted_first         search trust store first (default)
 -suiteB_128_only       Suite B 128-bit-only mode
 -suiteB_128            Suite B 128-bit mode allowing 192-bit algorithms
 -suiteB_192            Suite B 192-bit-only mode
 -partial_chain         accept chains anchored by intermediate trust-store CAs
 -no_alt_chains         (deprecated)
 -no_check_time         ignore certificate validity time
 -allow_proxy_certs     allow the use of proxy certificates
 -engine val            Use engine, possibly a hardware device
```

Figure 3.1: *openssl dgst --help*

Figure 3.2 shows the output for the following command:

```
openssl dgst --help
```

```
Usage: dgst [options] [file...]
  file... files to digest (default is stdin)
 -help               Display this summary
 -list               List digests
 -c                  Print the digest with separating colons
 -r                  Print the digest in coreutils format
 -out outfile        Output to filename rather than stdout
 -passin val         Input file pass phrase source
 -sign val           Sign digest using private key
 -verify val         Verify a signature using public key
 -prverify val       Verify a signature using private key
 -signature infile   File with signature to verify
 -keyform format     Key file format (PEM or ENGINE)
 -hex                Print as hex dump
 -binary             Print in binary form
 -d                  Print debug info
 -debug              Print debug info
 -fips-fingerprint   Compute HMAC with the key used in OpenSSL-FIPS fingerprint
 -hmac val           Create hashed MAC with key
 -mac val            Create MAC (not necessarily HMAC)
 -sigopt val         Signature parameter in n:v form
 -macopt val         MAC algorithm parameters in n:v form or key
 -*                  Any supported digest
 -rand val           Load the file(s) into the random number generator
 -writerand outfile  Write random data to the specified file
 -engine val         Use engine e, possibly a hardware device
 -engine_impl        Also use engine given by -engine for digest operations
```

***Figure 3.2**: openssl dgst --help*

Cryptographic Operations

This section covers how OpenSSL commands are used for various cryptographic operations. We will also cover use case examples wherever needed.

Encoding and Decoding

Base64 Encoding:

```
echo "Hello AVA" | openssl enc -base64  -out enc_out.txt
```

This command takes the string "**Hello AVA**" and encodes it in base64 format using OpenSSL. The echo "**Hello AVA**" part generates the input string. The **openssl enc -base64** part specifies that the encoding method is base64. The **-out enc_out.txt** part directs the output to a file named **enc_out.txt**, storing the base64-encoded result.

We can see encoded file contents:

```
cat enc_out.txt
SGVsbG8gQVZBCg==
```

Base64 Decoding:

```
openssl enc -base64 -d -in  /enc_out.txt -out /dec_out.txt
```

This command decodes a base64-encoded file using OpenSSL. The **`openssl enc -base64 -d`** part specifies that the decoding method is **base64**. The **`-in /enc_out.txt`** part indicates the input file that contains the base64-encoded data, named **`enc_out.txt`**. The **`-out /dec_out.txt`** part specifies the output file where the decoded result will be stored, named **`dec_out.txt`**.

We can see that we got our original text back after decoding:

```
cat dec_out.txt
Hello, AVA
```

Digest Commands

SHA-256 Hash for input text from stdin:

```
echo -n "Hello, AVA!" | openssl dgst -sha256 -out digest_out
```

This command generates a SHA-256 digest of the string **`"Hello, AVA!"`** using OpenSSL.

1. The **`echo -n "Hello, AVA!"`** part produces the input string without adding a newline at the end.
2. The **`openssl dgst -sha256`** part specifies that the SHA-256 hashing algorithm is to be used.
3. The **`-out digest_out`** part directs the resulting SHA-256 digest to be written to a file named **`digest_out`**.

```
cat digest_out
SHA2-256(stdin)= eb292370923be08e49b62045c1f21da2e11d919cd6fc-
cf86eecad669ddd5e6c1
```

Use Case Example(s)

Downloading files from the internet, you can verify their integrity by comparing the provided hash value with the hash value you generate.

```
openssl dgst -sha256 -out generated.sha256 downloaded.txt
```

Where,

1. **`-sha256`**: SHA-256 hash function.
2. **`-out generated.sha256`**: Writes the output hash to **`generated.sha256`**.
3. **`downloaded.txt`**: The file to be hashed.

`generated.sha256` should match with the hash given by file provider.

Verify Message Authenticity using HMAC-SHA256

Verifying an HMAC ensures that the message is authentic and has not been tampered with.

Generate HMAC

```
openssl dgst -sha256 -hmac "ava.key" -out out.hmac input.txt

cat out.hmac
HMAC-SHA2-256(input.txt)= c07f4ae334db83917aecf216ee7f3667d-
438c26b328663d327b2230d9e1710fc
```

Verify using HMAC

```
openssl dgst -sha256 -hmac "ava_key" input_file.txt

HMAC-SHA2-256(input.txt)= c07f4ae334db83917aecf216ee7f3667d-
438c26b328663d327b2230d9e1710fc
```

Compare this output with the previously saved **out.hmac** to ensure they match.

Encryption Decryption

OpenSSL command-based symmetric encryption and decryption are widely used for securing data at rest and in transit. Common use cases include encrypting files and sensitive data before storing them on disk or transmitting them over networks to ensure confidentiality. For instance, a file can be encrypted using Advanced Encryption Standard (AES) before being uploaded to cloud storage and later decrypted by authorized users. These operations are crucial for protecting sensitive information such as financial data, Personally Identifiable Information (PII), and confidential business documents.

AES-256-CBC Encryption:

```
cat plaintext.txt
Hello AVA!
openssl enc -aes-256-cbc -salt -in plaintext.txt -out encrypted.
txt
```

This command encrypts a file using the AES-256-CBC encryption algorithm with OpenSSL:

1. The **openssl enc -aes-256-cbc -salt** part specifies that the AES-256-CBC encryption algorithm should be used and that a random salt should be added to the encryption for added security.
2. The **-in plaintext.txt** part indicates the input file containing the plaintext data to be encrypted.

3. The **-out encrypted.txt** part specifies the output file where the encrypted data will be stored, named **encrypted.txt**.

AES-256-CBC Decryption:

```
openssl enc -d -aes-256-cbc -in encrypted.txt -out decrypted.txt
```

1. This command decrypts a file using the AES-256-CBC decryption algorithm with OpenSSL. The **openssl enc -d -aes-256-cbc** part specifies that the decryption method is AES-256-CBC.
2. The **-in encrypted.txt** part indicates the input file containing the encrypted data, named **encrypted.txt**.
3. The **-out decrypted.txt** part specifies the output file where the decrypted data will be stored, named **decrypted.txt**.

We can see that we got the plaintext back after decryption:

```
cat decrypted.txt
Hello AVA!
```

Use Case

Securely Storing Sensitive Information

Encrypting sensitive data such as personal financial information and companies secret files to ensure confidentiality. AES-256-CBC is a symmetric encryption algorithm that uses a 256-bit key and Cipher Block Chaining (CBC) mode for encryption. Keys need to be stored in a secure place for this.

1. **Generate a Secret Key and IV**:

   For AES-256-CBC, you need a 256-bit key (32 bytes) and an Initialization Vector (IV) of 128 bits (16 bytes). You can generate these using OpenSSL.

   Generate a 256-bit Key:

   ```
   openssl rand -hex 32 > aes256key.hex
   ```

   Generate a 128-bit IV:

   ```
   openssl rand -hex 16 > aes256iv.hex
   ```

Note: *IV is not the secret; this is for mitigating pattern analysis attacks. We need to make sure we provide a random IV each time when we encrypt data with the same key. IV can be stored along with encrypted data.*

2. **Encrypt the Sensitive Information File**:

   ```
   openssl enc -aes-256-cbc -in sensitive_info.txt -out encrypted_
   info.bin -K $(cat aes256key.hex) -iv $(cat aes256iv.hex)
   ```

Where,

a. **openssl enc -aes-256-cbc**: Specifies the AES-256-CBC encryption.

b. **-in sensitive_info.txt**: Input file to be encrypted.

c. **-out encrypted_info.bin**: Output file for the encrypted data.

d. **-K $(cat aes256key.hex):** Reads the encryption key from the generated key file.

e. **-iv $(cat aes256iv.hex):** Reads the IV from the generated IV file.

3. **Decrypt the File**

   To decrypt the encrypted file, use the same key and IV used in encryption.

```
openssl enc -d -aes-256-cbc -in encrypted_info.bin -out decrypted
_info.txt -K $(cat aes256key.hex) -iv $(cat aes256iv.hex)
```

Where,

a. **openssl enc -d -aes-256-cbc**: Indicates the AES-256-CBC decryption.

b. **-in encrypted_info.bin**: Input file to be decrypted.

c. **-out decrypted_info.txt:** Output file for the decrypted data.

d. **-K $(cat aes256key.hex):** Reads the decryption key from the generated key file.

e. **-iv $(cat aes256iv.hex):** Reads the IV from the generated IV file.

Common error:

```
Error: bad magic number
```

Root Cause:

- This error typically occurs if the input file is not in the expected format or if the wrong key/IV is used.
- **Solution**: Ensure that you use the correct key and IV for decryption and that the input file is the encrypted file.

Key and Certificate Management

OpenSSL-based key and certificate management has a variety of use cases across different domains. One primary use case is securing communications over the internet through TLS, where OpenSSL generates and manages keys and certificates to establish encrypted connections, such as HTTPS for websites. OpenSSL is also widely used in Virtual Private Networks (VPNs) to create secure tunnels for data transfer, ensuring confidentiality and integrity.

OpenSSL helps manage a Public Key Infrastructure (PKI), facilitating the issuance, renewal, and revocation of certificates for users and systems, enhancing overall security posture.

Key Generation

Generating an RSA Private Key:

```
openssl genpkey -algorithm RSA -out private.key -aes-256-cbc
```

This command generates a new RSA private key using OpenSSL.

1. The **`openssl genpkey -algorithm RSA`** part specifies that the RSA algorithm should be used to generate the private key.
2. The **`-out private.key`** part indicates that the generated private key should be saved to a file named **`private.key`**.
3. The **`-aes-256-cbc`** part specifies that the private key should be encrypted using the AES-256-CBC algorithm for added security.

Generating an EC Private Key (OpenSSL 3.0):

```
openssl genpkey -algorithm EC -out ecprivate.key -pkeyopt
ec_paramgen_curve:P-256
```

This command generates a new elliptic curve (**`EC`**) private key using OpenSSL.

1. The **`openssl genpkey -algorithm EC`** part specifies that the elliptic curve algorithm should be used to generate the private key.
2. The **`-out ecprivate.key`** part indicates that the generated private key should be saved to a file named **`ecprivate.key`**.
3. The **`-pkeyopt ec_paramgen_curve:P-256`** part specifies that the curve to be used for the elliptic curve key generation is **`P-256`**.

Certificate Signing Requests (CSR):

```
openssl req -new -key private.key -out request.csr
```

This command generates a new Certificate Signing Request (CSR) using OpenSSL:

1. The **`openssl req -new`** part specifies that a new CSR is being created.
2. The **`-key private.key`** part indicates the private key file to be used, named **`private.key`**.
3. The -out request.csr part specifies the output file where the generated CSR will be saved, named **`request.csr`**.

The CSR is then used to request a certificate from a Certificate Authority (CA).

Signing a CSR to Create a Certificate:

```
openssl x509 -req -in request.csr -signkey private.key -out
certificate.crt
```

This command generates a self-signed X.509 certificate using OpenSSL.

1. The **`openssl x509 -req`** part specifies that the input is a Certificate Signing Request (CSR).
2. The **`-in request.csr`** part indicates the CSR file to be used, named **`request.csr`**.
3. The **`-signkey private.key`** part specifies the private key file used to sign the certificate, named **`private.key`**.
4. The **`-out certificate.crt`** part specifies the output file where the generated certificate will be saved, named **`certificate.crt`**.
5. This self-signed certificate can be used for testing or internal purposes where a trusted third-party CA-signed certificate is not required.

Certificate Management:

Viewing a Certificate:

```
openssl x509 -in certificate.crt -text -noout
```

This command displays the textual representation of an X.509 certificate using OpenSSL.

1. The **`openssl x509 -in`** certificate.crt part specifies the input file containing the X.509 certificate to be examined, named certificate.crt.
2. The **`-text`** option instructs OpenSSL to display the certificate details in text format.
3. The **`-noout`** option ensures that only the textual representation is shown without any other output.

This command is useful for inspecting the contents of a certificate, including its subject, issuer, validity period, and public key details.

Verifying a Certificate:

```
openssl verify -CAfile ca.crt certificate.crt
```

This command verifies the validity of an X.509 certificate using OpenSSL:

1. The **`openssl verify -CAfile ca.crt`** part specifies that the verification should use the Certificate Authority (CA) certificate file named **`ca.crt`** as the trusted anchor.

2. The **certificate.crt** part indicates the certificate file to be verified against the CA.

OpenSSL checks if the certificate chains properly to the CA, ensuring its validity and authenticity according to the trust chain established by the CA certificate provided. This is crucial in validating certificates used in secure communications, ensuring they are issued by a trusted authority and have not been tampered with.

Here are some reasons why verification can fail along with example error messages:

- **Invalid Key Usage**:

  Error Message:

  `error 26 at 0 depth lookup:unsupported certificate purpose`

  The certificate is being used for a purpose not intended or allowed by its key usage extensions.

- **Mismatched Hostname**:

  Error Message:

  `error 62 at 0 depth lookup:Hostname mismatch`

  The hostname in the certificate does not match the hostname being verified.

- **Certificate Not Yet Valid**:

  Error Message:

  `error 9 at 0 depth lookup:certificate is not yet valid`

  The certificate's start date is in the future, making it not valid at the time of verification.

- **Certificate Expired:**

  Error Message:

  `error 10 at 0 depth lookup:certificate has expired`

  The certificate being verified has passed its validity period and is no longer valid.

- **Invalid CA Certificate**:

  Error Message:

  `error 18 at 0 depth lookup:self-signed certificate`

  The certificate chain includes a self-signed certificate that is not trusted because it is not in the CA file.

- **Certificate Revoked**:

  Error Message:

  `error 23 at 0 depth lookup:certificate revoked`

The certificate has been revoked and is listed in the Certificate Revocation List (CRL).

- **Untrusted Root CA**:

  Error Message:

  `error 20 at 0 depth lookup:unable to get local issuer certificate`

  The root CA certificate is not trusted or not included in the CA file, making it impossible to complete the certificate chain.

- **Intermediate Certificate Missing**:

  Error Message:

  `error 2 at 1 depth lookup:unable to get issuer certificate`

  An intermediate certificate required to complete the chain from the certificate to the root CA is missing.

- **Invalid Certificate Signature**:

  Error Message:

  `error 7 at 0 depth lookup:certificate signature failure`

  The signature on the certificate is invalid, possibly due to corruption or tampering.

- **Unsupported Algorithm**:

  Error Message:

  `error 65 at 0 depth lookup:unsupported algorithm`

  The certificate uses an algorithm that is not supported by the OpenSSL version being used.

Certificate Format Conversion:

OpenSSL supports various certificate formats such as Privacy Enhanced Mail (PEM), Distinguished Encoding Rules (DER), PKCS#7, and PKCS#12. We may need to convert the X.509 certificates from one format to another so that they can be effectively utilized across diverse environments, enhancing interoperability and security while meeting application-specific needs.

Example Commands

PEM to DER:

```
openssl x509 -in certificate.crt -outform der -out certificate.der
```

This command converts an X.509 certificate file (**`certificate.crt`**) from PEM format to DER format (**`certificate.der`**).

1. The **-outform der** option specifies the output format as DER, which is a binary format.

   This conversion is useful for applications or systems that require certificates in DER format, such as certain embedded devices or binary-based protocols.

PKCS#12 to PEM

```
openssl pkcs12 -in cert_in.pfx -out cert_out.pem -nodes
```

This command converts a PKCS#12 file (**cert_in.pfx**) containing certificates and possibly private keys into a PEM format file (**cert_out.pem**).

1. The **-nodes** option specifies that the private key should not be encrypted with a passphrase, ensuring it is in plain text within the PEM file.

   This is useful for applications that require PEM format certificates without encryption, such as some web servers or development environments.

Public Key Infrastructure (PKI)

By leveraging OpenSSL's robust features and capabilities, organizations can effectively establish and maintain a secure PKI, enabling encrypted communication, secure authentication, and reliable digital signatures across their networks and applications.

Let us see how we can achieve this using some example commands.

Creating a Certificate Authority (CA)

Setting up a CA:

```
openssl req -new -x509 -keyout ca.key -out ca.crt -days 3650
```

This command generates a self-signed X.509 certificate for a Certificate Authority (CA) using OpenSSL.

1. The **-new -x509** options specify that a new certificate request (**req**) should be created and self-signed (**x509**).
2. The **-keyout ca.key** option specifies the output file (**ca.key**) where the generated private key for the CA will be saved.
3. The **-out ca.crt** option specifies the output file (**ca.crt**) where the self-signed CA certificate will be saved.
4. The **-days 3650** option sets the validity period of the certificate to 10 years (3650 days), after which it expires unless renewed or reissued.

This command is essential for establishing a root CA certificate that can then be used to issue and sign other certificates within a PKI.

Issuing and Revoking Certificates

Issuing Certificates:

```
openssl ca -in request.csr -out certificate.crt -cert ca.crt -key-
file ca.key
```

This command processes a Certificate Signing Request (CSR) using OpenSSL's built-in CA functionality.

1. The **`-in request.csr`** specifies the input CSR file that contains the certificate request to be signed.
2. The **`-out certificate.crt`** specifies the output file where the signed certificate (**`certificate.crt`**) will be saved.
3. The **`-cert ca.crt`** specifies the CA certificate file (**`ca.crt`**) used to sign the CSR, establishing the trust chain.
4. The **`-keyfile ca.key`** specifies the private key file (**`ca.key`**) associated with the CA certificate, allowing OpenSSL to sign the certificate request securely.

This process is crucial in PKI environments for issuing trusted certificates signed by a designated Certificate Authority.

Revoking Certificates:

```
openssl ca -revoke certificate.crt -keyfile ca.key -cert ca.crt
```

1. **`openssl ca`**: Initiates the OpenSSL command for performing Certificate Authority (CA) operations.
2. **`-revoke certificate.crt`**: Specifies the certificate file (**`certificate.crt`**) to be revoked. This command marks the specified certificate as revoked in the CA's records.
3. **`-keyfile ca.key`**: Specifies the private key file (**`ca.key`**) associated with the CA certificate. This key file is used to authenticate and authorize the revocation operation.
4. **`-cert ca.crt`**: Specifies the CA certificate file (ca.crt) that signed the certificate being revoked. This file is used to validate the authority under which the certificate was issued, ensuring that only authorized entities can revoke certificates.

Using these parameters, the **`openssl ca -revoke`** command allows a Certificate Authority to maintain the integrity of its issued certificates by marking them as revoked, when necessary, thereby preventing their misuse after issuance.

Generating a CRL:

```
openssl ca -gencrl -out crl.pem -keyfile ca.key -cert ca.crt
```

1. **openssl ca**: Initiates the OpenSSL command for performing Certificate Authority (CA) operations.
2. **-gencrl**: Specifies that a Certificate Revocation List (CRL) should be generated. This command instructs OpenSSL to create a new CRL.
3. **-out crl.pem**: Specifies the output file (**crl.pem**) where the generated CRL will be saved. The CRL contains information about certificates that have been revoked by the CA.
4. **-keyfile ca.key**: Specifies the private key file (**ca.key**) associated with the CA certificate. This key file is used to sign the generated CRL, ensuring its authenticity and integrity.
5. **-cert ca.crt**: Specifies the CA certificate file (**ca.crt**) that signed the CRL. This file is used to validate the authority under which the CRL was issued, ensuring that it comes from a trusted source.

Using these parameters, the **openssl ca -gencrl** command allows a CA to generate a new Certificate Revocation List (CRL), which is essential for maintaining the security and trustworthiness of its certificate infrastructure by listing revoked certificates.

TLS Connections Testing

The **openssl s_client** command is used for testing and troubleshooting TLS connections. Following are practical examples demonstrating its various uses:

- **Testing TLS Connection to a Server:**

  ```
  openssl s_client -connect example.com:443
  ```

  This command connects to example.com on port 443 (HTTPS) and provides detailed information about the TLS handshake. It includes server certificate details, cipher suite negotiation, and protocol version, aiding in verifying server configuration and diagnosing connection issues.

- **Checking TLS Certificate Chain:**

  ```
  openssl s_client -connect example.com:443 -showcerts
  ```

  Adding -**showcerts** displays the complete certificate chain presented during the handshake. This includes all intermediate certificates up to the root CA certificate, ensuring the validity and correctness of the certificate chain.

- **Debugging SMTP/POP3/IMAP SSL/TLS Connections:**

  ```
  openssl s_client -connect mail.example.com:465 -crlf
  ```

This command connects to mail.example.com on port 465 (SMTPS) and converts line endings to CRLF format with **-crlf**. It aids in debugging TLS connections for secure email communications.

- **Testing TLS Version and Cipher Suites**:

```
openssl s_client -connect example.com:443 -tls1_2 -cipher AES256-SHA256
```

  Here, **-tls1_2** specifies TLS version 1.2, and **-cipher AES256-SHA256** specifies a cipher suite. This tests server support for specific TLS versions and cipher suites, ensuring compatibility and security configuration.

- **Extracting Server Certificate**:

```
openssl s_client -connect example.com:443 </dev/null 2>/dev/null | openssl x509 -outform PEM >server.crt
```

  This command connects to example.com on port **443**, suppresses interactive input, and pipes the server certificate to **openssl x509**. It converts the certificate to PEM format and saves it to **server.crt**, useful for further analysis or validation.

- **Testing TLS with Client Authentication**:

```
openssl s_client -connect example.com:443 -cert client.crt -key client.key
```

  Using **-cert client.crt** for the client certificate file and **-key client.key** for the private key file, this command tests TLS connections requiring client authentication. It facilitates mutual authentication where the client presents its certificate during the handshake.

Advanced Commands

We have so far covered all the commands that are commonly used across the security applications. In this topic, we will cover some advanced commands that are not frequently used but are very powerful for some specific applications.

S/MIME Operations

OpenSSL plays a crucial role in Secure/Multipurpose Internet Mail Extensions (S/MIME) operations, facilitating secure email communication through digital signatures and encryption. It supports the creation, signing, verification, and decryption of S/MIME messages using X.509 certificates and cryptographic algorithms. OpenSSL's functionalities include generating key pairs, managing certificates, and encoding messages in MIME format, ensuring confidentiality and integrity of email content. It is widely employed in email clients and servers to implement standards-compliant S/MIME solutions for safeguarding sensitive information exchanged via email.

Encrypting an Email:

```
openssl smime -encrypt -in plaintext.txt -out encrypted.txt
-outform PEM user.pem
```

1. **`-encrypt`**: Specifies that the command should encrypt the input data (**`plaintext.txt`**) using S/MIME encryption.
2. **`-in plaintext.txt`**: Specifies the input file (**`plaintext.txt`**) containing the plaintext data to be encrypted.
3. **`-out encrypted.txt`**: Specifies the output file (**`encrypted.txt`**) where the encrypted data will be saved.
4. **`-outform PEM`**: Specifies the output format (PEM) for the encrypted data. Privacy Enhanced Mail (PEM) is a Base64-encoded format commonly used for encoding cryptographic data.
5. **`user.pem`**: Specifies the recipient's public key file (**`user.pem`**) used for encryption. The data will be encrypted such that only the owner of **`user.pem`**'s corresponding private key can decrypt it.

This command encrypts **`plaintext.txt`** using the recipient's public key (**`user.pem`**), saves the encrypted data to **`encrypted.txt`** in PEM format, and ensures secure transmission or storage of sensitive information.

Decrypting an Email:

```
openssl smime -decrypt -in encrypted.txt -inform PEM -inkey
private.key
```

1. **`-decrypt`**: Specifies that the command should decrypt the input data (**`encrypted.txt`**) using S/MIME decryption.
2. **`-in encrypted.txt`**: Specifies the input file (**`encrypted.txt`**) containing the encrypted data to be decrypted.
3. **`-inform PEM`**: Specifies the input format (PEM) of the encrypted data. PEM is a Base64-encoded format commonly used for encoding cryptographic data.
4. **`-inkey private.key`**: Specifies the private key file (**`private.key`**) corresponding to the recipient's public key used for encryption. This private key is necessary to decrypt the data encrypted with the corresponding public key.

This command decrypts **`encrypted.txt`** using the private key (**`private.key`**), recovering the original plaintext data that was encrypted using S/MIME, ensuring confidentiality and integrity of the communication.

PKCS#12 Operations

Creating a PKCS#12 File:

```
openssl pkcs12 -export -out certificate.p12 -inkey private.key -in
certificate.crt
-certfile ca.crt
```

1. **`-export`**: Specifies that the command should create a new PKCS#12 file (**`certificate.p12`**) by exporting the specified certificates and private key into a single file.
2. **`-out certificate.p12`**: Specifies the output file (**`certificate.p12`**) where the PKCS#12 file will be saved.
3. **`-inkey private.key`**: Specifies the input file (**`private.key`**) containing the private key associated with certificate.crt. This private key is necessary for inclusion in the PKCS#12 file.
4. **`-in certificate.crt`**: Specifies the input file (**`certificate.crt`**) containing the certificate to be included in the PKCS#12 file.
5. **`-certfile ca.crt`**: Specifies an additional file (**`ca.crt`**) containing CA certificates that may be necessary for certificate chain validation.

This command creates a new PKCS#12 file (**`certificate.p12`**) that includes the private key (**`private.key`**), the certificate (**`certificate.crt`**), and any necessary CA certificates (**`ca.crt`**). PKCS#12 files are commonly used to securely store and transport certificates and private keys, often used in scenarios such as secure email client configurations or certificate distribution.

Online Certificate Status Protocol (OCSP) Commands

OCSP Request: OCSP requests play a vital role in ensuring that certificates used in TLS connections, email encryption, code signing, and other secure communications are valid and have not been revoked, contributing to the trust and reliability of digital interactions on the internet.

Example of OpenSSL command to check the status of the certificate:

```
openssl ocsp -issuer ca.crt -cert certificate.crt -url http://
ocsp.example.com
```

1. **`-issuer ca.crt`**: Specifies the issuer's certificate file (**`ca.crt`**) that issued the certificate (certificate.crt) being checked. This helps OpenSSL find the correct Certificate Authority (CA) to verify the certificate's validity.
2. **`-cert certificate.crt`**: Specifies the certificate file (**`certificate.crt`**) for which the OCSP request will be generated. This is the certificate whose status (valid, revoked, or unknown) will be checked.

3. **-url http://ocsp.example.com**: Specifies the URL (**http://ocsp.example.com**) of the OCSP responder. This is where OpenSSL sends the OCSP request to check the status of certificate.crt.

This command sends an OCSP request to the specified OCSP responder (http://ocsp.example.com) to check the validity status of certificate.crt issued by the CA (**ca.crt**). OCSP is used to determine if a certificate is currently valid or has been revoked, providing real-time certificate status information for secure communications and trust validation in PKI environments.

Miscellaneous Utilities

This section covers miscellaneous utilities, including random number generation and time operations.

Random Number Generation

Generating Random Bytes:

```
openssl rand -base64 32
```

1. **-base64**: Specifies that the output should be encoded in Base64 format. This encoding converts binary data into a text format, making it easier to handle and transfer.
2. **32**: Specifies the number of bytes (or characters in Base64 encoding) to generate. In this case, it generates 32 bytes of random data.

This command generates **32** random bytes and outputs them in Base64-encoded format. It is commonly used to generate cryptographic keys, initialization vectors, or any other random data required for secure operations in applications such as encryption, authentication, and digital signatures.

Time Operations

Converting and manipulating ASN.1 Time:

```
openssl asn1parse -in asn1time.der
```

1. **-in asn1time.der**: Specifies the input file (**asn1time.der**) containing **ASN.1** encoded data. Distinguished Encoding Rules (DER) is a binary encoding format used for **ASN.1** data.

This command parses the **ASN.1** encoded data in asn1time.der, displaying its structure and content. **ASN.1** is a notation used to describe data structures independent of machine-specific encoding, often used in cryptographic protocols, certificates, and other data formats requiring structured representation.

Using Scripts for OpenSSL Commands

Using scripts with OpenSSL commands enhances productivity, security, and reliability in cryptographic operations, making them an essential tool for administrators and security professionals.

Benefits:

- **Automation:** Scripts automate repetitive tasks, reducing the risk of human error and saving time.

  They can be scheduled to run at specific times, ensuring regular tasks are performed consistently without manual intervention.

- **Consistency:** Scripts ensure that the same commands are executed with the same parameters every time, providing uniform results.

  They help maintain consistency in operations, especially in environments where multiple administrators might be performing tasks.

- **Efficiency:** Scripts can handle multiple files or operations in a batch, making processes more efficient.

  They streamline complex sequences of commands, reducing the overall time and effort required for cryptographic operations.

- **Error Handling:** Scripts can include error-checking mechanisms to handle and log errors, providing feedback and ensuring issues are addressed promptly.

  They can be designed to perform actions based on the success or failure of previous commands, improving robustness.

- **Reproducibility:** Scripts ensure that procedures are reproducible, which is crucial for debugging and verifying cryptographic operations.

  They allow for the exact replication of tasks in different environments or systems.

- **Scalability:** Scripts can be easily modified to scale operations up or down, making it simple to adapt to changing requirements.

  They can handle large-scale operations across multiple systems or environments efficiently.

Following are some examples that will show you how to write scripts based on use cases.

There are a lot of use cases for the script, but we will see only two examples here.

Script to Check Expired Certificates in the Directory

```
#!/bin/bash

# Usage function to display help
usage() {
    echo "Usage: $0 -d <cert_directory> -a <alert_days>"
    exit 1
}

# Parse command-line arguments
while getopts ":d:a:" opt; do
    case $opt in
        d) CERT_DIR="$OPTARG"
        ;;
        a) ALERT_DAYS="$OPTARG"
        ;;
        *) usage
        ;;
    esac
done

# Check if both arguments are provided
if [ -z "$CERT_DIR" ] || [ -z "$ALERT_DAYS" ]; then
    usage
fi

# Check if the certificate directory valid
if [ ! -d "$CERT_DIR" ]; then
    echo "Error: Directory $CERT_DIR does not exist."
    exit 1
fi

# Check if the alert days is a valid number
if ! [[ "$ALERT_DAYS" =~ ^[0-9]+$ ]]; then
    echo "Error: Alert days must be a valid number."
    exit 1
fi

# Check certificate expiration dates for all certificates in the
provided directory
for CERT in "$CERT_DIR"/*.crt; do
    if openssl x509 -checkend $((ALERT_DAYS * 86400)) -noout -in
"$CERT"; then
```

```
            echo "Certificate $(basename "$CERT") is still valid."
        else
            echo "ALERT: Certificate $(basename "$CERT") is expiring 
within $ALERT_DAYS days!"
        fi
done
```

To use this script, you would run it with the -d option for the certificate directory and the -a option for the alert days.

Example: This example will check for expiry status of certificates in current directory (expiring in 30 days).

```
./check_expiry.sh -d ava_book/ -a 30
```

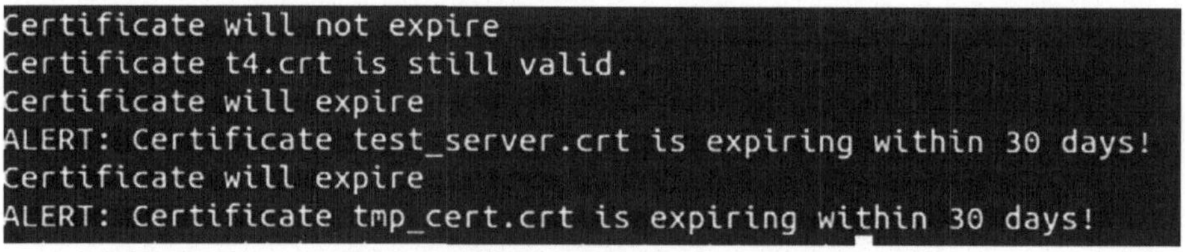

Figure 3.3: *Expiry status of certificates*

Script for Creating Digital Signature and Verification

```
#!/bin/bash

# Usage function

usage() {
    echo "Usage: $0 {sign|verify} filename -k <keyfile>"
    exit 1
}

# Parse command-line arguments
OPERATION=$1
FILE=$2
shift 2

while getopts ":k:" opt; do
    case $opt in
        k) KEYFILE="$OPTARG"
        ;;
        *) usage
        ;;
    esac
done

# Check if the key file argument is provided
```

```
if [ -z "$KEYFILE" ]; then
    usage
fi

# Sign or verify the file based on the action
if [ "$OPERATION" == "sign" ]; then
    openssl dgst -sha256 -sign "$KEYFILE" -out "${FILE}.sig" "$FILE"
    if [ $? -eq 0 ]; then
        echo "File signed, signature stored in ${FILE}.sig"
    else
        echo "Error signing file."
        exit 1
    fi
elif [ "$OPERATION" == "verify" ]; then
    openssl dgst -sha256 -verify "$KEYFILE" -signature "${FILE}.sig" "$FILE"
    if [ $? -eq 0 ]; then
        echo "Signature verified successfully."
    else
        echo "Signature verification failed."
        exit 1
    fi
else
    usage
fi
```

Example:

```
./digital_signature.sh sign testfile -k private_key.pem
```

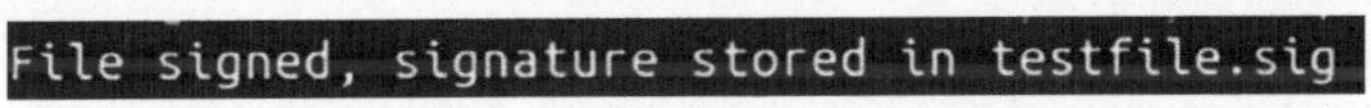

Figure 3.4: *Creating digital signature*

```
./digital_signature.sh verify testfile -k public_key.pem
```

Figure 3.5: *Verification*

Conclusion

In this chapter, we covered important commands along with some useful examples. These commands will be your quick reference. We have not covered all the possible combinations and parameters from the commands. You can experiment with those by referring to help command.

By categorizing commands based on practical use cases, this chapter has offered a structured approach to understanding and utilizing OpenSSL efficiently. The inclusion of real-world examples and troubleshooting guidance ensures that users can confidently apply these commands in various scenarios. With a strong foundation in OpenSSL CLI, you are now well-equipped to integrate these tools into security workflows, automate cryptographic tasks, and effectively manage PKI environments.

In the next chapter, we will cover OpenSSL from a coding perspective. This will help you to integrate OpenSSL operations into your application.

CHAPTER 4
OpenSSL C library APIs

Introduction

The OpenSSL library provides a powerful set of C APIs that allow developers to implement cryptographic functionality and secure communications in their applications. These APIs are critical for achieving tasks such as encryption, decryption, digital signatures, key exchange, secure data transmission, and so on.

If OpenSSL is installed on your machine, you should be able to use those libraries just by doing #include for the correct header file in your code. If you want to check the source code and example code, you can check the following GitHub link:

https://github.com/openssl/openssl

Though a lot of example code and support pages are available on the internet, this section will give you an overview of APIs in an organized way along with related examples.

This diagram shows OpenSSL 3.0 C library organization. We will discuss all these modules in the subsequent section.

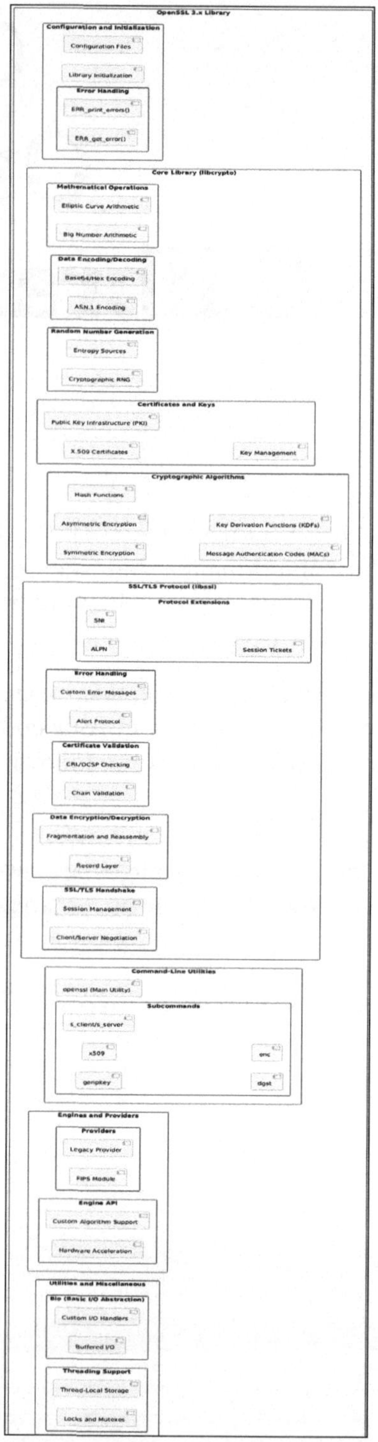

Figure 4.1: *OpenSSL 3.0 C Library Organization*

Structure

In this chapter, we will cover the following topics:

- Library Initialization
- Core Library (**libcrypto**)
- SSL/TLS Communication
- Engine and Providers
- Utilities and Miscellaneous

Library Initialization

OpenSSL (**libssl** and **libcrypto**) allocates various resources during startup that need to be properly freed when the library is shut down. In multi-threaded applications, additional resources are allocated for each thread, and these must be freed before the thread terminates.

Initialization logic has somewhat changed between the versions, so we have to be careful while upgrading to newer versions or writing the code where only older versions are supported.

- **Pre-OpenSSL 1.1.0 (Before 2016):** In versions prior to OpenSSL 1.1.0, applications needed to manually initialize the libraries using functions such as **SSL_library_init()** for the SSL/TLS library (**libssl**) and **OpenSSL_add_all_algorithms()** for the cryptographic encryption algorithms library (**libcrypto**). **OpenSSL_add_all_ciphers()** and **OpenSSL_add_all_digests()** used to load ciphers and digests.

  Initialization was not automatically handled by the library, so failing to call these functions would result in incorrect or incomplete setup.

- **OpenSSL 1.1.0 and Later:** With the release of OpenSSL 1.1.0, **OPENSSL_init_ssl()** was introduced to streamline the initialization process. It unified the initialization of both libssl and **libcrypto** into a single function call, simplifying the setup for applications.

  Automatic Initialization: Starting in OpenSSL 1.1.0, the need for explicit initialization using **OPENSSL_init_ssl()** became less strict because OpenSSL started automatically initializing itself when the first SSL-related function was called. However, explicit initialization is still recommended, especially in complex applications where control over the initialization process is required. Important changes are **SSL_library_init()**, **SSL_load_error_strings()**, and others that are now no-ops or deprecated. No need to call any cleanup functions.

For use case example:

```
#include <openssl/ssl.h>

// Just use SSL functions, no explicit initialization needed
SSL_CTX *ctx = SSL_CTX_new(TLS_client_method());
```

Key differences are shown in *Table* 4.1:

Version	**Changes**
Pre-OpenSSL 1.1.0 (Before 2016):	Manual Initialization and cleanup required
OpenSSL 1.1.0 and Later or 3.x	Initialization and cleanup are automatic

Table 4.1: *Key Differences*

SSL Library Initialization

The recommended way to initialize the SSL Library in OpenSSL 1.1.x and later, including version 3.x.

```
#include <openssl/ssl.h>

int OPENSSL_init_ssl(uint64_t opts, const OPENSSL_INIT_SETTINGS
*settings);
```

- **`opts`**: specify initialization options.
- **`settings`**: For advanced configuration, "**`NULL`**" can be used for default settings.

While **`OPENSSL_init_ssl(0, NULL)`** can be called for the most common use cases, there are situations where custom parameters are necessary to control specific aspects of OpenSSL's initialization process. Some examples are provided as follows:

FIPS Mode Activation

Scenario: You need to ensure that your application is compliant with the Federal Information Processing Standards (FIPS), which require using only FIPS-approved cryptographic algorithms and processes.

Custom Parameter:

```
OPENSSL_INIT_LOAD_CONFIG | OPENSSL_INIT_ENGINE_ALL_BUILTIN |
OPENSSL_INIT_NO_LOAD_CRYPTO_STRINGS
```

Explanation: In OpenSSL 3.0, the FIPS module is provided as a provider. To enable FIPS mode, you might need to load a specific configuration file that initializes the FIPS provider. You can pass the **`OPENSSL_INIT_LOAD_CONFIG`** flag to ensure that the OpenSSL configuration is loaded, which may include settings to enable the FIPS mode.

```
#include <stdio.h>
      #include <openssl/evp.h>
      #include <openssl/provider.h>
      #include <openssl/conf.h>

      int main() {
          // Initialize OpenSSL with configuration loading enabled
          if (OPENSSL_init_ssl(OPENSSL_INIT_LOAD_CONFIG, NULL) != 1) {
              fprintf(stderr, "Error initializing OpenSSL with
      configuration\n");
              return 1;
          }

          // Load the FIPS provider
          OSSL_PROVIDER *fips = OSSL_PROVIDER_load(NULL, "fips");
          if (fips == NULL) {
              fprintf(stderr, "Failed to load FIPS provider\n");
              ERR_print_errors_fp(stderr);
              return 1;
          }

          printf("FIPS mode enabled successfully.\n");

          // Perform cryptographic operations here

          // Cleanup: Unload the FIPS provider
          OSSL_PROVIDER_unload(fips);

          return 0;
      }
```

Custom Engine Initialization

Scenario: You want to use a custom cryptographic engine (for example, hardware accelerators or specific cryptographic modules) instead of the default software implementations provided by OpenSSL.

Custom Parameter:

```
OPENSSL_INIT_ENGINE_ALL_BUILTIN
```

Explanation: By passing the **OPENSSL_INIT_ENGINE_ALL_BUILTIN** flag, you ensure that all built-in cryptographic engines are initialized. If your application relies on specific hardware acceleration for cryptographic operations, this flag is necessary.

API call example:

```
if (OPENSSL_init_ssl(OPENSSL_INIT_ENGINE_ALL_BUILTIN, NULL) != 1)
{
    // Handle initialization failure
}
```

Disabling Auto-Loading of Strings

Scenario: Your application runs in a resource-constrained environment, such as an embedded system, and you want to minimize memory usage by preventing OpenSSL from loading human-readable error strings.

Custom Parameter:

```
OPENSSL_INIT_NO_LOAD_CRYPTO_STRINGS
```

Explanation:

By passing the **OPENSSL_INIT_NO_LOAD_CRYPTO_STRINGS** flag, you prevent OpenSSL from loading the error strings that translate error codes into human-readable text. This saves memory but may make debugging more difficult.

API call example:

```
if (OPENSSL_init_ssl(OPENSSL_INIT_NO_LOAD_CRYPTO_STRINGS, NULL)
!= 1) {
    // Handle initialization failure
}
```

Manual Configuration of Cryptographic Algorithms

Scenario: You want to ensure that only a specific set of cryptographic algorithms or providers are available to your application, either for compliance reasons or to reduce the attack surface.

Custom Parameter:

```
OPENSSL_INIT_NO_ADD_ALL_CIPHERS | OPENSSL_INIT_NO_ADD_ALL_DIGESTS
```

Explanation: Passing these flags prevents OpenSSL from automatically adding all ciphers and digests, allowing you to manually control which algorithms are available. This can be important in security-critical environments where you need to restrict the algorithms in use.

API call example:

```
if (OPENSSL_init_ssl(OPENSSL_INIT_NO_ADD_ALL_CIPHERS | OPENSSL_
INIT_NO_ADD_ALL_DIGESTS, NULL) != 1) {
    // Handle initialization failure
}
```

Custom Configuration File Loading

Scenario: You have a custom OpenSSL configuration file that defines specific providers, algorithms, or settings, and you need to load this configuration during initialization.

Custom Parameter:

```
OPENSSL_INIT_LOAD_CONFIG
```

Explanation: The `OPENSSL_INIT_LOAD_CONFIG` flag ensures that OpenSSL loads its configuration from a file, typically `openssl.cnf`. This file can define provider settings, enable FIPS mode, set specific cipher suites, and so on. This is especially useful if your application needs to initialize specific settings without hard-coding them in the source code.

API call example:

```
if (OPENSSL_init_ssl(OPENSSL_INIT_LOAD_CONFIG, NULL) != 1) {
    // Handle initialization failure
}
```

Pre-Initialization Hooks

Scenario: You need to perform certain operations before the initialization of OpenSSL, such as setting up custom memory management functions or configuring environment-specific settings.

Custom Parameter:

Custom initialization flags combined with `OPENSSL_INIT_SETTINGS`.

Explanation: You may need to set custom initialization parameters that are not covered by the predefined flags. By setting up your own pre-initialization routines, you can modify how OpenSSL allocates memory or handles its internal state.

API call example:

```
OPENSSL_INIT_SETTINGS *settings = OPENSSL_INIT_new();
// Custom settings can be applied here
OPENSSL_init_ssl(0, settings);
```

Crypto Library Initialization

Starting from version 1.1.x, OpenSSL automatically handles the allocation of all necessary resources, eliminating the need for explicit initialization. Likewise, it will automatically perform deinitialization when required.

However, there are cases where explicit initialization may be preferred or necessary, such as when non-default initialization settings are required. The function **OPENSSL_init_crypto()** can be used for this purpose to initialize:

```
int OPENSSL_init_crypto(uint64_t opts, const OPENSSL_INIT_SET-
TINGS *settings);
```

One more thing, if you have already initialized the SSL library using **OPENSSL_init_ssl()**, then it internally initializes the crypto library, and hence you do not need to explicitly call this API again.

The parameters for custom initialization using this API are the same as those of **OPENSSL_init_ssl()**, hence will not be repeated here.

Loading Custom Configuration File

The OpenSSL library uses the configuration from **openssl.cnf** by default, which is available at the default path based on installation.

But we can load configuration from a custom configuration file if needed in a particular application.

```
int CONF_modules_load_file(const char *filename, const char
*appname,
                                        unsigned long flags);
```

Example for loading from a file:

```
    const char *custom_configuration_file = "/path/to/your/custom_
openssl.cnf";

    if (CONF_modules_load_file(custom_configuration_file, NULL, 0)
<= 0) {
        fprintf(stderr, "Error loading custom OpenSSL
configuration file: %s\n", custom_configuration_file);
        ERR_print_errors_fp(stderr);
        return -1;
    }
```

There is another way to load configuration from the **CONF** structure:

```
int CONF_modules_load(const CONF *cnf, const char *appname,
                                unsigned long flags);
```

This can be used when you want to modify configuration loaded from a file and then apply it.

Example:

```
    CONF *conf = NCONF_new(NULL);
      if (conf == NULL) {
          fprintf(stderr, "CONF structurecreation failed\n");
```

```
        ERR_print_errors_fp(stderr);
        return -1;
    }

    const char *config_file = "/path/to/your/custom_openssl.cnf";
    long errorline = 0;

   // Load CONF structure with configuration file data
    if (NCONF_load(conf, config_file, &errorline) <= 0) {
        fprintf(stderr, "Error loading configuration file at line
%ld\n", errorline);
        ERR_print_errors_fp(stderr);
        NCONF_free(conf);
        return -1;
    }

    const char *appname = NULL;  // Specify an application name
if needed, otherwise NULL
    unsigned long flags = 0;     // You can use flags if needded

//// You can modify the context of CONF here

// Load the configuration from CONF strucure
    if (CONF_modules_load(conf, appname, flags) <= 0) {
        fprintf(stderr, "Error loading and processing configura-
tion modules\n");
        ERR_print_errors_fp(stderr);
        NCONF_free(conf);
        return -1;
    }
```

This table summarizes differences between the two mentioned approaches:

	CONF_load()	**CONF_modules_load_file()**
Level	Low-level (manual configuration handling)	High-level (automatic module initialization)
Functionality	Loads a configuration file into a CONF structure	Loads and processes a configuration file, initializes modules
Module Initialization	No	Yes
Use Case	Manual parsing and processing of configuration data	Automatic setup of OpenSSL environment from config
Typical Scenario	Custom parsing of configuration settings	Applying OpenSSL configurations such as providers and engines

Control	Provides fine-grained control over configuration handling	Simplifies configuration by automatically processing OpenSSL-specific settings

Table 4.2: *Loading configurations methods comparison*

Core Library (`libcrypto`)

`libcrypto` is the core library of OpenSSL, offering a comprehensive suite of cryptographic operations essential for securing data. It provides the fundamental building blocks for cryptographic applications, including encryption, decryption, key generation, hashing, and random number generation. **`libcrypto`** is designed to support a wide variety of cryptographic algorithms, such as symmetric ciphers (for example, AES, DES), asymmetric ciphers (for example, RSA, ECC), and hashing algorithms (for example, SHA-256). Additionally, it enables developers to manage digital certificates, generate cryptographic keys, sign and verify data, and handle various cryptographic protocols.

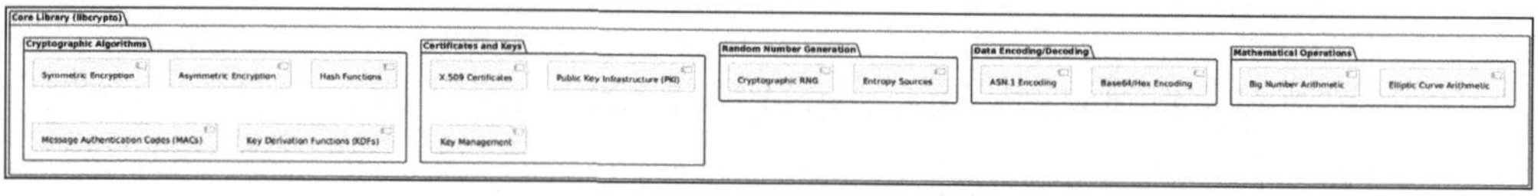

Figure 4.2: *Libcrypto organization*

This section provides some key APIs for reference. We will cover details for some of these functionalities commonly used in the field in a separate section.

We have already covered initialization APIs in previous sections. We will not repeat it here.

Message Digests (Hashing)

Hash functions transform input data into a fixed-size string of bytes. Hashing is essential for data integrity, password storage, and digital signatures.

Key APIs:

- **`EVP_DigestInit()`**: Initializes a digest context.
- **`EVP_DigestUpdate()`**: Adds data to the digest.
- **`EVP_DigestFinal()`**: Finalizes the digest and retrieves the hash value.

Example code snippet:

```
EVP_MD_CTX *mdctx = EVP_MD_CTX_new();
unsigned char hash[EVP_MAX_MD_SIZE];
unsigned int hash_len;
```

```
EVP_DigestInit(mdctx, EVP_sha256());
EVP_DigestUpdate(mdctx, "Hello, World!", 13);
EVP_DigestFinal(mdctx, hash, &hash_len);

EVP_MD_CTX_free(mdctx);
```

Use Cases:

Verifying the integrity of data.

Creating hashes for digital signatures.

Symmetric Encryption

Symmetric encryption uses a single key for both encryption and decryption. OpenSSL provides support for algorithms such as AES and DES.

Key APIs:

- **`EVP_EncryptInit()`**: Initializes the encryption context.
- **`EVP_EncryptUpdate()`**: Encrypts data.
- **`EVP_EncryptFinal()`**: Finalizes the encryption process.

Example code snippet:

```
EVP_CIPHER_CTX *ctx = EVP_CIPHER_CTX_new();
unsigned char key[32], iv[16], ciphertext[128];
int len;

EVP_EncryptInit(ctx, EVP_aes_256_cbc(), key, iv);
EVP_EncryptUpdate(ctx, ciphertext, &len, plaintext, plaintext_
len);
EVP_EncryptFinal(ctx, ciphertext + len, &len);

EVP_CIPHER_CTX_free(ctx);
```

Use Cases:

- Encrypting sensitive data for storage.
- Securing communications between parties.

Asymmetric Encryption (Public-Key Cryptography)

Asymmetric encryption uses a pair of keys, that is, a public key for encryption and a private key for decryption. It is widely used for secure key exchanges and digital signatures.

Key APIs:

- **RSA_public_encrypt()**: Encrypts data with a public key.
- **RSA_private_decrypt()**: Decrypts data with a private key.

Example code snippet:

```
RSA *rsa = RSA_new();
unsigned char ciphertext[256];
int ciphertext_len;

ciphertext_len = RSA_public_encrypt(data_len, data, ciphertext,
rsa, RSA_PKCS1_OAEP_PADDING);
```

Use Cases:

- Secure key exchange in SSL/TLS.
- Encrypting data for transmission to a specific recipient.

Key Management

Managing cryptographic keys is a critical aspect of secure systems. OpenSSL provides functions to generate, store, and manipulate keys.

Key APIs:

- **EVP_PKEY_new()**: Creates a new key object.
- **EVP_PKEY_free()**: Frees the key object.
- **EVP_PKEY_generate()**: Generates a key pair.

Example code snippet:

```
EVP_PKEY_CTX *ctx = EVP_PKEY_CTX_new_id(EVP_PKEY_RSA, NULL);
EVP_PKEY *pkey = NULL;

EVP_PKEY_keygen_init(ctx);
EVP_PKEY_keygen(ctx, &pkey);
```

Use Cases:

- Generating RSA or ECC key pairs for SSL/TLS.
- Managing keys in a secure key storage system.

Digital Signatures

Digital signatures provide a way to verify the authenticity and integrity of data. OpenSSL supports signing and verifying data using public-key cryptography.

Key APIs:

- **`EVP_SignInit()`**: Initializes the signing context.
- **`EVP_SignUpdate()`**: Adds data to the signature.
- **`EVP_SignFinal()`**: Finalizes the signature.

Example code snippet (not the full code):

```
// Initialize signing operation with SHA-256
    if (EVP_SignInit(mdctx, EVP_sha256()) != 1) {
        fprintf(stderr, "Error initializing signing\n");
        EVP_MD_CTX_free(mdctx);
        EVP_PKEY_free(pkey);
        return 1;
    }

    // Add data to be signed
    if (EVP_SignUpdate(mdctx, data, data_len) != 1) {
        fprintf(stderr, "Error updating signing data\n");
        EVP_MD_CTX_free(mdctx);
        EVP_PKEY_free(pkey);
        return 1;
    }

    // Finalize the signing process and obtain the signature
    if (EVP_SignFinal(mdctx, sig, &sig_len, pkey) != 1) {
        fprintf(stderr, "Error finalizing signing process\n");
        EVP_MD_CTX_free(mdctx);
        EVP_PKEY_free(pkey);
        return 1;
    }
```

Random Number Generation (RNG)

Random numbers are critical for cryptographic operations, such as generating cryptographic keys and nonces. OpenSSL provides a robust RNG system, ensuring cryptographic randomness.

Key APIs:

- **`RAND_bytes()`**: Generates cryptographically secure random bytes.
- **`RAND_priv_bytes()`**: Generates random bytes suitable for private use (for example, key generation).

Example code snippet:

```
unsigned char random_bytes[32];
if (RAND_bytes(random_bytes, sizeof(random_bytes)) != 1) {
```

```
        // Handle error
        ERR_print_errors_fp(stderr);
    }
```

Use Cases:

- Generating initialization vectors (IVs) for encryption.
- Creating random keys for symmetric encryption.

TLS Communication

The **libssl** library, part of the OpenSSL suite, is specifically designed to implement the SSL and TLS protocols, enabling secure communication over networks. It offers a rich set of features for establishing encrypted connections and ensuring data integrity. The **libssl** supports various encryption algorithms, key exchange mechanisms, and certificate handling, making it a critical component for building secure applications and services.

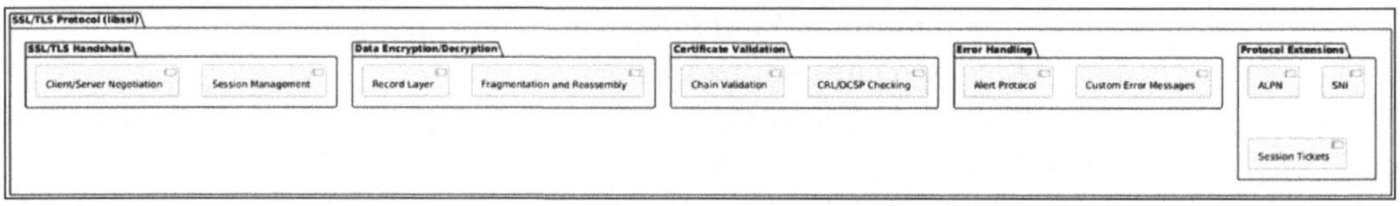

Figure 4.3: *libssl organization*

The following sections cover the core aspects of the SSL/TLS protocol as implemented in **libssl**, including handshake management, data encryption, certificate validation, error handling, and protocol extensions.

SSL/TLS Handshake

The SSL/TLS handshake is the initial phase of the protocol, where the client and server negotiate security parameters, exchange keys, and authenticate each other. This process establishes the foundation for secure communication.

Client/Server Negotiation

Client/Server negotiation involves selecting the cryptographic algorithms, key exchange mechanisms, and protocol versions supported by both the client and the server. This negotiation ensures that both parties agree on a secure method of communication.

C Code Example: Client/Server Negotiation

```
#include <openssl/ssl.h>

SSL_CTX *ctx = SSL_CTX_new(TLS_client_method());
```

```
SSL *ssl = SSL_new(ctx);
SSL_set_fd(ssl, socket_fd);

if (SSL_connect(ssl) <= 0) {
    ERR_print_errors_fp(stderr);
} else {
    printf("SSL/TLS handshake successful\n");
}
```

Significant Enhancement in OpenSSL 3.0

Provider Support: OpenSSL 3.0 enables applications to dynamically load and switch between different providers, making it easier to add or update cryptographic algorithms without modifying the core OpenSSL library.

Updated C Code example with `PROVIDER` context:

```
OSSL_PROVIDER *deflt = OSSL_PROVIDER_load(NULL, "default");
SSL_CTX *ctx = SSL_CTX_new(TLS_client_method());
SSL *ssl = SSL_new(ctx);
SSL_set_fd(ssl, socket_fd);

if (SSL_connect(ssl) <= 0) {
    ERR_print_errors_fp(stderr);
} else {
    printf("SSL/TLS handshake successful\n");
}

OSSL_PROVIDER_unload(deflt);
```

Session Management

Session management enables the reuse of session parameters in subsequent connections, improving performance by avoiding a full handshake. OpenSSL provides session resumption features, including session IDs and session tickets.

Code snippet for session management

```
SSL_SESSION *session = SSL_get1_session(ssl);

// Later, for resuming the session
SSL_set_session(ssl, session);
SSL_connect(ssl);
```

Data Encryption/Decryption

Once the handshake is complete, data encryption and decryption take place in the record layer. This layer is responsible for securing the communication by encrypting outgoing data and decrypting incoming data.

Significant Enhancement in OpenSSL 3.0:

Support for New Algorithms: OpenSSL 3.0 introduces support for newer cryptographic algorithms such as SM4, X25519, and Ed25519, ensuring stronger security and compatibility with modern standards.

Record Layer

The record layer handles data transmission, ensuring confidentiality and integrity. It fragments application data, encrypts it, and transmits it securely.

C Code example: Sending encrypted data

```
const char *msg = "Hello, Secure World!";
SSL_write(ssl, msg, strlen(msg));
```

Fragmentation and Reassembly

Due to the maximum transmission unit (MTU) limits, large messages are fragmented into smaller parts. The record layer handles fragmentation and ensures the correct reassembly of messages on the receiving end.

Certificate Validation

Certificate validation is a critical step in SSL/TLS, ensuring that the certificates presented during the handshake are trustworthy. The validation process involves checking the certificate chain and verifying revocation status using mechanisms such as Certificate Revocation List (CRL) and Online Certificate Status Protocol (OCSP).

Certificate Chain Validation

OpenSSL verifies the chain of certificates, ensuring that each certificate is signed by a trusted certificate authority (CA).

Code snippet for certificate Chain Validation:

```
X509 *cert = SSL_get_peer_certificate(ssl);
if (cert) {
    long verify_result = SSL_get_verify_result(ssl);
    if (verify_result == X509_V_OK) {
        printf("Certificate chain is valid.\n");
    }
    X509_free(cert);
}
```

CRL/OCSP Checking

CRL and OCSP are used to check if the certificates have been revoked. OpenSSL supports both methods for revocation checking, allowing applications to verify the validity of certificates in real-time.

Error Handling

Error handling in SSL/TLS is crucial for identifying and responding to issues that occur during the handshake, data transmission, or certificate validation processes. OpenSSL provides detailed error messages and implements the Alert Protocol for communicating errors between the client and server.

Alert Protocol

The Alert Protocol is used to signal errors and other important conditions. Alerts are categorized as warnings or fatal errors, with fatal errors terminating the connection.

Code snippet for handling SSL Alerts:

```
int ret = SSL_read(ssl, buffer, sizeof(buffer));
if (ret <= 0) {
    int error_code = SSL_get_error(ssl, ret);
    if (error_code == SSL_ERROR_SSL) {
        printf("SSL error: %s\n", ERR_reason_error_string(ERR_
get_error()));
    }
}
```

Custom Error Messages

Applications can define custom error messages for more user-friendly error reporting, improving the debugging and troubleshooting processes.

Protocol Extensions

SSL/TLS supports various protocol extensions that enhance its functionality, such as Application-Layer Protocol Negotiation (ALPN), Server Name Indication (SNI), and session tickets for session resumption.

Application Layer Protocol Negotiation (ALPN)

ALPN allows the client and server to negotiate the application protocol to be used over the secure connection. This is commonly used in HTTP/2 and other protocols.

Code snippet for setting ALPN Protocols:

```
const unsigned char *alpn_protos = (unsigned char *)"\x02h2\
x08http/1.1";
SSL_CTX_set_alpn_protos(ctx, alpn_protos, 10);
```

Server Name Indication (SNI)

SNI enables the client to specify the hostname it is trying to connect to during the handshake, allowing the server to present the appropriate certificate for that hostname.

API:

```
SSL_set_tlsext_host_name(ssl, "example.com");
```

Session Tickets

Session tickets are a mechanism introduced in TLS to optimize the performance of secure connections by enabling session resumption without requiring full handshakes. When session tickets are used, the server encapsulates the session state (session keys, algorithms, and so on) into a ticket and sends it to the client. The client can then store this ticket and present it in future connections, allowing the server to resume the session without performing a full handshake. This reduces the overhead of establishing secure connections, especially in scenarios where many short-lived connections are made.

- **Initial Full Handshake:** During the initial handshake, the server generates a session ticket that encapsulates the session parameters (for example, cryptographic keys and algorithms negotiated during the handshake). This ticket is encrypted and sent to the client.
- **Session Resumption:** The client stores the session ticket and, during subsequent connections, sends it back to the server in the **`ClientHello`** message. If the server accepts the ticket, it resumes the session using the encrypted session state, avoiding a full handshake. Only a brief exchange (known as an abbreviated handshake) is needed to resume the session.
- **Server-Side State Reduction:** One of the main benefits of session tickets is that they eliminate the need for servers to store session state. Unlike traditional session IDs, which require the server to maintain a mapping of session IDs to session data, session tickets offload this responsibility to the client. This is particularly useful in large-scale systems where maintaining session state for many clients can be resource-intensive.
- **OpenSSL Session Ticket API:** OpenSSL provides several functions for working with session tickets. By default, session tickets are enabled in OpenSSL. However, they can be controlled and configured using specific options.

- **Enabling/Disabling Session Tickets**: You can control session ticket usage with the **SSL_CTX_set_options()** function.

  ```
  // Disable session tickets
  SSL_CTX_set_options(ctx, SSL_OP_NO_TICKET);
  ```

  When session tickets are disabled using the **SSL_OP_NO_TICKET** option, the server will rely on session IDs for session resumption, which require the server to store session state.

- **Customizing Ticket Behavior**: OpenSSL also allows for more advanced customization, such as generating custom session tickets or handling ticket encryption manually, using callbacks such as **SSL_CTX_set_tlsext_ticket_key_cb()**.

  ```
  SSL_CTX_set_tlsext_ticket_key_cb(ctx, my_ticket_key_callback);
  ```

  This **callback** function allows developers to implement their own logic for encrypting and decrypting session tickets, providing greater control over the security of session resumption.

Benefits of Session Tickets:

- **Performance Improvement**: Session tickets enable abbreviated handshakes, reducing the overhead of re-establishing secure connections. This is particularly useful in high-traffic environments such as web servers and APIs with frequent short-lived connections.
- **Scalability**: By eliminating the need for server-side session state, session tickets improve scalability and reduce memory usage, which is especially beneficial in distributed systems.
- **Flexibility**: Session tickets work better than session IDs in load-balanced environments, removing the need for sticky sessions or shared session state across multiple servers.

Security Considerations:

- **Ticket Lifetime**: Reusing session tickets over long periods can reduce security. To prevent this, set ticket expiration times and rotate session keys regularly.
- **Ticket Encryption**: Since tickets contain sensitive data, they must be securely encrypted before being sent to the client to avoid security vulnerabilities such as session hijacking.
- **Forward Secrecy**: Ensure session tickets are generated with new ephemeral keys to maintain forward secrecy, even when resuming sessions.

Engines and Providers

The OpenSSL library supports both Engines and Providers to enhance cryptographic functionality. These abstractions allow the integration of hardware acceleration, custom algorithms, and modular cryptographic operations into the OpenSSL framework.

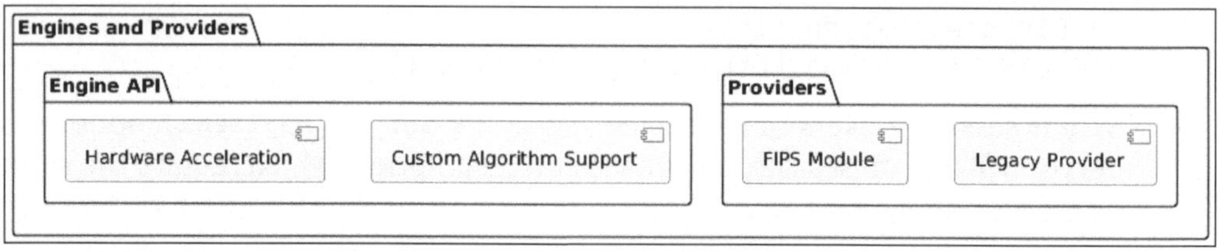

***Figure 4.4**: Engines and Providers*

Engines

The Engine API in OpenSSL provides an interface to offload cryptographic operations to external devices, such as hardware accelerators, or to support custom cryptographic algorithms. Engines serve as a bridge between the core OpenSSL functions and external cryptographic modules.

Key Features:

- **Hardware Acceleration**: Engines allow OpenSSL to offload cryptographic computations, such as AES encryption or SHA hashing, to specialized hardware for improved performance.

  Example of Using Engines for Hardware Acceleration:

  ```
  #include <openssl/engine.h>

  ENGINE *engine;
  ENGINE_load_builtin_engines();
  engine = ENGINE_by_id("dynamic");

  // Load hardware acceleration engine, e.g., Intel AES-NI
  if (!ENGINE_init(engine)) {
      // handle error
  }
  ENGINE_set_default(engine, ENGINE_METHOD_ALL);
  ```

  In this example, the Engine API is used to load and initialize a hardware-based cryptographic engine, such as Intel's AES-NI, which speeds up AES encryption by using processor-specific instructions.

  We will cover OpensSSL engine for hardware acceleration in detail in a separate section of this book.

- **Custom Algorithm Support**: Custom cryptographic algorithms, which are not available in the default OpenSSL implementation, can be supported via Engines.

Providers

Providers were introduced in OpenSSL 3.0 as a new way to offer cryptographic algorithms and modules. They are designed to replace engines in future versions and provide a more flexible, modular way to access cryptographic functionality.

Key Features:

- **FIPS Module**: The Federal Information Processing Standards (FIPS) module, available as a provider, ensures compliance with US government security standards. The FIPS provider delivers only FIPS 140-2 validated cryptographic algorithms.
- **Legacy Provider**: The legacy provider includes older cryptographic algorithms that are not part of the default provider, such as MD2 or RC4.

  Example of Loading a FIPS Provider:

  ```
  #include <openssl/provider.h>

  OSSL_PROVIDER *fips_provider;

  fips_provider = OSSL_PROVIDER_load(NULL, "fips");
  if (!fips_provider) {
      // handle error
  }

  // Now, OpenSSL is using FIPS-validated cryptographic operations
  ```

Here, the FIPS provider is loaded to ensure all cryptographic operations comply with FIPS 140-2 standards. Providers allow switching between various cryptographic modules as per the application's needs.

FIPS Details

The FIPS module plays a pivotal role in OpenSSL, offering a suite of cryptographic algorithms that have been rigorously validated under the FIPS 140-2 standard. This validation is a critical requirement for government entities and various regulated industries, ensuring that cryptographic operations adhere to strict security protocols. The FIPS module guarantees that cryptographic algorithms are correctly implemented and thoroughly tested, providing a high level of security assurance.

Purpose of the FIPS Module

The primary objective of the FIPS module is to deliver cryptographic functionality that complies with the US government's FIPS 140-2 and 140-3 standards. This compliance is vital for organizations that handle sensitive or classified data, such as financial institutions, healthcare providers, and government agencies. Implementing a FIPS-compliant module ensures that applications meet stringent security criteria, enabling them to be certified according to regulatory security requirements. This makes the FIPS module indispensable in environments where strong data protection and regulatory compliance are mandatory.

Key Features of the FIPS Module:

- **FIPS-Validated Algorithms:** The FIPS module restricts the available cryptographic algorithms to those that are validated under FIPS. This includes:
  - Advanced Encryption Standard (AES)
  - Secure Hash Algorithms (SHA-2) family
  - Rivest–Shamir–Adleman (RSA) for key generation, encryption, and signing
  - Hash-based Message Authentication Code (HMAC)
  - Deterministic Random Bit Generator (DRBG) for secure random number generation
- **Module Integrity**: A key aspect of FIPS certification is ensuring that the cryptographic module operates correctly and has not been tampered with. OpenSSL's FIPS module performs a self-integrity test upon loading to confirm that its binary has not been altered.
- **Strict API Usage**: When the FIPS module is enabled, the application is limited to using only FIPS-validated cryptographic operations. Any non-FIPS algorithms (such as MD5 or RC4) are not available through the FIPS provider. This ensures strict compliance with the standard.
- **Continuous Monitoring**: To maintain compliance, the FIPS module constantly monitors certain operations, such as ensuring that the random number generator (RNG) functions correctly. It performs health tests on startup and periodically during use.
- **Separation from Non-FIPS Operations**: When using the FIPS provider, applications must ensure that they do not mix FIPS-validated operations with non-FIPS algorithms. This separation is maintained via the provider mechanism in OpenSSL 3.0.

Enable and Use the FIPS Module

To enable the FIPS module in OpenSSL 3.0, the FIPS provider must be loaded explicitly. Once loaded, the FIPS provider takes over all cryptographic operations, and only FIPS-compliant algorithms are allowed.

Here is a step-by-step guide to loading and using the FIPS module:

1. **Install the FIPS Module**: The FIPS module must be separately installed and configured. It is often packaged with OpenSSL in versions designed for FIPS use, or it can be built following specific instructions from OpenSSL.

2. **Load the FIPS Provider**: Using the OpenSSL API, you can explicitly load the FIPS provider during runtime.

   Example C Code:

```
#include <openssl/provider.h>
#include <openssl/evp.h>

OSSL_PROVIDER *fips_provider;

// Load the FIPS provider
fips_provider = OSSL_PROVIDER_load(NULL, "fips");
if (!fips_provider) {
    // handle error: FIPS provider failed to load
}
```

Set the Default Provider to FIPS:

Once the FIPS provider is loaded, it should be set as the default provider to ensure that all cryptographic operations use only FIPS-validated algorithms.

Example:

```
EVP_default_properties_enable_fips(NULL, 1);  // Enable FIPS mode
globally
```

Confirm FIPS Compliance: After the FIPS provider is loaded, you can query OpenSSL to check if FIPS mode is active.

Example:

```
#include <openssl/fips.h>

if (FIPS_mode()) {
    printf("FIPS mode is active.\n");
} else {
    printf("FIPS mode is not active.\n");
}
```

Here is an example of performing a FIPS-compliant SHA-256 hash operation. This example demonstrates how to perform a SHA-256 hash using the FIPS provider, ensuring that the operation is FIPS-compliant.

```
#include <openssl/evp.h>
#include <openssl/provider.h>
#include <stdio.h>
#include <string.h>

int main() {
    // Load the FIPS provider
    OSSL_PROVIDER *fips = OSSL_PROVIDER_load(NULL, "fips");
```

```
    if (!fips) {
        fprintf(stderr, "Failed to load FIPS provider\n");
        return 1;
    }

    EVP_MD_CTX *mdctx = EVP_MD_CTX_new();
    if (!mdctx) {
        fprintf(stderr, "Failed to create MD context\n");
        return 1;
    }

    const EVP_MD *sha256 = EVP_sha256();
    if (!EVP_DigestInit_ex(mdctx, sha256, NULL)) {
        fprintf(stderr, "Digest initialization failed\n");
        return 1;
    }

    const char *msg = "FIPS compliant message";
    EVP_DigestUpdate(mdctx, msg, strlen(msg));

    unsigned char digest[EVP_MAX_MD_SIZE];
    unsigned int digest_len;

    EVP_DigestFinal_ex(mdctx, digest, &digest_len);

    printf("SHA-256 Digest: ");
    for (int i = 0; i < digest_len; i++) {
        printf("%02x", digest[i]);
    }
    printf("\n");

    EVP_MD_CTX_free(mdctx);
    OSSL_PROVIDER_unload(fips);
    return 0;
}
```

Utilities and Miscellaneous

The Utilities and Miscellaneous section of OpenSSL offers various helper functions and mechanisms to support the development of OpenSSL-based applications. These utilities address common needs such as memory management, threading, and input/output (I/O) handling, making the OpenSSL library easier to integrate, especially in complex, multithreaded, or high-performance environments.

Figure 4.5: *Utilities and miscellaneous*

Memory Management

OpenSSL provides its own memory management functions to enhance security and prevent issues such as memory leaks, particularly in the handling of cryptographic data. OpenSSL's memory management utilities wrap around standard system functions, offering additional features such as automatic memory zeroization to ensure sensitive data is not left behind in the memory after it is no longer needed.

- **`OPENSSL_malloc()`**: A wrapper around the standard malloc() function that includes additional error checking and diagnostics. This function is designed to ensure that OpenSSL is aware of all memory allocations for debugging and secure memory management.

  Example:

  ```
  #include <openssl/crypto.h>

  void *ptr = OPENSSL_malloc(1024);  // Allocate 1024 bytes
  if (!ptr) {
      // handle error
  }

  OPENSSL_free(ptr);  // Free the memory when done
  ```

- **Memory Zeroization**: OpenSSL provides functions to securely wipe sensitive data from memory to prevent it from being recoverable. This is particularly useful when handling cryptographic keys or sensitive application data.

  Example (Memory Zeroization):

  ```
  #include <openssl/crypto.h>

  unsigned char key[32];  // Example sensitive data (AES key)

  // After using the key...
  OPENSSL_cleanse(key, sizeof(key));  // Securely erase the key
  from memory
  OPENSSL_cleanse() ensures that sensitive data is wiped from memory
  and cannot be recovered, even if the memory is later accessed.
  ```

Threading Support

In a multithreaded application, OpenSSL needs to ensure that shared resources are accessed safely. To achieve this, OpenSSL provides thread-safe utilities, including locks, mutexes, and support for thread-local storage.

- **Locks and Mutexes**: OpenSSL provides functions for managing locks in multithreaded applications, ensuring thread-safe access to internal data structures.

  Example:

  ```
  #include <openssl/crypto.h>

  CRYPTO_RWLOCK *lock = CRYPTO_THREAD_lock_new();  // Create a new
  lock

  CRYPTO_THREAD_write_lock(lock);  // Acquire a write lock
  // Critical section: perform thread-sensitive operations
  CRYPTO_THREAD_unlock(lock);  // Release the lock

  CRYPTO_THREAD_lock_free(lock);  // Clean up the lock
  ```

- **Thread-Local Storage**: OpenSSL provides mechanisms for thread-local storage (TLS), allowing each thread to have its own independent instance of certain data, reducing contention between threads.

  Example (Thread-Local Storage):

  ```
  #include <openssl/crypto.h>

  static CRYPTO_THREAD_LOCAL thread_key;

  void init_thread_local() {
      if (!CRYPTO_THREAD_init_local(&thread_key, NULL)) {
          // handle error
      }
  }

  void set_thread_local_data(void *data) {
      CRYPTO_THREAD_set_local(&thread_key, data);
  }

  void *get_thread_local_data() {
      return CRYPTO_THREAD_get_local(&thread_key);
  }
  ```

Thread-local storage is useful when each thread needs its own copy of data (for example, a cryptographic context), reducing the need for locks and improving performance.

Basic I/O (BIO) Abstraction

The BIO abstraction in OpenSSL is a flexible system for managing input and output operations. BIOs offer a buffered I/O mechanism and allow for custom implementations of I/O handling, making them suitable for a wide range of use cases, including network communication and file operations.

- **Buffered I/O:** BIOs provide automatic buffering of input/output operations, which helps optimize performance when dealing with large volumes of data. This is particularly useful for network communication where data might arrive in smaller chunks.

  Example (Buffered I/O):

  ```
  #include <openssl/bio.h>

  BIO *bio = BIO_new(BIO_s_mem());  // Create a memory BIO (buffered
  I/O)

  const char *data = "Hello, OpenSSL!";
  BIO_write(bio, data, strlen(data));  // Write data to the BIO

  char buffer[128];
  int bytes_read = BIO_read(bio, buffer, sizeof(buffer));  // Read
  the data back
  buffer[bytes_read] = '\0';
  printf("Read from BIO: %s\n", buffer);

  BIO_free(bio);  // Clean up
  ```

  In this example, a memory BIO is used to buffer data. You can perform similar operations with file-based or socket-based BIOs, enabling efficient I/O across various communication channels.

- **Custom I/O Handlers:** OpenSSL allows you to create custom BIO methods that define how input and output operations are handled. This enables integration with custom I/O systems, such as specialized network protocols or hardware interfaces.

  Example (Custom I/O Handler):

  ```
  #include <openssl/bio.h>

  static int custom_write(BIO *b, const char *buf, int len) {
  ```

```
    // Custom write function (e.g., write to hardware)
    return len;  // Assume all data was written
}

BIO_METHOD *custom_method;
BIO *bio;

custom_method = BIO_meth_new(BIO_TYPE_SOURCE_SINK, "custom BIO");
BIO_meth_set_write(custom_method, custom_write);

bio = BIO_new(custom_method);  // Create a BIO with custom handler

BIO_write(bio, "Custom I/O", 10);  // Use the custom BIO for I/O
operations

BIO_free(bio);
BIO_meth_free(custom_method);
```

This example defines a custom BIO that uses a custom write function. You can similarly define read, control, and other I/O operations to handle complex or specialized I/O cases.

Conclusion

In this chapter, we introduced the fundamental concepts of OpenSSL's C library APIs, focusing on the core functionalities and common use cases to establish a solid foundation. We covered essential cryptographic operations, initialization, and configuration APIs, providing practical examples to help readers understand their implementation.

While we have touched on key areas, this chapter serves as an overview, setting the stage for a deeper dive into specific OpenSSL APIs and advanced topics in subsequent chapters. In the following chapters, we will explore additional APIs in greater depth, discussing intricate details, specialized use cases, and performance considerations. This structured approach will help readers build a comprehensive understanding of OpenSSL and its powerful toolkit for cryptography and secure communication.

Chapter 5
Public Key Infrastructure with OpenSSL

Introduction

In *Chapter 1, Cryptography Basics and Network Security*, we explored the foundational concepts of cryptography, covering essential topics such as encryption, hashing, and digital signatures. We also laid out the core principles needed to understand Public Key Infrastructure (PKI) in a secure system. Building on that foundation, this chapter dives deeper into PKI, focusing on practical applications and hands-on examples using C APIs. Here, we will guide you through setting up a certificate authority, generating and managing certificates, and integrating PKI into real-world applications. By the end of this chapter, you will gain experience with OpenSSL's C APIs for PKI operations, equipping you to implement and troubleshoot PKI in complex environments.

In *Chapter 3, OpenSSL Command Line Interface*, we have covered PKI-related OpenSSL commands with some examples. In this chapter, we will deep dive into the various PKI operations using OpenSSL APIs and wherever needed we will mention related OpenSSL commands. We may skip the initialization part in some cases to avoid repetition as we have already covered it in *Chapter 3, OpenSSL Command Line Interface.*

Structure

In this chapter, we will cover the following topics:

- Setting Up a Simple Certificate Authority with OpenSSL's C APIs
- Generating and Using Certificate Signing Requests
- Issuing and Managing Certificates
- Managing Certificate Lifecycle

- Creating Certificate Chains and Intermediate Certificate Authorities
- Validating Certificate and Setting Up Revocation Mechanisms
- Validating a Certificate Against a Certificate Revocation List
- Setting Up and Validating with Online Certificate Status Protocol
- Applying PKI to Secure a Web Application (or Network Service)

Setting Up a Simple Certificate Authority with OpenSSL's C APIs

In this section, we will walk through setting up a basic Certificate Authority (CA) using OpenSSL's C APIs. A CA is a trusted entity responsible for issuing and signing digital certificates. This example demonstrates how to generate a CA's private key, create a self-signed certificate, and configure OpenSSL for CA operations. Equivalent OpenSSL commands are provided to relate the code with familiar tools.

Step 1: Generating the CA Private Key

The first step in creating a CA is generating a secure private key. In OpenSSL C APIs, the private key is typically generated using the **EVP_PKEY** and RSA functions.

```
#include <openssl/evp.h>
#include <openssl/pem.h>
#include <openssl/rsa.h>
#include <openssl/err.h>
#include <stdio.h>

// Function to generate the CA's private key and save it to a file
void generate_ca_private_key(const char *filename) {
    // Create a new EVP_PKEY structure to hold the private key
    EVP_PKEY *pkey = EVP_PKEY_new();
    if (!pkey) {
        fprintf(stderr, "Error allocating EVP_PKEY structure\n");
        return;
    }

    // Generate a 2048-bit RSA key pair
    RSA *rsa = RSA_generate_key(2048, RSA_F4, NULL, NULL);
    if (!rsa) {
        fprintf(stderr, "Error generating RSA key\n");
        EVP_PKEY_free(pkey);
        return;
    }

    // Assign the generated RSA key to the EVP_PKEY structure
```

```
    EVP_PKEY_assign_RSA(pkey, rsa);

    // Open the output file for writing the private key
    FILE *file = fopen(filename, "wb");
    if (file) {
        // Write the private key in PEM format
        PEM_write_PrivateKey(file, pkey, NULL, NULL, 0, NULL,
NULL);
        fclose(file);
        printf("CA private key saved to %s\n", filename);
    } else {
        fprintf(stderr, "Error saving private key to file\n");
    }

    // Free the EVP_PKEY structure (RSA is freed automatically)
    EVP_PKEY_free(pkey);
}
```

Equivalent OpenSSL command:

```
openssl genpkey -algorithm RSA -out ca_private_key.pem -pkeyopt
rsa_keygen_bits:2048
```

Step 2: Creating a Self-Signed Certificate

A self-signed certificate acts as the CA's own identity and the root of trust for the certificates it issues. OpenSSL's X.509 API is used to create and sign the certificate.

```
#include <openssl/x509.h>
void create_self_signed_cert(const char *key_file, const char
*cert_file) {
    FILE *key_fp = fopen(key_file, "rb");
    EVP_PKEY *pkey = PEM_read_PrivateKey(key_fp, NULL, NULL,
NULL);
    fclose(key_fp);

    if (!pkey) {
        fprintf(stderr, "Error reading private key\n");
        return;
    }

    X509 *x509 = X509_new();
    X509_set_version(x509, 2); // Set X.509 version (v3)

    ASN1_INTEGER_set(X509_get_serialNumber(x509), 1); // Serial
number
    X509_gmtime_adj(X509_get_notBefore(x509), 0);      // Valid
from now
    X509_gmtime_adj(X509_get_notAfter(x509), 365 * 24 * 60 * 60);
```

```
// 1 year validity

    X509_set_pubkey(x509, pkey);

    X509_NAME *name = X509_get_subject_name(x509);
    X509_NAME_add_entry_by_txt(name, "C", MBSTRING_ASC, (unsigned
char *)"US", -1, -1, 0);
    X509_NAME_add_entry_by_txt(name, "O", MBSTRING_ASC, (unsigned
char *)"My CA", -1, -1, 0);
    X509_NAME_add_entry_by_txt(name, "CN", MBSTRING_ASC, (un-
signed char *)"Root CA", -1, -1, 0);

    X509_set_issuer_name(x509, name);

    if (!X509_sign(x509, pkey, EVP_sha256())) {
        fprintf(stderr, "Error signing the certificate\n");
        X509_free(x509);
        EVP_PKEY_free(pkey);
        return;
    }

    FILE *cert_fp = fopen(cert_file, "wb");
    if (cert_fp) {
        PEM_write_X509(cert_fp, x509);
        fclose(cert_fp);
        printf("Self-signed certificate saved to %s\n", cert_file);
    } else {
        fprintf(stderr, "Error saving certificate\n");
    }
    X509_free(x509);
    EVP_PKEY_free(pkey);
}
```

Equivalent OpenSSL command:

```
openssl req -x509 -new -nodes -key ca_private_key.pem -sha256
-days 365 -out ca_cert.pem -subj "/C=US/O=My CA/CN=Root CA"
```

Note: *Always handle errors by checking the return values of OpenSSL functions and using* ***`ERR_print_errors_fp(stderr)`*** *for diagnostics. Protect private keys with encryption or secure hardware modules such as HSMs or TPMs. For advanced features, such as adding Subject Alternative Names (SANs), leverage the X.509v3 API.*

By the end of this setup, you will have a functional root CA ready to issue certificates for various applications.

Generating and Using Certificate Signing Requests

A Certificate Signing Request (CSR) is a request sent to a Certificate Authority (CA) to issue a certificate. It contains the applicant's public key and information such as the Common Name (CN) and Subject Alternative Names (SANs). In this section, we demonstrate how to create a CSR using OpenSSL C APIs, focusing on setting fields such as CN and SAN.

```
#include <openssl/x509.h>
#include <openssl/x509v3.h>
#include <openssl/pem.h>
#include <stdio.h>

// Function to create a new CSR and save it to a file
void create_csr(const char *key_file, const char *csr_file, const
char *common_name, const char *alt_names) {
    // Read the private key from the file
    FILE *key_fp = fopen(key_file, "rb");
    if (!key_fp) {
        fprintf(stderr, "Error opening private key file: %s\n",
key_file);
        return;
    }

    EVP_PKEY *pkey = PEM_read_PrivateKey(key_fp, NULL, NULL,
NULL);
    fclose(key_fp);

    if (!pkey) {
        fprintf(stderr, "Error reading private key\n");
        return;
    }

    // Create a new X509_REQ (CSR) structure
    X509_REQ *req = X509_REQ_new();
    if (!req) {
        fprintf(stderr, "Error creating X509_REQ structure\n");
        EVP_PKEY_free(pkey);
        return;
    }

    // Set the public key for the CSR
    X509_REQ_set_pubkey(req, pkey);
```

```
    // Set the subject name for the CSR
    X509_NAME *name = X509_NAME_new();
    if (!name) {
        fprintf(stderr, "Error creating X509_NAME structure\n");
        X509_REQ_free(req);
        EVP_PKEY_free(pkey);
        return;
    }

    // Add Common Name (CN) to the subject name
    X509_NAME_add_entry_by_txt(name, "CN", MBSTRING_ASC,
(unsigned char *)common_name, -1, -1, 0);

    // Set the subject name in the CSR
    X509_REQ_set_subject_name(req, name);
    X509_NAME_free(name); // Free the name structure as it's no
longer needed
    // Add Subject Alternative Name (SAN) extension
    if (alt_names) {
        X509_EXTENSION *san_ext = NULL;
        STACK_OF(X509_EXTENSION) *exts = sk_X509_EXTENSION_new_
null();

        // Format the SANs as a comma-separated string
        san_ext = X509V3_EXT_conf_nid(NULL, NULL, NID_subject_
alt_name, alt_names);
        if (san_ext) {
            sk_X509_EXTENSION_push(exts, san_ext);
            X509_REQ_add_extensions(req, exts);
            sk_X509_EXTENSION_pop_free(exts, X509_EXTENSION_
free);
        } else {
            fprintf(stderr, "Error creating SAN extension\n");
        }
    }

    // Sign the CSR with the private key
    if (!X509_REQ_sign(req, pkey, EVP_sha256())) {
        fprintf(stderr, "Error signing the CSR\n");
        X509_REQ_free(req);
        EVP_PKEY_free(pkey);
        return;
    }

    // Write the CSR to a file in PEM format
    FILE *csr_fp = fopen(csr_file, "wb");
    if (csr_fp) {
```

```
        PEM_write_X509_REQ(csr_fp, req);
        fclose(csr_fp);
        printf("CSR saved to %s\n", csr_file);
    } else {
        fprintf(stderr, "Error saving CSR to file\n");
    }

    // Free resources
    X509_REQ_free(req);
    EVP_PKEY_free(pkey);
}
```

Key Points in the Code:

1. **Reading the Private Key**: The private key is required to sign the CSR. The **`PEM_read_PrivateKey`** function reads the private key from the provided file.

2. **Creating the CSR Structure**: **`X509_REQ_new`** initializes the structure for the CSR. This structure will later hold the public key, subject name, and extensions.

3. **Setting the Common Name (CN)**: The CN field is mandatory for a CSR and usually contains the domain name of the entity. We use **`X509_NAME_add_entry_by_txt`** to add this field to the subject name.

4. **Adding SAN Extensions**: The **`X509V3_EXT_conf_nid`** function creates a Subject Alternative Name (SAN) extension. SANs are additional domain names or IPs associated with the certificate.

5. **Signing the CSR**: The **`X509_REQ_sign`** function signs the CSR using the private key and a specified digest algorithm (SHA-256 in this case).

6. **Writing the CSR to a File**: The CSR is saved in PEM format using **`PEM_write_X509_REQ`**.

Equivalent OpenSSL command

```
openssl req -new -key private_key.pem -out request.csr -subj "/
CN=example.com"  -addext "subjectAltName=DNS:example.com,DNS:www.
example.com"
```

By the end of this process, you will have a CSR file ready to be submitted to a CA for certificate issuance. This example equips you to generate CSRs programmatically for various entities in your application.

Issuing and Managing Certificates

This section focuses on using OpenSSL C APIs to issue certificates from a Certificate

Authority (CA) and manage their lifecycle, including renewal and revocation. Alongside, equivalent OpenSSL commands will be provided for reference.

```
#include <openssl/x509.h>
#include <openssl/x509v3.h>
#include <openssl/pem.h>
#include <stdio.h>
// Function to issue a certificate signed by the CA
void issue_certificate(const char *ca_cert_file, const char *ca_
key_file, const char *csr_file, const char *issued_cert_file) {
    // Read the CA's private key
    FILE *key_fp = fopen(ca_key_file, "rb");
    if (!key_fp) {
        fprintf(stderr, "Error opening CA private key file: %s\n",
ca_key_file);
        return;
    }

    EVP_PKEY *ca_pkey = PEM_read_PrivateKey(key_fp, NULL, NULL,
NULL);
    fclose(key_fp);

    if (!ca_pkey) {
        fprintf(stderr, "Error reading CA private key\n");
        return;
    }

    // Read the CA's certificate
    FILE *ca_cert_fp = fopen(ca_cert_file, "rb");
    if (!ca_cert_fp) {
        fprintf(stderr, "Error opening CA certificate file: %s\n",
ca_cert_file);
        EVP_PKEY_free(ca_pkey);
        return;
    }

    X509 *ca_cert = PEM_read_X509(ca_cert_fp, NULL, NULL, NULL);
    fclose(ca_cert_fp);

    if (!ca_cert) {
        fprintf(stderr, "Error reading CA certificate\n");
        EVP_PKEY_free(ca_pkey);
        return;
    }

    // Read the CSR
    FILE *csr_fp = fopen(csr_file, "rb");
```

```
    if (!csr_fp) {
        fprintf(stderr, "Error opening CSR file: %s\n", csr_file);
        X509_free(ca_cert);
        EVP_PKEY_free(ca_pkey);
        return;
    }

    X509_REQ *csr = PEM_read_X509_REQ(csr_fp, NULL, NULL, NULL);
    fclose(csr_fp);

    if (!csr) {
        fprintf(stderr, "Error reading CSR\n");
        X509_free(ca_cert);
        EVP_PKEY_free(ca_pkey);
        return;
    }

    // Create a new certificate
    X509 *cert = X509_new();
    if (!cert) {
        fprintf(stderr, "Error creating certificate\n");
        X509_REQ_free(csr);
        X509_free(ca_cert);
        EVP_PKEY_free(ca_pkey);
        return;
    }

    // Set the serial number for the certificate
    ASN1_INTEGER_set(X509_get_serialNumber(cert), 1); // Incre-
ment for each issued certificate

    // Set the validity period
    X509_gmtime_adj(X509_get_notBefore(cert), 0);          //
Valid from now
    X509_gmtime_adj(X509_get_notAfter(cert), 365 * 24 * 60 * 60);
// Valid for 1 year

    // Set the subject from the CSR
    X509_set_subject_name(cert, X509_REQ_get_subject_name(csr));

    // Set the issuer from the CA certificate
    X509_set_issuer_name(cert, X509_get_subject_name(ca_cert));

    // Attach the public key from the CSR
    EVP_PKEY *pubkey = X509_REQ_get_pubkey(csr);
    X509_set_pubkey(cert, pubkey);
    EVP_PKEY_free(pubkey);
```

```
    // Add any additional extensions (for example, basic
constraints, key usage)
    X509_EXTENSION *ext = X509V3_EXT_conf_nid(NULL, NULL, NID_
basic_constraints, "CA:FALSE");
    X509_add_ext(cert, ext, -1);
    X509_EXTENSION_free(ext);
    // Sign the certificate with the CA's private key
    if (!X509_sign(cert, ca_pkey, EVP_sha256())) {
        fprintf(stderr, "Error signing certificate\n");
        X509_free(cert);
        X509_REQ_free(csr);
        X509_free(ca_cert);
        EVP_PKEY_free(ca_pkey);
        return;
    }

    // Save the issued certificate to a file
    FILE *cert_fp = fopen(issued_cert_file, "wb");
    if (cert_fp) {
        PEM_write_X509(cert_fp, cert);
        fclose(cert_fp);
        printf("Certificate issued and saved to %s\n", issued_
cert_file);
    } else {
        fprintf(stderr, "Error saving certificate to file\n");
    }
    // Free resources
    X509_free(cert);
    X509_REQ_free(csr);
    X509_free(ca_cert);
    EVP_PKEY_free(ca_pkey);
}
```

Managing Certificate Lifecycle

Renewal: Renewal involves creating a new certificate for an entity using the same or updated details. This can be achieved by reusing the entity's CSR or generating a new certificate

Revocation: Revocation marks a certificate as invalid before its expiry. This is done by adding it to the Certificate Revocation List (CRL).

```
#include <openssl/x509.h>
#include <openssl/pem.h>
#include <openssl/x509v3.h>
```

```
void revoke_certificate(const char *ca_cert_file, const char *ca_
key_file, const char *crl_file) {
    FILE *ca_fp = fopen(ca_cert_file, "rb");
    if (!ca_fp) {
        fprintf(stderr, "Error opening CA certificate\n");
        return;
    }
    X509 *ca_cert = PEM_read_X509(ca_fp, NULL, NULL, NULL);
    fclose(ca_fp);

    FILE *key_fp = fopen(ca_key_file, "rb");
    EVP_PKEY *ca_key = PEM_read_PrivateKey(key_fp, NULL, NULL,
NULL);
    fclose(key_fp);

    X509_CRL *crl = X509_CRL_new();
    X509_CRL_set_issuer_name(crl, X509_get_subject_name(ca_
cert));
    X509_gmtime_adj(X509_CRL_get_lastUpdate(crl), 0);
    X509_gmtime_adj(X509_CRL_get_nextUpdate(crl), 7 * 24 * 60 *
60); // Next update in 1 week

    X509_REVOKED *revoked = X509_REVOKED_new();
    ASN1_INTEGER_set(X509_REVOKED_get_serialNumber(revoked), 1);
// Serial of revoked cert
    X509_gmtime_adj(X509_REVOKED_get_revocationDate(revoked), 0);
    X509_CRL_add0_revoked(crl, revoked);

    if (X509_CRL_sign(crl, ca_key, EVP_sha256())) {
        FILE *crl_fp = fopen(crl_file, "wb");
        PEM_write_X509_CRL(crl_fp, crl);
        fclose(crl_fp);
        printf("CRL saved to %s\n", crl_file);
    } else {
        fprintf(stderr, "Error signing CRL\n");
    }

    X509_free(ca_cert);
    EVP_PKEY_free(ca_key);
    X509_CRL_free(crl);
}
```

Equivalent OpenSSL commands

Issue:

```
openssl x509 -req -in request.csr -CA ca_cert.pem -CAkey ca_pri-
vate_key.pem  -CAcreateserial -out issued_cert.pem -days 365 -sha256
```

Revoke:

```
openssl ca -revoke issued_cert.pem
openssl ca -gencrl -out ca_crl.pem
```

By following this process, readers can issue, renew, and revoke certificates programmatically and manage their lifecycle effectively.

Creating Certificate Chains and Intermediate Certificate Authorities

Certificate chains and intermediate CAs are crucial components of real-world Public Key Infrastructure (PKI). They enable a hierarchical trust model where a Root CA delegates signing authority to Intermediate CAs, which, in turn, sign entity certificates.

This section demonstrates how to create an intermediate CA and build a certificate chain using OpenSSL C APIs. Equivalent OpenSSL commands are also provided for clarity.

Overview of the Process:

1. **Create a Root CA Certificate**:
    a. Generate a private key and a self-signed certificate for the Root CA.
2. **Create an Intermediate CA Certificate**:
    a. Generate a private key and CSR for the Intermediate CA.
    b. Sign the Intermediate CA certificate with the Root CA's private key.
3. **Issue an Entity Certificate**:
    a. Generate a private key and CSR for the entity.
    b. Sign the entity certificate using the Intermediate CA.
4. **Bundle Certificates into a Chain**:
    a. Combine the Root CA and Intermediate CA certificates in a file to represent the chain.

```
#include <openssl/x509.h>
#include <openssl/x509v3.h>
#include <openssl/pem.h>
#include <stdio.h>

// Function to generate a self-signed certificate for a Root CA
void create_root_ca(const char *root_key_file, const char *root_
cert_file) {
```

```
    // Generate private key
    EVP_PKEY *pkey = EVP_PKEY_new();
    RSA *rsa = RSA_generate_key(2048, RSA_F4, NULL, NULL);
    EVP_PKEY_assign_RSA(pkey, rsa);

    // Create a new X509 certificate
    X509 *cert = X509_new();
    X509_set_version(cert, 2); // X.509 v3
    ASN1_INTEGER_set(X509_get_serialNumber(cert), 1);

    // Set validity period
    X509_gmtime_adj(X509_get_notBefore(cert), 0);
    X509_gmtime_adj(X509_get_notAfter(cert), 365 * 24 * 60 * 60);

    // Set subject and issuer (self-signed)
    X509_NAME *name = X509_get_subject_name(cert);
    X509_NAME_add_entry_by_txt(name, "CN", MBSTRING_ASC,
(unsigned char *)"Root CA", -1, -1, 0);
    X509_set_issuer_name(cert, name);

    // Set public key
    X509_set_pubkey(cert, pkey);

    // Add basic constraints extension
    X509_EXTENSION *ext = X509V3_EXT_conf_nid(NULL, NULL, NID_
basic_constraints, "CA:TRUE");
    X509_add_ext(cert, ext, -1);
    X509_EXTENSION_free(ext);

    // Sign the certificate
    X509_sign(cert, pkey, EVP_sha256());

    // Write private key and certificate to files
    FILE *key_fp = fopen(root_key_file, "wb");
    PEM_write_PrivateKey(key_fp, pkey, NULL, NULL, 0, NULL,
NULL);
    fclose(key_fp);

    FILE *cert_fp = fopen(root_cert_file, "wb");
    PEM_write_X509(cert_fp, cert);
    fclose(cert_fp);

    // Free resources
    X509_free(cert);
    EVP_PKEY_free(pkey);
```

```
    printf("Root CA created successfully.\n");
}

// Function to create an Intermediate CA certificate signed by the
Root CA
void create_intermediate_ca(const char *root_key_file, const char
*root_cert_file, const char *inter_key_file, const char *inter_
cert_file) {
    // Generate private key for Intermediate CA
    EVP_PKEY *pkey = EVP_PKEY_new();
    RSA *rsa = RSA_generate_key(2048, RSA_F4, NULL, NULL);
    EVP_PKEY_assign_RSA(pkey, rsa);

    // Write the private key to a file
    FILE *key_fp = fopen(inter_key_file, "wb");
    PEM_write_PrivateKey(key_fp, pkey, NULL, NULL, 0, NULL,
NULL);
    fclose(key_fp);

    // Create a CSR for the Intermediate CA
    X509_REQ *req = X509_REQ_new();
    X509_REQ_set_pubkey(req, pkey);

    // Set the subject name for the Intermediate CA
    X509_NAME *name = X509_NAME_new();
    X509_NAME_add_entry_by_txt(name, "CN", MBSTRING_ASC,
(unsigned char *)"Intermediate CA", -1, -1, 0);
    X509_REQ_set_subject_name(req, name);
    X509_NAME_free(name);

    // Sign the CSR
    X509_REQ_sign(req, pkey, EVP_sha256());

    // Read the Root CA certificate and private key
    FILE *root_cert_fp = fopen(root_cert_file, "rb");
    X509 *root_cert = PEM_read_X509(root_cert_fp, NULL, NULL,
NULL);
    fclose(root_cert_fp);

    FILE *root_key_fp = fopen(root_key_file, "rb");
    EVP_PKEY *root_key = PEM_read_PrivateKey(root_key_fp, NULL,
NULL, NULL);
    fclose(root_key_fp);

    // Create a certificate for the Intermediate CA
    X509 *cert = X509_new();
    X509_set_version(cert, 2);
```

```
    ASN1_INTEGER_set(X509_get_serialNumber(cert), 2);

    // Set validity period
    X509_gmtime_adj(X509_get_notBefore(cert), 0);
    X509_gmtime_adj(X509_get_notAfter(cert), 365 * 24 * 60 * 60);

    // Set subject and issuer
    X509_set_subject_name(cert, X509_REQ_get_subject_name(req));
    X509_set_issuer_name(cert, X509_get_subject_name(root_cert));

    // Set public key
    EVP_PKEY *pubkey = X509_REQ_get_pubkey(req);
    X509_set_pubkey(cert, pubkey);
    EVP_PKEY_free(pubkey);

    // Add basic constraints extension
    X509_EXTENSION *ext = X509V3_EXT_conf_nid(NULL, NULL, NID_
basic_constraints, "CA:TRUE");
    X509_add_ext(cert, ext, -1);
    X509_EXTENSION_free(ext);

    // Sign the Intermediate CA certificate with the Root CA's
private key
    X509_sign(cert, root_key, EVP_sha256());

    // Write the Intermediate CA certificate to a file
    FILE *cert_fp = fopen(inter_cert_file, "wb");
    PEM_write_X509(cert_fp, cert);
    fclose(cert_fp);

    // Free resources
    X509_free(cert);
    X509_REQ_free(req);
    X509_free(root_cert);
    EVP_PKEY_free(root_key);
    EVP_PKEY_free(pkey);

    printf("Intermediate CA created successfully.\n");
}

int main() {
    // Create Root CA
    create_root_ca("root_key.pem", "root_cert.pem");

    // Create Intermediate CA
    create_intermediate_ca("root_key.pem", "root_cert.pem",
```

```
"inter_key.pem", "inter_cert.pem");

    return 0;
}
```

Equivalent OpenSSL Commands

Generate Root CA

```
openssl genrsa -out root_key.pem 2048
openssl req -x509 -new -nodes -key root_key.pem -sha256 -days 365
-out root_cert.pem -subj "/CN=Root CA"
```

Generate Intermediate CA

```
openssl genrsa -out inter_key.pem 2048
openssl req -new -key inter_key.pem -out inter.csr -subj
"/CN=Intermediate CA"
openssl x509 -req -in inter.csr -CA root_cert.pem -CAkey root_
key.pem -CAcreateserial -out inter_cert.pem -days 365 -sha256
```

Validating Certificates and Setting Up Revocation Mechanisms

Certificate validation is a critical process in Public Key Infrastructure (PKI) that ensures the trustworthiness of certificates by verifying their authenticity, validity, and revocation status. This section explores how to validate certificates and manage revocation using Certificate Revocation Lists (CRLs) and Online Certificate Status Protocol (OCSP) with OpenSSL C APIs. We will also provide equivalent OpenSSL commands where applicable.

Key Concepts:

- **Certificate Validation**:
  - Verifies the certificate's signature, expiration date, and trust chain up to a trusted Root CA.
- **Certificate Revocation**:
  - Certificates can be revoked by the issuing CA when compromised or no longer valid.
  - Two primary mechanisms for checking revocation:
    - **CRLs**: A list of revoked certificates published by the CA.
    - **OCSP**: A real-time protocol for querying the status of a certificate.

Code Implementation

The following code demonstrates:

Validating a Certificate Chain

```
#include <openssl/x509.h>
#include <openssl/x509_vfy.h>
#include <openssl/pem.h>
#include <stdio.h>

// Function to validate a certificate chain
int validate_certificate(const char *cert_file, const char *ca_
cert_file, const char *inter_cert_file) {
    // Load the certificate to be validated
    FILE *cert_fp = fopen(cert_file, "r");
    if (!cert_fp) {
        perror("Error opening certificate file");
        return -1;
    }
    X509 *cert = PEM_read_X509(cert_fp, NULL, NULL, NULL);
    fclose(cert_fp);

    // Create a certificate store and add the CA certificate
    X509_STORE *store = X509_STORE_new();
    FILE *ca_fp = fopen(ca_cert_file, "r");
    if (!ca_fp) {
        perror("Error opening CA certificate file");
        X509_free(cert);
        return -1;
    }
    X509 *ca_cert = PEM_read_X509(ca_fp, NULL, NULL, NULL);
    fclose(ca_fp);
    X509_STORE_add_cert(store, ca_cert);

    // Add Intermediate Certificate to the store
    FILE *inter_fp = fopen(inter_cert_file, "r");
    if (!inter_fp) {
        perror("Error opening Intermediate certificate file");
        X509_free(cert);
        X509_free(ca_cert);
        X509_STORE_free(store);
        return -1;
    }
    X509 *inter_cert = PEM_read_X509(inter_fp, NULL, NULL, NULL);
    fclose(inter_fp);
    X509_STORE_add_cert(store, inter_cert);
```

```
    // Create a certificate store context
    X509_STORE_CTX *ctx = X509_STORE_CTX_new();
    X509_STORE_CTX_init(ctx, store, cert, NULL);

    // Validate the certificate
    int ret = X509_verify_cert(ctx);
    if (ret == 1) {
        printf("Certificate validation successful.\n");
    } else {
        printf("Certificate validation failed: %s\n", X509_
verify_cert_error_string(X509_STORE_CTX_get_error(ctx)));
    }

    // Free resources
    X509_free(cert);
    X509_free(ca_cert);
    X509_free(inter_cert);
    X509_STORE_CTX_free(ctx);
    X509_STORE_free(store);

    return ret;
}
```

Generating and Checking CRLs.

```
#include <openssl/x509.h>
#include <openssl/x509_vfy.h>
#include <openssl/pem.h>
#include <openssl/x509v3.h>

void generate_crl(const char *ca_key_file, const char *ca_cert_
file, const char *crl_file) {
    FILE *ca_key_fp = fopen(ca_key_file, "r");
    EVP_PKEY *ca_key = PEM_read_PrivateKey(ca_key_fp, NULL, NULL,
NULL);
    fclose(ca_key_fp);

    FILE *ca_cert_fp = fopen(ca_cert_file, "r");
    X509 *ca_cert = PEM_read_X509(ca_cert_fp, NULL, NULL, NULL);
    fclose(ca_cert_fp);

    // Create CRL
    X509_CRL *crl = X509_CRL_new();
    X509_CRL_set_version(crl, 1); // v2 CRL
    X509_CRL_set_issuer_name(crl, X509_get_subject_name(ca_cert));
```

```
    // Set CRL last update and next update times
    X509_gmtime_adj(X509_CRL_get_lastUpdate(crl), 0);
    X509_gmtime_adj(X509_CRL_get_nextUpdate(crl), 7 * 24 * 60 *
60); // 7 days validity
    // Add a revoked certificate to the CRL
    X509_REVOKED *revoked = X509_REVOKED_new();
    ASN1_INTEGER_set(X509_REVOKED_get0_serialNumber(revoked),
12345); // Example serial number
    X509_gmtime_adj(X509_REVOKED_get0_revocationDate(revoked),
0);
    X509_CRL_add0_revoked(crl, revoked);

    // Sign the CRL with the CA's private key
    X509_CRL_sign(crl, ca_key, EVP_sha256());

    // Write CRL to file
    FILE *crl_fp = fopen(crl_file, "wb");
    PEM_write_X509_CRL(crl_fp, crl);
    fclose(crl_fp);
    printf("CRL generated successfully.\n");

    // Free resources
    X509_CRL_free(crl);
    X509_free(ca_cert);
    EVP_PKEY_free(ca_key);
}
```

Equivalent command

```
openssl ca -gencrl -out crl.pem -keyfile root_key.pem -cert root_
cert.pem
```

Validating a Certificate Against a Certificate Revocation List

A Certificate Revocation List (CRL) is a mechanism used in PKI to revoke and list certificates that are no longer valid. To validate a certificate against a CRL, the following steps are performed:

1. **CRL Basics**:
    - A CRL is issued by the Certificate Authority (CA).
    - It contains a list of revoked certificates (identified by their serial numbers) along with the reason for revocation and the revocation date.

2. **Use of `X509_STORE` in OpenSSL:**
   - **`X509_STORE`** is a structure in OpenSSL that represents the trust store, containing trusted CA certificates and other validation information (such as CRLs).
   - By adding a CRL to the **`X509_STORE`**, OpenSSL can validate certificates against the revocation list during the certificate chain verification process.

Code example

```
#include <openssl/x509.h>
#include <openssl/x509_vfy.h>
#include <openssl/pem.h>
#include <stdio.h>

int validate_cert_with_crl(const char *cert_file, const char
*ca_cert_file, const char *crl_file) {
    // Load the certificate to be validated
    FILE *cert_fp = fopen(cert_file, "r");
    if (!cert_fp) {
        perror("Error opening certificate file");
        return -1;
    }
    X509 *cert = PEM_read_X509(cert_fp, NULL, NULL, NULL);
    fclose(cert_fp);

    // Load the CA certificate
    FILE *ca_cert_fp = fopen(ca_cert_file, "r");
    if (!ca_cert_fp) {
        perror("Error opening CA certificate file");
        X509_free(cert);
        return -1;
    }
    X509 *ca_cert = PEM_read_X509(ca_cert_fp, NULL, NULL, NULL);
    fclose(ca_cert_fp);

    // Load the CRL
    FILE *crl_fp = fopen(crl_file, "r");
    if (!crl_fp) {
        perror("Error opening CRL file");
        X509_free(cert);
        X509_free(ca_cert);
        return -1;
    }
    X509_CRL *crl = PEM_read_X509_CRL(crl_fp, NULL, NULL, NULL);
    fclose(crl_fp);
```

```
    // Create a trust store and add the CA certificate
    X509_STORE *store = X509_STORE_new();
    if (X509_STORE_add_cert(store, ca_cert) != 1) {
        fprintf(stderr, "Error adding CA certificate to trust
store.\n");
        X509_free(cert);
        X509_free(ca_cert);
        X509_CRL_free(crl);
        X509_STORE_free(store);
        return -1;
    }

    // Add the CRL to the trust store
    if (X509_STORE_add_crl(store, crl) != 1) {
        fprintf(stderr, "Error adding CRL to trust store.\n");
        X509_free(cert);
        X509_free(ca_cert);
        X509_CRL_free(crl);
        X509_STORE_free(store);
        return -1;
    }

    // Set flags to enable CRL checking
    X509_STORE_set_flags(store, X509_V_FLAG_CRL_CHECK | X509_V_
FLAG_CRL_CHECK_ALL);

    // Create a store context and initialize it with the certifi-
cate and store
    X509_STORE_CTX *ctx = X509_STORE_CTX_new();
    if (!ctx || X509_STORE_CTX_init(ctx, store, cert, NULL) != 1)
{
        fprintf(stderr, "Error initializing store context.\n");
        X509_free(cert);
        X509_free(ca_cert);
        X509_CRL_free(crl);
        X509_STORE_free(store);
        if (ctx) X509_STORE_CTX_free(ctx);
        return -1;
    }

    // Verify the certificate
    int ret = X509_verify_cert(ctx);
    if (ret == 1) {
        printf("Certificate validation successful.\n");
    } else {
        printf("Certificate validation failed: %s\n", X509_
verify_cert_error_string(X509_STORE_CTX_get_error(ctx)));
```

```
    }

    // Free resources
    X509_free(cert);
    X509_free(ca_cert);
    X509_CRL_free(crl);
    X509_STORE_CTX_free(ctx);
    X509_STORE_free(store);

    return ret;
}
```

Setting Up and Validating with OCSP

The Online Certificate Status Protocol (OCSP) provides a real-time mechanism to check the revocation status of a certificate. Unlike Certificate Revocation Lists (CRLs), which are periodically updated and downloaded, OCSP queries are performed on-demand, making them more efficient for scenarios requiring immediate revocation checks.

In OpenSSL, this process involves two primary structures:

- **`OCSP_REQUEST`**: Represents the request sent to an OCSP responder to query the status of a certificate.
- **`OCSP_RESPONSE`**: Represents the response from the OCSP responder, indicating whether the certificate is valid, revoked, or unknown.

Step-by-Step Process

Here is a detailed explanation of how to create and process OCSP requests using OpenSSL's C APIs:

1. **Create the OCSP Request**
    - The OCSP request includes the certificate you want to verify and its issuing CA certificate.
    - These are used to identify the certificate's status.
2. **Send the Request to the OCSP Responder**
    - The OCSP responder is typically provided by the Certificate Authority (CA) that issued the certificate.
    - The responder's URL is usually embedded in the certificate under the Authority Information Access (AIA) extension.

3. **Process the OCSP Response**
   - The response from the OCSP responder contains the status of the certificate:
     - **Good**: The certificate is valid.
     - **Revoked**: The certificate has been revoked.
     - **Unknown**: The responder does not recognize the certificate.

Code example

Here is an example that demonstrates querying the OCSP status of a certificate using OpenSSL C APIs:

```
#include <openssl/ocsp.h>
#include <openssl/x509.h>
#include <openssl/pem.h>
#include <openssl/bio.h>
#include <openssl/err.h>
#include <stdio.h>

int query_ocsp_status(const char *cert_file, const char *issuer_
cert_file, const char *ocsp_url) {
    // Load the certificate to be verified
    FILE *cert_fp = fopen(cert_file, "r");
    if (!cert_fp) {
        perror("Error opening certificate file");
        return -1;
    }
    X509 *cert = PEM_read_X509(cert_fp, NULL, NULL, NULL);
    fclose(cert_fp);

    // Load the issuing CA certificate
    FILE *issuer_fp = fopen(issuer_cert_file, "r");
    if (!issuer_fp) {
        perror("Error opening issuer certificate file");
        X509_free(cert);
        return -1;
    }
    X509 *issuer_cert = PEM_read_X509(issuer_fp, NULL, NULL,
NULL);
    fclose(issuer_fp);

    // Create an OCSP_REQUEST
    OCSP_REQUEST *ocsp_req = OCSP_REQUEST_new();
    if (!ocsp_req) {
        fprintf(stderr, "Error creating OCSP request.\n");
        X509_free(cert);
```

```
        X509_free(issuer_cert);
        return -1;
    }

    // Add the certificate ID to the request
    OCSP_CERTID *cert_id = OCSP_cert_to_id(NULL, cert, issuer_
cert);
    if (!cert_id) {
        fprintf(stderr, "Error creating certificate ID.\n");
        OCSP_REQUEST_free(ocsp_req);
        X509_free(cert);
        X509_free(issuer_cert);
        return -1;
    }
    OCSP_request_add0_id(ocsp_req, cert_id);

    // Send the OCSP request to the responder
    BIO *bio = BIO_new_connect(ocsp_url); // e.g., "ocsp.example.
com:80"
    if (!bio || BIO_do_connect(bio) <= 0) {
        fprintf(stderr, "Error connecting to OCSP responder.\n");
        OCSP_REQUEST_free(ocsp_req);
        X509_free(cert);
        X509_free(issuer_cert);
        BIO_free_all(bio);
        return -1;
    }

    OCSP_RESPONSE *ocsp_resp = OCSP_sendreq_bio(bio, "/ocsp",
ocsp_req);
    if (!ocsp_resp) {
        fprintf(stderr, "Error sending OCSP request.\n");
        OCSP_REQUEST_free(ocsp_req);
        X509_free(cert);
        X509_free(issuer_cert);
        BIO_free_all(bio);
        return -1;
    }

    // Analyze the OCSP response
    int status = OCSP_response_status(ocsp_resp);
    if (status != OCSP_RESPONSE_STATUS_SUCCESSFUL) {
        fprintf(stderr, "OCSP responder error: %s\n", OCSP_
response_status_str(status));
    } else {
        OCSP_BASICRESP *basic_resp = OCSP_response_get1_basic
(ocsp_resp);
```

```
        if (basic_resp) {
            int cert_status, crl_reason;
            ASN1_GENERALIZEDTIME *revtime, *thisupd, *nextupd;

            if (OCSP_resp_find_status(basic_resp, cert_id, &cert_
status, &crl_reason, &revtime, &thisupd, &nextupd)) {
                if (cert_status == V_OCSP_CERTSTATUS_GOOD) {
                    printf("Certificate status: GOOD\n");
                } else if (cert_status == V_OCSP_CERTSTATUS_RE-
VOKED) {
                    printf("Certificate status: REVOKED\n");
                } else if (cert_status == V_OCSP_CERTSTATUS_UN-
KNOWN) {
                    printf("Certificate status: UNKNOWN\n");
                }
            } else {
                fprintf(stderr, "Error retrieving certificate
status.\n");
            }

            OCSP_BASICRESP_free(basic_resp);
        }
    }

    // Free resources
    OCSP_RESPONSE_free(ocsp_resp);
    OCSP_REQUEST_free(ocsp_req);
    X509_free(cert);
    X509_free(issuer_cert);
    BIO_free_all(bio);

    return status;
}
```

Applying PKI to Secure a Web Application (or Network Service)

In this section, we will demonstrate how PKI can be used to secure a web application or network service by configuring certificates for HTTPS and enabling Mutual TLS (mTLS) for added security. mTLS ensures both the client and server verify each other's certificates, providing strong authentication and encryption.

Steps to Apply PKI for a Web Application

1. **Generate a Certificate Authority (CA)**

   a. The CA is responsible for issuing certificates for the server and clients.

   b. Use the following OpenSSL command to generate a self-signed CA certificate:

   ```
   # Generate the CA private key
   openssl genrsa -out ca.key 4096
   ```

Note: *As CA certificates have a larger lifetime in the order of years, key size is chosen here as the largest available size for the CA key as a recommendation from various sources. Example: https://cloud.google.com/certificate-authority-service/docs/choosing-key-algorithm*

```
# Create a self-signed CA certificate
openssl req -x509 -new -nodes -key ca.key -sha256 -days 365 -out ca.crt \
    -subj "/C=US/ST=California/L=San Francisco/O=Example CA/CN=example.com"
```

2. **Generate a Server Certificate**

   a. The server certificate is used to secure the web application and authenticate it to clients.

```
# Generate the server private key
openssl genrsa -out server.key 2048
```

Note: *For server/client keys, we can use 2048 size as the server/client lifetime is comparatively short.*

```
# Create a Certificate Signing Request (CSR) for the server
openssl req -new -key server.key -out server.csr \
    -subj "/C=US/ST=California/L=San Francisco/O=Example Server/CN=server.example.com"

# Sign the server certificate with the CA
openssl x509 -req -in server.csr -CA ca.crt -CAkey ca.key -CAcreateserial \
    -out server.crt -days 365 -sha256
```

The **`server.crt`** and **`server.key`** will be used to configure the server.

3. **Generate Client Certificates (for mTLS)**

   a. Each client accessing the service will have its own certificate for mutual authentication.

```
# Generate the client private key
openssl genrsa -out client.key 2048

# Create a Certificate Signing Request (CSR) for the client
openssl req -new -key client.key -out client.csr \
    -subj "/C=US/ST=California/L=San Francisco/O=Example Client/
CN=client.example.com"

# Sign the client certificate with the CA
openssl x509 -req -in client.csr -CA ca.crt -CAkey ca.key
-CAcreateserial \
    -out client.crt -days 365 -sha256
```

The **`client.crt`** and **`client.key`** will be used by the client.

4. **Configure the Web Server for HTTPS**

   a. Use the server certificate and private key (**`server.crt`** and **`server.key`**) to enable HTTPS on the web server.

   For NGINX: Add the following to your NGINX configuration file:

```
server {
    listen 443 ssl;
    server_name server.example.com;

    ssl_certificate     /path/to/server.crt;
    ssl_certificate_key /path/to/server.key;

    ssl_protocols        TLSv1.2 TLSv1.3;
    ssl_ciphers          HIGH:!aNULL:!MD5;

    location / {
        root /usr/share/nginx/html;
        index index.html;
    }
}
```

5. **Enable Mutual TLS (mTLS)**

   a. Configure the server to request and verify client certificates.

   For NGINX: Update the NGINX configuration to include client certificate verification:

```
server {
    listen 443 ssl;
    server_name server.example.com;

    ssl_certificate     /path/to/server.crt;
```

```
    ssl_certificate_key /path/to/server.key;

    ssl_client_certificate /path/to/ca.crt; # CA certificate to
verify clients
    ssl_verify_client on;                   # Enforce client
certificate validation

    ssl_protocols       TLSv1.2 TLSv1.3;
    ssl_ciphers         HIGH:!aNULL:!MD5;

    location / {
        root /usr/share/nginx/html;
        index index.html;
    }
}
```

b. In this configuration, the server checks that the client certificate is valid and signed by the CA (**ca.crt**).

6. **Test the Configuration**

   a. Use tools such as **curl** or a browser to test the server's HTTPS and mTLS setup.

   Testing HTTPS:

   ```
   curl -k https://server.example.com
   ```

   Testing mTLS (with a client certificate):

   ```
   curl --key client.key --cert client.crt --cacert ca.crt https://
   server.example.com
   ```

   i. The **--key** and **--cert** options specify the client's private key and certificate.

   ii. The **--cacert** option ensures the server certificate is verified using the CA.

Conclusion

In this chapter, we explored the practical application of PKI to secure web applications and network services. Starting with the creation of a Certificate Authority (CA), we demonstrated how to issue server and client certificates, followed by configuring HTTPS and enabling Mutual TLS (mTLS) for robust authentication. We walked through the steps to generate and manage certificates, including their lifecycle through renewal and revocation, and emphasized the importance of using strong keys and secure TLS settings. By integrating PKI with real-world scenarios, such as web server configurations, we showcased how PKI establishes trust and enhances security in modern systems. These foundations provide a solid framework for implementing and maintaining a secure, scalable, and trustworthy PKI ecosystem.

In the next chapter, we will cover details of symmetric key cryptography with some practical references using OpenSSL.

CHAPTER 6
Symmetric Key Cryptography with OpenSSL

Introduction

In *Chapter 1, Cryptography Basics and Network Security*, we explored the theoretical foundations of cryptography, including the fundamental principles of symmetric key cryptography. We discussed how symmetric key algorithms function, their strengths and limitations, and their critical role in ensuring data confidentiality and integrity in secure communication systems. Building upon that theoretical knowledge, this chapter shifts focus to a hands-on, practical approach.

In this chapter, we will delve into the implementation of symmetric key cryptography using OpenSSL, one of the most widely used cryptographic libraries. The chapter is designed to provide step-by-step guidance on how to encrypt and decrypt data, manage cryptographic keys, and secure files using symmetric algorithms such as AES and DES. By the end, you will have a comprehensive understanding of how to effectively use OpenSSL's APIs and command-line tools to address real-world security challenges.

Let us transition from theory to practice, where we will unlock the full potential of OpenSSL to implement secure and efficient cryptographic solutions.

Structure

In this chapter, we will cover the following topics:

- Setting Up OpenSSL for Symmetric Key Cryptography
- Using Symmetric Ciphers in OpenSSL
- Key and IV Management

- File Encryption and Decryption
- Authenticated Encryption (AEAD) with OpenSSL

Setting Up OpenSSL for Symmetric Key Cryptography

When writing C programs using OpenSSL for symmetric key cryptography, include the appropriate libraries and header files in your project.

- **Libraries to Link**

  Ensure your program links against the following libraries during compilation:

  - **`libcrypto`**: The core cryptographic library that includes symmetric cipher implementations.
  - **`libssl` (optional)**: Provides SSL/TLS functionality but may not be required for standalone symmetric cryptography.
  - Ensure OpenSSL is properly installed on your system using the following commands:
    - **`openssl version`**
    - compile with **`-wall`** flag to enable all computer warnings, helping catch potential issues.

  ```
  gcc -Wall -o symmetric_example symmetric_example.c -lcrypto -ldl
  ```

  Note: *`-idl` flag is often needed on linux system to handle dynamic linking for **`openssl`***

  Example compilation command:

  ```
  gcc -o symmetric_example symmetric_example.c -lcrypto
  ```

- **Header Files to Include**

  Use the following header files in your code for symmetric cryptography:

  - **`<openssl/evp.h>`**: The high-level cryptographic API for encryption and decryption.
  - **`<openssl/rand.h>`**: For generating secure random keys and IVs.
  - **`<openssl/err.h>`**: For error handling and debugging.

  Example:

  ```
  #include <openssl/evp.h>
  #include <openssl/rand.h>
  #include <openssl/err.h>
  ```

- **Environment Setup**

  Make sure the library paths are correctly set if OpenSSL is installed in a non-default location. Use `-I` for include paths and `-L` for library paths:

  ```
  gcc -o symmetric_example symmetric_example.c -I/usr/local/include
  -L/usr/local/lib -lcrypto
  ```

Using Symmetric Ciphers in OpenSSL

Symmetric ciphers are widely used for encrypting data efficiently and securely. OpenSSL provides extensive support for symmetric encryption algorithms such as **AES, ChaCha20, and legacy ciphers such as 3DES**, along with multiple cipher modes such as **Cipher Block Chaining (CBC)**, **Galois/Counter Mode (GCM)**, and **XTS (used for disk encryption)**. This section covers practical examples of these ciphers, detailed code snippets for encryption and decryption, and explanations of cipher modes.

- **Examples of Symmetric Ciphers**
  - **Advanced Encryption Standard (AES)**: The most popular and secure symmetric cipher, supporting 128, 192, and 256-bit keys.
  - **Triple DES (3DES)**: A legacy encryption method that applies DES three times, still used in older systems but deprecated in modern cryptography.
  - **ChaCha20**: A modern, high-speed stream cipher, optimized for software performance, used in TLS 1.3 and mobile encryption.
- **Code Snippets for Encryption and Decryption**

OpenSSL's EVP API is the recommended high-level interface for symmetric encryption. Following are examples for AES encryption and decryption in CBC mode.

Generation of key and IV used in this example are explained in the next section .

1. **Encryption with AES in CBC Mode**

```
#include <openssl/evp.h>
#include <openssl/rand.h>
#include <string.h>
#include <stdio.h>

// Function to handle errors by printing OpenSSL error messages
and aborting the program
void handleErrors() {
    ERR_print_errors_fp(stderr);
    abort();
}

/*
 * Function to perform AES-256-CBC encryption.
```

```
 *
 * Parameters:
 * - plaintext: Pointer to the data to be encrypted
 * - plaintext_len: Length of the plaintext
 * - key: Pointer to the 256-bit encryption key
 * - iv: Pointer to the 128-bit initialization vector (IV)
 * - ciphertext: Buffer to store the encrypted data
 *
 * Returns:
 * - The length of the encrypted ciphertext
 */
int encrypt(const unsigned char *plaintext, int plaintext_len,
const unsigned char *key,
            const unsigned char *iv, unsigned char *ciphertext) {

    EVP_CIPHER_CTX *ctx = EVP_CIPHER_CTX_new(); // Create a new
cipher context
    if (!ctx) handleErrors(); // Check for allocation failure

    // Initialize the encryption operation with AES-256-CBC
    if (EVP_EncryptInit_ex(ctx, EVP_aes_256_cbc(), NULL, key, iv)
!= 1)
        handleErrors();

    int len, ciphertext_len;

    // Encrypt the plaintext in blocks
    if (EVP_EncryptUpdate(ctx, ciphertext, &len, plaintext,
plaintext_len) != 1)
        handleErrors();
    ciphertext_len = len; // Store the length of the first
encrypted block

    // Finalize encryption: Handles padding and final block
encryption
    if (EVP_EncryptFinal_ex(ctx, ciphertext + len, &len) != 1)
        handleErrors();
    ciphertext_len += len; // Add the final block length to total
ciphertext length

    EVP_CIPHER_CTX_free(ctx); // Free the cipher context
    return ciphertext_len; // Return the total length of the
encrypted data
}
```

2. **Decryption with AES in CBC Mode**

```
/*
 * Function to perform AES-256-CBC decryption.
 *
 * Parameters:
 * - ciphertext: Pointer to the encrypted data
 * - ciphertext_len: Length of the ciphertext
 * - key: Pointer to the 256-bit decryption key
 * - iv: Pointer to the 128-bit initialization vector (IV)
 * - plaintext: Buffer to store the decrypted data
 *
 * Returns:
 * - The length of the decrypted plaintext
 */

int decrypt(const unsigned char *ciphertext, int ciphertext_len,
const unsigned char *key,
            const unsigned char *iv, unsigned char *plaintext) {

    // Create a new cipher context
    EVP_CIPHER_CTX *ctx = EVP_CIPHER_CTX_new();
    if (!ctx) handleErrors(); // Check for allocation failure

    // Initialize the decryption operation with AES-256-CBC
    if (EVP_DecryptInit_ex(ctx, EVP_aes_256_cbc(), NULL, key, iv)
!= 1)
        handleErrors();

    int len, plaintext_len;

    // Decrypt the ciphertext in blocks
    if (EVP_DecryptUpdate(ctx, plaintext, &len, ciphertext,
ciphertext_len) != 1)
        handleErrors();
    plaintext_len = len; // Store the length of the first
decrypted block

    // Finalize decryption: Handles removal of padding and
processes the final block
    if (EVP_DecryptFinal_ex(ctx, plaintext + len, &len) != 1)
        handleErrors();
    plaintext_len += len; // Add the final block length to total
plaintext length
```

```
    EVP_CIPHER_CTX_free(ctx); // Free the cipher context
    return plaintext_len; // Return the total length of the
decrypted data
}
```

- **Explanation of AES Cipher Modes**
  - **Cipher Block Chaining (CBC)**:
    - Splits plaintext into fixed-size blocks.
    - Each block is XORed with the previous ciphertext block before encryption.
    - Requires an Initialization Vector (IV) for the first block.
    - Vulnerable to padding oracle attacks if not implemented correctly.

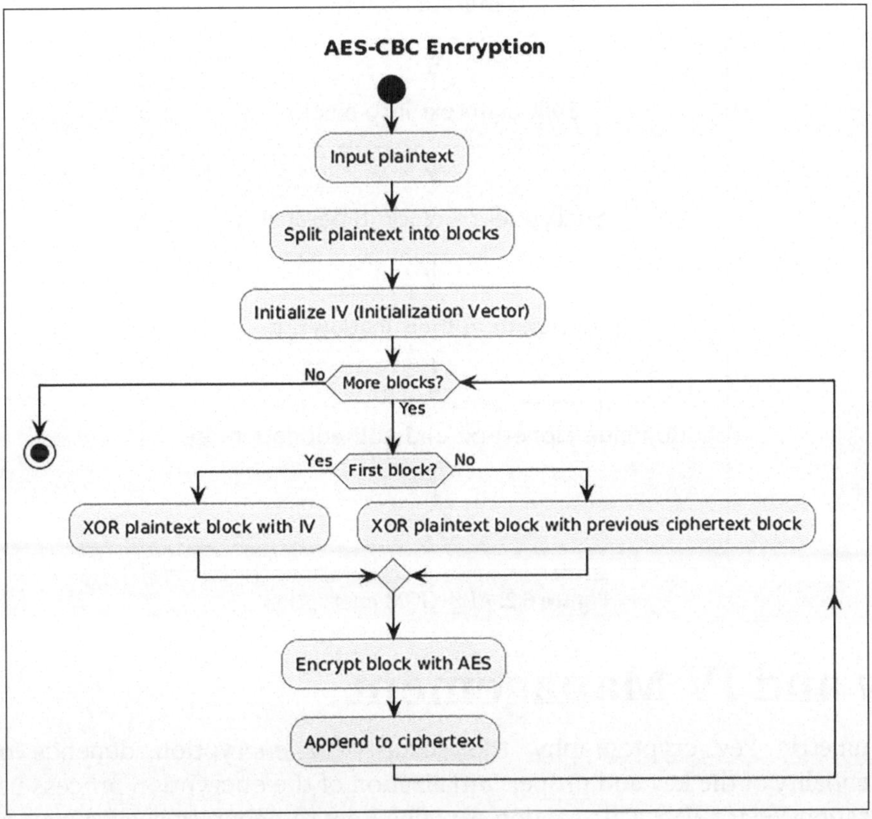

***Figure 6.1**: AES-CBC encryption*

  - **GCM (Galois/Counter Mode)**:
    - Combines encryption with authentication for better security.
    - Provides confidentiality, integrity, and authenticity in one step.
    - Faster than CBC in parallel implementations.

- **ChaCha20-Poly1305**: A stream cipher with authentication, faster than AES-GCM on software-only platforms.
- **AES-XTS**: Used in disk encryption (BitLocker, LUKS).

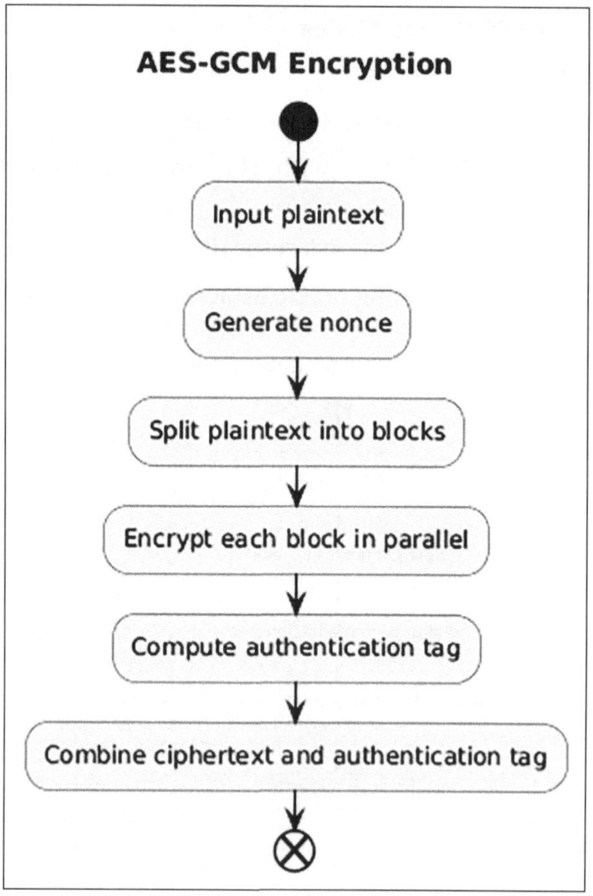

***Figure 6.2**: AES-GCM encryption*

Key and IV Management

In symmetric key cryptography, the security of encryption depends on the confidentiality of the key and proper initialization of the encryption process using an Initialization Vector (IV). This section explains how to generate secure keys and IVs using OpenSSL APIs, and discusses best practices for securely storing and retrieving them.

1. **Generating Random Keys and IVs Using OpenSSL APIs**:

   OpenSSL provides the **`RAND_bytes`** API for generating cryptographically secure random bytes, which can be used to create keys and IVs.

   Code Snippet: Generating Random Keys and IVs

```
#include <openssl/rand.h>
#include <stdio.h>
#include <string.h>
#include <stdlib.h>

#define KEY_SIZE 32   // 256 bits for AES-256 encryption
#define IV_SIZE 16    // 128 bits for AES block size

/*
 * Function to generate a random key and IV for AES encryption.
 *
 * Parameters:
 * - key: Pointer to a buffer where the generated 256-bit key will
be stored.
 * - iv: Pointer to a buffer where the generated 128-bit IV will
be stored.
 */
void generate_key_and_iv(unsigned char *key, unsigned char *iv) {
    // Generate a cryptographically secure random key
    if (RAND_bytes(key, KEY_SIZE) != 1) {
        fprintf(stderr, "Error generating random key\n");
        exit(EXIT_FAILURE); // Exit if key generation fails
    }

    // Generate a cryptographically secure random IV
    if (RAND_bytes(iv, IV_SIZE) != 1) {
        fprintf(stderr, "Error generating random IV\n");
        exit(EXIT_FAILURE); // Exit if IV generation fails
    }
}
```

2. **Secure Key Storage and Retrieval**

   Storing and retrieving cryptographic keys securely is critical to maintaining the confidentiality of encrypted data. Following are some methods for secure key management:

   - **Hardware Security Modules (HSMs)**: Use dedicated hardware to store keys securely.
   - **Trusted Platform Module (TPM)**: Utilize TPM chips for secure storage. We will see more details of this in a separate chapter of OpenSSL engine.

- **Key Management Services (KMS)**: Services such as AWS KMS or Azure Key Vault can store keys securely in the cloud.
- **Encrypted Files**: Store keys in files encrypted with a strong passphrase. OpenSSL provides tools for encrypting and decrypting files.

Code Snippet: Encrypting and Storing a Key in a File:

```
#include <openssl/evp.h>
#include <openssl/aes.h>
#include <stdio.h>
#include <string.h>
#include <stdlib.h>

/*
 * Function to encrypt an AES key using a passphrase and store it
in a file.
 *
 * Parameters:
 * - key: Pointer to the 256-bit (32-byte) AES key to be encrypted
 * - filename: Name of the file where the encrypted key will be
stored
 * - passphrase: User-provided passphrase used for key encryption
 */
void save_encrypted_key_to_file(const unsigned char *key, const
char *filename, const char *passphrase) {

    // Open the file in binary write mode
    FILE *file = fopen(filename, "wb");
    if (!file) {
        perror("Error opening file");
        exit(EXIT_FAILURE);
    }

    // Generate an 8-byte random salt for key derivation
    unsigned char salt[8];
    RAND_bytes(salt, sizeof(salt));

    // Derive encryption key and IV using the passphrase and salt
    unsigned char derived_key[32], iv[16];
    EVP_BytesToKey(EVP_aes_256_cbc(), EVP_sha256(), salt,
                   (unsigned char *)passphrase, strlen(pass-
phrase), 1, derived_key, iv);

    // Create a new encryption context
    EVP_CIPHER_CTX *ctx = EVP_CIPHER_CTX_new();
    EVP_EncryptInit_ex(ctx, EVP_aes_256_cbc(), NULL, derived_key,
iv);
```

```
    unsigned char ciphertext[256];  // Buffer to store the encrypted
key
    int len, ciphertext_len = 0;

    // Encrypt the key (assumed to be 32 bytes long for AES-256)
    EVP_EncryptUpdate(ctx, ciphertext, &len, key, 32);
    ciphertext_len = len;

    // Finalize encryption (handles padding if needed)
    EVP_EncryptFinal_ex(ctx, ciphertext + len, &len);
    ciphertext_len += len;

    // Write salt and encrypted key to the file
    fwrite(salt, 1, sizeof(salt), file);  // Write salt (8 bytes)
    fwrite(ciphertext, 1, ciphertext_len, file);  // Write encrypted
key

    // Close the file and free the encryption context
    fclose(file);
    EVP_CIPHER_CTX_free(ctx);

    printf("Key securely saved to %s\n", filename);
}
```

This example encrypts a key using a passphrase and writes it to a file, including a salt for key derivation.

File Encryption and Decryption

File encryption and decryption are critical for protecting sensitive data at rest. OpenSSL provides robust APIs for encrypting and decrypting files using symmetric encryption algorithms such as AES. This section covers a step-by-step guide for file encryption and decryption, along with error handling to ensure reliability during file operations.

Step-by-Step Example: Encrypting and Decrypting Files

1. **Encryption of a File:** The following example encrypts the contents of an input file and writes the ciphertext to an output file using AES in CBC mode.

   Code Snippet: File Encryption

   ```
   #include <openssl/evp.h>
   #include <openssl/rand.h>
   ```

```
#include <stdio.h>
#include <stdlib.h>
#include <string.h>

#define KEY_SIZE 32    // 256 bits AES key
#define IV_SIZE 16     // 128 bits IV (AES block size)

/*
 * Function to handle errors by printing a message and exiting
the program.
 *
 * Parameters:
 * - message: A string describing the error.
 */
void handleErrors(const char *message) {
    perror(message);
    exit(EXIT_FAILURE);
}

/*
 * Function to encrypt a file using AES-256-CBC and save the
encrypted content to a new file.
 *
 * Parameters:
 * - input_file: Name of the file to be encrypted.
 * - output_file: Name of the file where encrypted data will be
stored.
 * - key: Pointer to a 256-bit AES encryption key.
 */
void encrypt_file(const char *input_file, const char *output_file,
const unsigned char *key) {
    // Open the input file in read-binary mode
    FILE *in = fopen(input_file, "rb");
    if (!in) handleErrors("Error opening input file");

    // Open the output file in write-binary mode
    FILE *out = fopen(output_file, "wb");
    if (!out) handleErrors("Error opening output file");

    unsigned char iv[IV_SIZE]; // Buffer to store the IV

    // Generate a random IV for encryption
    if (RAND_bytes(iv, IV_SIZE) != 1)
        handleErrors("Error generating IV");

    // Write IV to the beginning of the output file (needed for
decryption)
```

```
    fwrite(iv, 1, IV_SIZE, out);

    // Create and initialize an OpenSSL encryption context
    EVP_CIPHER_CTX *ctx = EVP_CIPHER_CTX_new();
    if (!ctx) handleErrors("Error creating cipher context");

    // Initialize AES-256-CBC encryption with the key and IV
    if (EVP_EncryptInit_ex(ctx, EVP_aes_256_cbc(), NULL, key, iv)
!= 1)
        handleErrors("Error initializing encryption");

    unsigned char buffer[1024];  // Buffer for reading input file in
chunks
    unsigned char ciphertext[1024 + EVP_MAX_BLOCK_LENGTH];  //
Buffer for encrypted output
    int bytes_read, len;

    // Read input file and encrypt each chunk
    while ((bytes_read = fread(buffer, 1, sizeof(buffer), in)) > 0)
{
        if (EVP_EncryptUpdate(ctx, ciphertext, &len, buffer,
bytes_read) != 1)
            handleErrors("Error during encryption");
        fwrite(ciphertext, 1, len, out); // Write encrypted data
to output file
    }

    // Finalize encryption (handles padding for the last block)
    if (EVP_EncryptFinal_ex(ctx, ciphertext, &len) != 1)
        handleErrors("Error finalizing encryption");
    fwrite(ciphertext, 1, len, out); // Write final encrypted
block

    // Close files and free encryption context
    fclose(in);
    fclose(out);
    EVP_CIPHER_CTX_free(ctx);
}
```

2. **Decryption of a File:** The following example decrypts the contents of an encrypted file and writes the plaintext to an output file.

   Code Snippet: File Decryption

```
#include <openssl/evp.h>
#include <openssl/rand.h>
#include <stdio.h>
#include <stdlib.h>
```

```
#include <string.h>

#define KEY_SIZE 32   // 256-bit AES key
#define IV_SIZE 16    // 128-bit IV (AES block size)

/*
 * Function to decrypt a file encrypted using AES-256-CBC.
 *
 * Parameters:
 * - input_file: Name of the file containing encrypted data.
 * - output_file: Name of the file where decrypted data will be
stored.
 * - key: Pointer to a 256-bit AES decryption key.
 */
void decrypt_file(const char *input_file, const char *output_file,
const unsigned char *key) {
    // Open the encrypted input file in binary read mode
    FILE *in = fopen(input_file, "rb");
    if (!in) handleErrors("Error opening input file");

    // Open the output file in binary write mode
    FILE *out = fopen(output_file, "wb");
    if (!out) handleErrors("Error opening output file");

    unsigned char iv[IV_SIZE];  // Buffer to store the IV

    // Read the IV from the beginning of the input file
    if (fread(iv, 1, IV_SIZE, in) != IV_SIZE)
        handleErrors("Error reading IV");

    // Create and initialize a decryption context
    EVP_CIPHER_CTX *ctx = EVP_CIPHER_CTX_new();
    if (!ctx) handleErrors("Error creating cipher context");

    // Initialize AES-256-CBC decryption with the retrieved IV
    if (EVP_DecryptInit_ex(ctx, EVP_aes_256_cbc(), NULL, key, iv)
!= 1)
        handleErrors("Error initializing decryption");

    unsigned char buffer[1024 + EVP_MAX_BLOCK_LENGTH];  // Buffer
for reading encrypted chunks
    unsigned char plaintext[1024];  // Buffer to store decrypted
data
    int bytes_read, len;
```

```
    // Read encrypted data from input file and decrypt it in
chunks
    while ((bytes_read = fread(buffer, 1, sizeof(buffer), in)) > 0)
{
        if (EVP_DecryptUpdate(ctx, plaintext, &len, buffer,
bytes_read) != 1)
            handleErrors("Error during decryption");
        fwrite(plaintext, 1, len, out); // Write decrypted data
to output file
    }

    // Finalize decryption (handles padding removal)
    if (EVP_DecryptFinal_ex(ctx, plaintext, &len) != 1)
        handleErrors("Error finalizing decryption");
    fwrite(plaintext, 1, len, out); // Write final decrypted block

    // Close files and free decryption context
    fclose(in);
    fclose(out);
    EVP_CIPHER_CTX_free(ctx);
}
```

We have already checked the key and IV generation earlier. We need to use same for passing as parameter in the preceding functions.

Error Handling During File Operations

Error handling is crucial for ensuring reliability in file encryption and decryption. Here are some practices for robust error management:

1. **File Open Errors**: Check if the file pointer is **NULL** after calling **fopen**.
2. **File Read/Write Errors**: Use **ferror** to detect read or write errors during **fread** or **fwrite**.
3. **Cryptographic Errors**: Use **EVP_* API** return values to check for failures. For more detailed error messages, call **ERR_print_errors_fp(stderr)** from OpenSSL's error-handling library.
4. **Resource Management**: Always close files and free resources (for example, **EVP_CIPHER_CTX_free**) to avoid memory leaks.

With these detailed steps, you can implement reliable file encryption and decryption using OpenSSL, ensuring the security of sensitive data at rest.

Authenticated Encryption (AEAD) with OpenSSL

Authenticated Encryption with Associated Data (AEAD) provides both encryption and authentication in a single operation, ensuring the confidentiality, integrity, and authenticity of data.

AEAD modes such as AES-GCM (Galois/Counter Mode) and ChaCha20-Poly1305 are widely used in secure communication protocols such as TLS 1.3, IPsec, and QUIC.

Overview of AEAD:

- **Encryption:** Encrypts plaintext while generating an **authentication tag** to ensure data integrity.
- **Decryption:** Decrypts ciphertext **only if the authentication tag is valid**, preventing unauthorized modifications.
- **Authentication Failure:** If decryption fails due to an invalid tag, the **plaintext is never revealed**, improving security.
- **Associated Data (AAD):** Data that is **not encrypted** but is **authenticated** (for example, headers in TLS or IPsec).

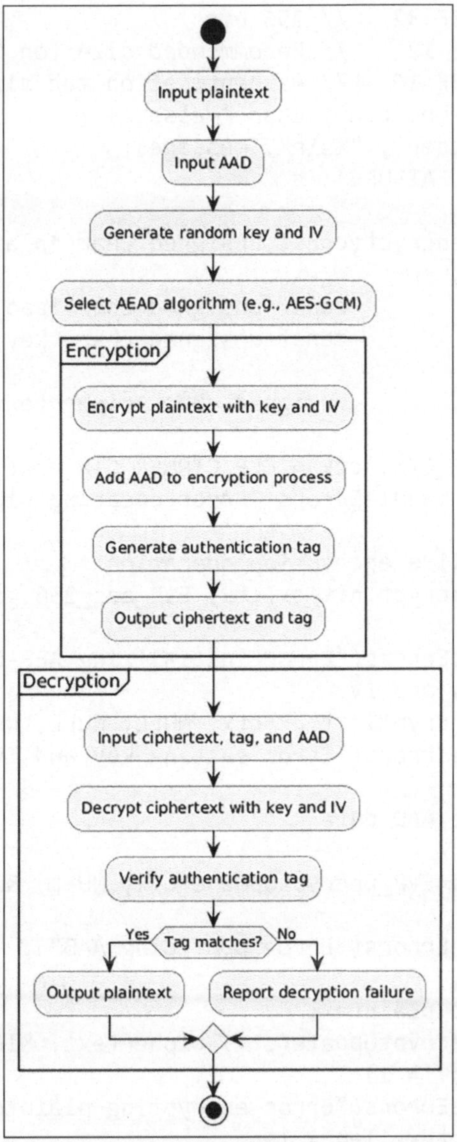

Figure 6.3: AEAD *encryption decryption flow*

Code Snippet: AEAD Encryption and Decryption with AES-GCM

1. **Encryption with AEAD (AES-GCM):** The encryption process encrypts the plaintext, generates a ciphertext, and outputs an authentication tag.

```
#include <openssl/evp.h>
#include <stdio.h>
#include <string.h>
#include <stdlib.h>
```

```
#define KEY_SIZE 32   // 256 bits
#define IV_SIZE 12    // Recommended size for GCM
#define TAG_SIZE 16   // Authentication tag size
void handleErrors(const char *message) {
    fprintf(stderr, "%s\n", message);
    exit(EXIT_FAILURE);
}
void aes_gcm_encrypt(const unsigned char *plaintext, int
plaintext_len,
                     const unsigned char *aad, int aad_len,
                     const unsigned char *key, const unsigned
char *iv,
                     unsigned char *ciphertext, unsigned char
*tag) {
    EVP_CIPHER_CTX *ctx = EVP_CIPHER_CTX_new();
    if (!ctx) handleErrors("Error creating cipher context");

    // Initialize encryption operation
    if (EVP_EncryptInit_ex(ctx, EVP_aes_256_gcm(), NULL, NULL,
NULL) != 1)
        handleErrors("Error initializing AES-GCM encryption");
    // Set key and IV
    if (EVP_EncryptInit_ex(ctx, NULL, NULL, key, iv) != 1)
        handleErrors("Error setting key and IV");

    // Provide AAD data
    int len;
    if (aad && EVP_EncryptUpdate(ctx, NULL, &len, aad, aad_len)
!= 1)
        handleErrors("Error providing AAD");

    // Encrypt plaintext
    if (EVP_EncryptUpdate(ctx, ciphertext, &len, plaintext,
plaintext_len) != 1)
        handleErrors("Error encrypting plaintext");
    int ciphertext_len = len;

    // Finalize encryption
    if (EVP_EncryptFinal_ex(ctx, ciphertext + len, &len) != 1)
        handleErrors("Error finalizing encryption");
    ciphertext_len += len;

    // Get authentication tag
    if (EVP_CIPHER_CTX_ctrl(ctx, EVP_CTRL_GCM_GET_TAG, TAG_SIZE,
```

```
tag) != 1)
        handleErrors("Error getting authentication tag");

    EVP_CIPHER_CTX_free(ctx);
}
```

2. **Decryption with AEAD (AES-GCM):** The decryption process decrypts the ciphertext only if the authentication tag matches.

```
void aes_gcm_decrypt(const unsigned char *ciphertext, int
ciphertext_len,
                     const unsigned char *aad, int aad_len,
                     const unsigned char *key, const unsigned
char *iv,
                     const unsigned char *tag, unsigned char
*plaintext) {
    EVP_CIPHER_CTX *ctx = EVP_CIPHER_CTX_new();
    if (!ctx) handleErrors("Error creating cipher context");

    // Initialize decryption operation
    if (EVP_DecryptInit_ex(ctx, EVP_aes_256_gcm(), NULL, NULL,
NULL) != 1)
        handleErrors("Error initializing AES-GCM decryption");

    // Set key and IV
    if (EVP_DecryptInit_ex(ctx, NULL, NULL, key, iv) != 1)
        handleErrors("Error setting key and IV");

    // Provide AAD data
    int len;
    if (aad && EVP_DecryptUpdate(ctx, NULL, &len, aad, aad_len)
!= 1)
        handleErrors("Error providing AAD");

    // Decrypt ciphertext
    if (EVP_DecryptUpdate(ctx, plaintext, &len, ciphertext,
ciphertext_len) != 1)
        handleErrors("Error decrypting ciphertext");
    int plaintext_len = len;

    // Set expected authentication tag
    if (EVP_CIPHER_CTX_ctrl(ctx, EVP_CTRL_GCM_SET_TAG, TAG_SIZE,
(void *)tag) != 1)
        handleErrors("Error setting authentication tag");

    // Finalize decryption (fails if tag verification fails)
    if (EVP_DecryptFinal_ex(ctx, plaintext + len, &len) != 1) {
        handleErrors("Decryption failed: Tag mismatch");
```

```
        }
        plaintext_len += len;

        EVP_CIPHER_CTX_free(ctx);
    }
```

Conclusion

In this chapter, we explored the practical aspects of symmetric key cryptography using OpenSSL, focusing on essential operations such as encryption, decryption, key and IV management, file encryption, and authenticated encryption (AEAD). These examples demonstrated how OpenSSL provides a powerful and flexible API for implementing secure cryptographic operations in real-world applications. By combining encryption techniques with proper error handling and secure key management, developers can build robust systems to protect sensitive data.

Looking ahead, the next chapter will delve into OpenSSL Engine methods, which enhance cryptographic operations by leveraging hardware-based acceleration and custom cryptographic implementations. These methods are particularly beneficial for high-performance use cases, enabling faster symmetric encryption and decryption while offloading computation from the CPU. Understanding how to integrate OpenSSL Engines into the workflows discussed in this chapter will further optimize and secure your cryptographic applications.

CHAPTER 7

OpenSSL Engine for Security Hardware

Introduction

As cryptographic applications grow more sophisticated, the demand for secure, high-performance solutions becomes increasingly critical. OpenSSL provides extensive support for integrating hardware-based cryptographic accelerators through its Engine framework, enabling developers to leverage dedicated security hardware for offloading cryptographic operations, isolating sensitive keys, and enhancing performance. This chapter explores the practical use of OpenSSL Engines with security hardware, focusing on Atmel's `CryptoAuthLib` and hardware such as the ATECC608B, which offers secure key storage, hardware-accelerated encryption, and authenticated communication.

Building on the concepts introduced in the previous chapters, this chapter focuses on configuring OpenSSL with security hardware to perform cryptographic operations such as encryption, decryption, and key management. Through step-by-step examples and detailed explanations, you will learn how to integrate Atmel's security hardware with OpenSSL for real-world applications, such as secure TLS connections and hardware-accelerated symmetric encryption. By the end of this chapter, you will be equipped to enhance the security and performance of your cryptographic implementations using OpenSSL Engines and specialized hardware.

We will also cover how the Provider Framework added in OpenSSL 3.0 can be used for security hardware integration.

Structure

In this chapter, we will cover the following topics:

- Introduction to OpenSSL Engine
- Overview of Security Hardware
- Setting Up OpenSSL for Security Hardware

- Key Management with Security Hardware
- Accelerating Cryptographic Operations
- Real-World Application: Secure TLS with Atmel Hardware
- Provider Framework for Security Hardware Integration

Introduction to OpenSSL Engine

The **OpenSSL Engine** framework provides a standardized mechanism for integrating OpenSSL with external cryptographic hardware or software implementations. While OpenSSL Engines were more prominent in earlier OpenSSL versions (pre-3.0), they are still relevant for specific hardware integrations that have not yet transitioned to the **Provider Framework** in OpenSSL 3.0.

The OpenSSL Engine framework acts as an abstraction layer between OpenSSL and cryptographic hardware, such as:

- **Hardware Security Modules (HSMs)**: Devices that perform cryptographic operations and securely store keys.
- **Trusted Platform Modules (TPMs)**: Security chips used for device authentication and secure key storage.
- **Smart Cards**: Tokens for secure identity management and cryptographic operations.

The OpenSSL Engine framework enables OpenSSL to:

- Offload cryptographic operations (for example, RSA, AES) to hardware, improving performance.
- Ensure key isolation, where private keys remain securely stored in hardware, never exposed to software or system memory.
- Support custom cryptographic algorithms implemented in external libraries or hardware.

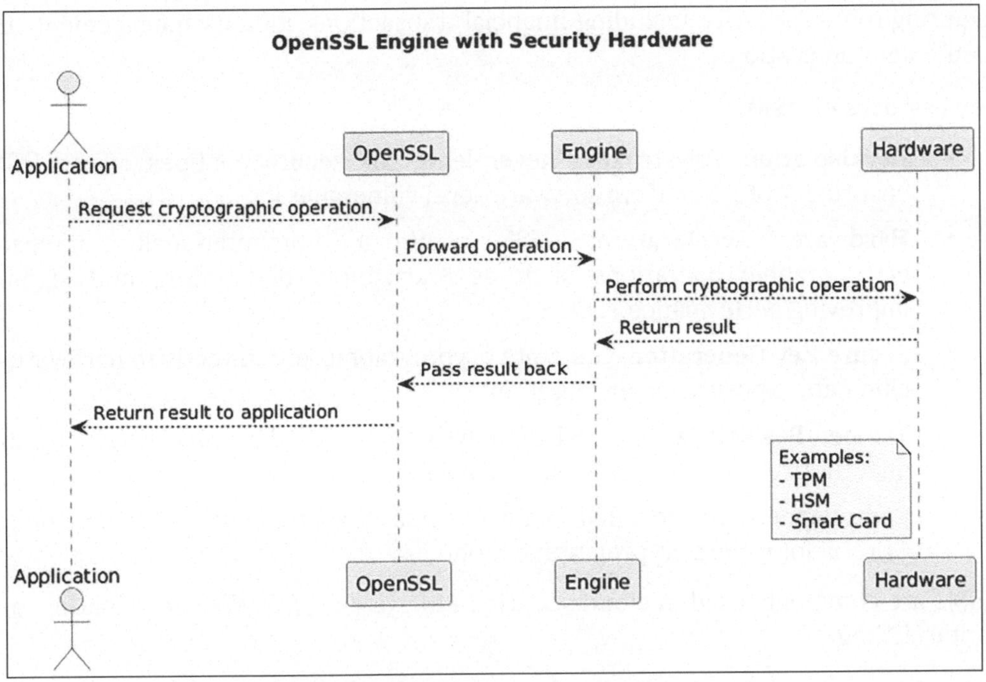

***Figure 7.1:** OpenSSL engine with Security Hardware*

Benefits of Using Security Hardware with OpenSSL Engine

- **Performance Improvement**: Offloading computationally expensive operations such as RSA or ECC to dedicated hardware accelerators.
- **Enhanced Security**: Isolating private keys from system memory reduces the attack surface for malware or memory-based attacks.
- **Regulatory Compliance**: Facilitates compliance with regulations requiring secure key storage, such as FIPS 140-2.
- **Scalability**: Hardware offloading frees up CPU resources for other application-level tasks.

Overview of Security Hardware

There are different types of security hardware that we can integrate with OpenSSL.

We will cover a few important types here and elaborate more wherever needed.

Hardware Security Module (HSM)

A Hardware Security Module (HSM) is a dedicated physical device designed to securely manage, store, and process cryptographic keys. HSMs are used in applications requiring robust security, including financial transactions, identity management, and secure communications.

Key Features of HSMs:

- **Key Isolation**: Private keys never leave the secure confines of the HSM, ensuring protection from software-level vulnerabilities.
- **Hardware Acceleration**: HSMs offload computationally intensive cryptographic operations such as encryption, decryption, and signing, improving performance.
- **Secure Key Generation**: Generate cryptographic keys directly in hardware to eliminate exposure during creation.
- **Tamper Resistance**: Physical tamper-resistant mechanisms protect against unauthorized access or reverse engineering.
- **Compliance**: Often certified to meet standards such as FIPS 140-2 or Common Criteria for secure cryptographic modules.

HSMs are commonly used in cloud security, PKI systems, SSL/TLS termination, and digital signing.

For a deeper dive into security hardware, we will take an example hardware chip, Atmel's ATECC608B, and cover more details on the integration process. We can use similar mechanism for other security hardware.

Atmel `CryptoAuthLib` and ATECC608B

`CryptoAuthLib` is a library developed by Microchip Technology to facilitate secure communication with Microchip's security hardware, such as the ATECC608B Secure Element. This library provides a simple API for implementing cryptographic functions such as key storage, secure authentication, and data encryption.

The ATECC608B is a secure element chip designed for cryptographic operations, providing strong security in IoT, automotive, and industrial applications.

Features of ATECC608B:

- **Secure Key Storage**: Store up to 16 private keys securely within the chip.
- **Asymmetric Cryptography**: Support for ECC algorithms (for example, ECDSA and ECDH).
- **Symmetric Cryptography**: Support for AES-128 encryption and decryption.
- **Random Number Generation**: Onboard cryptographic-grade random number generator (RNG).

- **Counter and Timestamp Support**: Secure counters for time-limited operations.
- **Tamper Resistance**: Protection against physical attacks, including voltage or temperature manipulation.

`CryptoAuthLib` with ATECC608B: The **`CryptoAuthLib`** library provides APIs to communicate with the ATECC608B over an I²C or SPI interface. It abstracts the hardware's complexity, allowing developers to easily use cryptographic features.

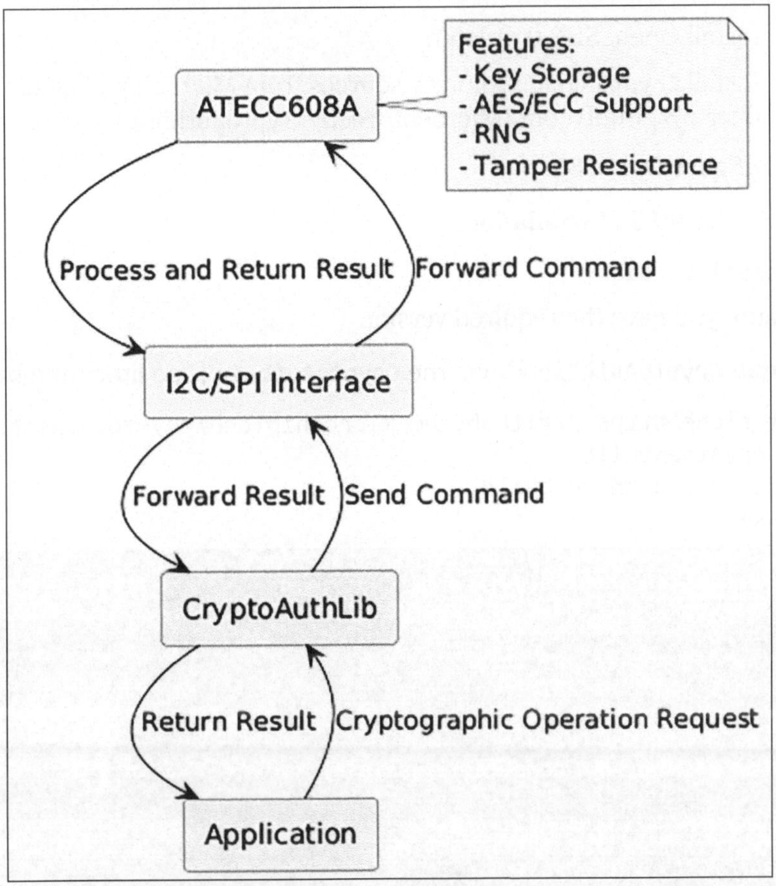

Figure 7.2: *Cryptoauthlib/ATECC608B/Application integration*

Setting Up OpenSSL for Security Hardware

This section focuses on configuring OpenSSL with the **`CryptoAuthLib`** engine to enable hardware-accelerated cryptographic operations using Atmel/Microchip secure elements such as the ATECC608B. Following is a detailed guide covering the installation, configuration, and integration process.

Installing and Configuring OpenSSL with the `CryptoAuthLib` Engine

Prerequisites:

- **Development Tools**: Ensure you have **`gcc`**, **`make`**, and **`cmake`** installed.
- **Dependencies**:
  - Install OpenSSL 3.0 or later.
  - Install **`CryptoAuthLib`** library sources from Microchip's GitHub repository (https://github.com/MicrochipTech/cryptoauthlib).

Steps to Configure OpenSSL:

1. **Verify OpenSSL Installation**:

   ```
   openssl version
   ```

   Ensure you have the required version.

2. **Install `CryptoAuthLib`**: Clone the **`CryptoAuthLib`** repository and build it.

   ```
   git clone https://github.com/MicrochipTech/cryptoauthlib.git
   cd cryptoauthlib
   mkdir build && cd build
   cmake ..
   ```

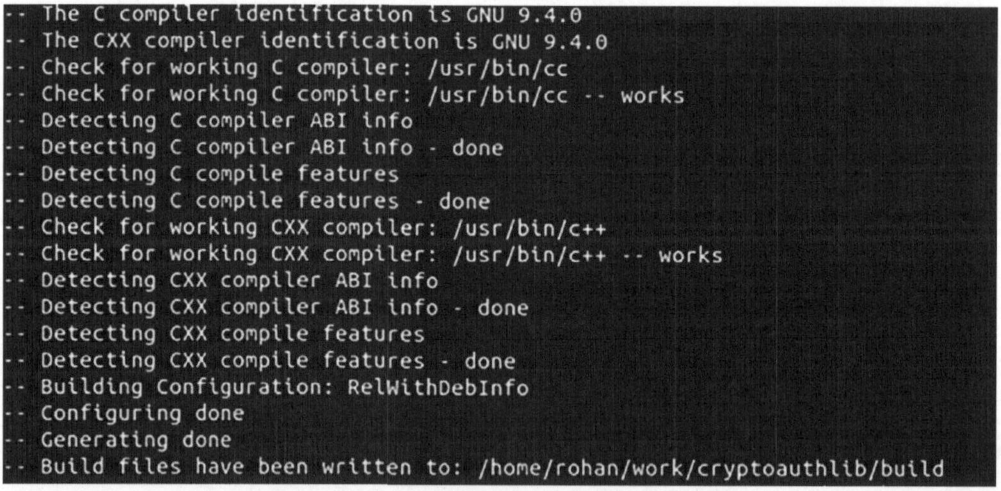

Figure 7.3: *Building CryptoAuthLib repository*

   ```
   make
   sudo make install
   ```

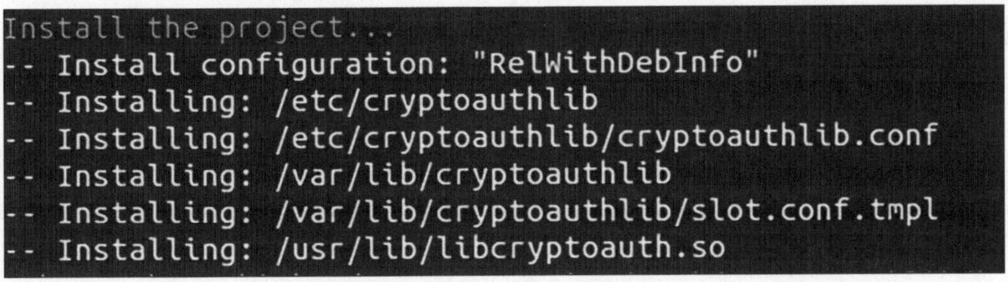

Figure 7.4: *Installing CryptoAuthLib*

3. **Set Up the `CryptoAuthLib` Engine**: Configure OpenSSL to load the **`CryptoAuthLib`** engine by updating the OpenSSL configuration file (**`openssl.cnf`**).

```
[engine_section]
cryptoauthlib = cryptoauthlib_engine
[cryptoauthlib_engine]
engine_id = cryptoauthlib
init = 1
```

   This informs OpenSSL to use the **`CryptoAuthLib`** engine for cryptographic operations.

Building `CryptoAuthLib` with OpenSSL

To integrate **`CryptoAuthLib`** with OpenSSL, follow these steps:

Step 1: Configure the `CryptoAuthLib` Build

Ensure **`CryptoAuthLib`** is built with support for your hardware interface (for example, I²C or SPI). Use **`cmake`** with the appropriate flags:

```
cmake -DATCA_HAL_I2C=ON -DATCA_HAL_SPI=OFF ..
```

Step 2: Link `CryptoAuthLib` to OpenSSL

While building **`CryptoAuthLib`**, ensure that the engine directory in OpenSSL is updated with the **`CryptoAuthLib`** plugin. This step might require creating a custom shared object file (**`.so`**) for **`CryptoAuthLib`**.

Example command:

```
gcc -fPIC -shared -o cryptoauthlib_engine.so -I/path/to/openssl/
include -L/path/to/openssl/lib -lcrypto
```

Linking the Hardware to OpenSSL

To complete the setup, connect the hardware to the system and verify the integration:

1. **Connect the Secure Element**:
   a. Use I²C or SPI to connect the ATECC608B to your host system.
   b. Ensure you have the correct pin connections for power, ground, data, and clock.
2. **Verify Hardware Communication**: Use the **`cryptotool`** utility from **`CryptoAuthLib`** to test the hardware connection:

   ```
   cryptotool info
   ```

   This command should display details of the connected ATECC608B.
3. **Test OpenSSL with `CryptoAuthLib`**: Verify that OpenSSL recognizes the **`CryptoAuthLib`** engine:

   ```
   openssl engine -t -c
   ```

   Output:

   ```
   (cryptoauthlib) CryptoAuthLib Engine
   [ available ]
   ```

Key Management with Security Hardware

Key management is a critical aspect of cryptographic systems, ensuring that cryptographic keys are securely generated, stored, and used without exposing them to vulnerabilities. This section focuses on leveraging Atmel/Microchip secure elements such as the ATECC608B for secure key management using the **`CryptoAuthLib`** library and integrating these keys with OpenSSL.

Generating, Storing, and Retrieving Keys on ATECC608B

Step 1: Generate a Key Pair on ATECC608B

Using **`CryptoAuthLib`**, you can generate an ECC key pair directly on the ATECC608B.

C Code Example: Generating a Key Pair

```
#include "cryptoauthlib.h"
void generate_key_pair() {
    ATCA_STATUS status;
    uint8_t public_key[64]; // ECC public key size (P-256)
```

```
    // Initialize the CryptoAuthLib library and configure the device
    status = atcab_init(&cfg_ateccx08a_i2c_default);
    if (status != ATCA_SUCCESS) {
        printf("Failed to initialize CryptoAuthLib: %d\n", status);
        return;
    }

    // Generate an ECC key pair in a specific slot (for example,
slot 0)
    // The private key is stored securely within the ATECC608B,
and the public key is returned
    status = atcab_genkey(0, public_key);
    if (status == ATCA_SUCCESS) {
        printf("Key pair generated successfully. Public Key:\n");

        // Print the generated public key in hexadecimal format
        for (int i = 0; i < 64; i++) {
            printf("%02X", public_key[i]);
        }
        printf("\n");
    } else {
        printf("Failed to generate key pair: %d\n", status);
    }

    // Release CryptoAuthLib resources to free up memory
    atcab_release();
}
```

Step 2: Store and Use the Private Key

The private key is securely stored in a designated slot inside the ATECC608B. The key is referenced by its slot ID during cryptographic operations (for example, signing, decryption).

Using Hardware-Stored Keys for OpenSSL Operations

To integrate hardware-stored keys with OpenSSL, you can use the `CryptoAuthLib` engine or a custom OpenSSL provider to offload operations.

C Code Example: Signing Data with Hardware Key

```
#include "cryptoauthlib.h"

void sign_data() {
    ATCA_STATUS status;
    uint8_t message[32] = { /* 32-byte SHA256 hash */ }; //
```

```
Placeholder for the message hash to be signed
    uint8_t signature[64]; // ECC signature size for P-256 (64
bytes)

    // Initialize CryptoAuthLib and configure communication with
ATECC608B
    status = atcab_init(&cfg_ateccx08a_i2c_default);
    if (status != ATCA_SUCCESS) {
        printf("Failed to initialize CryptoAuthLib: %d\n", status);
        return;
    }

    // Sign the 32-byte message hash using the private key stored
in slot 0 of the ATECC608B
    status = atcab_sign(0, message, signature);
    if (status == ATCA_SUCCESS) {
        printf("Message signed successfully. Signature:\n");

        // Print the generated ECC signature in hexadecimal format
        for (int i = 0; i < 64; i++) {
            printf("%02X", signature[i]);
        }
        printf("\n");
    } else {
        printf("Failed to sign data: %d\n", status);
    }

    // Release CryptoAuthLib resources before exiting
    atcab_release();
}
```

Using Hardware to Isolate Private Keys

The private key stored in the ATECC608B is inaccessible to the host application. All cryptographic operations involving the private key (for example, signing or decryption) are performed inside the hardware. This ensures the key is never exposed to software vulnerabilities.

Integration with OpenSSL

To use hardware-managed keys with OpenSSL, you can:

1. Configure the **CryptoAuthLib** engine or provider.
2. Reference the key slot in OpenSSL commands.

Accelerating Cryptographic Operations

Offloading cryptographic computations to hardware offers significant performance and security advantages over software-only solutions. This section explores the benefits of hardware acceleration for cryptographic operations, demonstrates how to perform signing and verification using the ATECC608B secure element with OpenSSL, and compares software-based and hardware-accelerated workflows.

Benefits of Hardware Acceleration:

- **Performance Improvements**: Hardware modules such as the ATECC608B are optimized for cryptographic computations, enabling faster operations compared to software implementations.
- **Enhanced Security**: Cryptographic keys never leave the hardware, reducing the risk of key exposure and protecting against software-based attacks.
- **Power Efficiency**: Dedicated cryptographic hardware consumes less power than general-purpose CPUs performing the same operations.

Example: Signing and Verifying Data Using ATECC608B and OpenSSL

Step 1: Signing Data Using ATECC608B

The private key used for signing is securely stored in the ATECC608B. The signing process involves the following steps:

a. Initialize the **`CryptoAuthLib`** library.

b. Load the private key slot in the ATECC608B.

c. Sign the data using the key stored in hardware.

C Code Example: Signing Data

```
#include "cryptoauthlib.h"
#include <stdio.h>

void sign_data_with_ATECC608B() {
    ATCA_STATUS status;
    uint8_t message[32] = { /* Precomputed SHA256 hash */ };
    uint8_t signature[64]; // ECC signature (P-256)

    // Initialize the CryptoAuthLib library
    status = atcab_init(&cfg_ateccx08a_i2c_default);
    if (status != ATCA_SUCCESS) {
        printf("Failed to initialize CryptoAuthLib: %d\n", status);
        return;
    }
```

```
    // Sign the message using the private key in slot 0
    status = atcab_sign(0, message, signature);
    if (status == ATCA_SUCCESS) {
        printf("Signature generated successfully:\n");
        for (int i = 0; i < 64; i++) {
            printf("%02X", signature[i]);
        }
        printf("\n");
    } else {
        printf("Failed to sign data: %d\n", status);
    }

    // Release the library
    atcab_release();
}
```

Step 2: Verifying Data Using OpenSSL

Verification can be performed in software using the public key retrieved from the hardware. This ensures compatibility with OpenSSL-based applications.

C Code Example: Verifying Data

```
#include <openssl/ec.h>
#include <openssl/evp.h>
#include <openssl/sha.h>
#include <stdio.h>

void verify_signature_with_openssl() {
    const char *public_key_hex = "04..."; // Public key from
ATECC608B (hex-encoded)
    uint8_t signature[64] = { /* ECC signature */ };
    uint8_t message[32] = { /* Precomputed SHA256 hash */ };

    EC_KEY *ec_key = NULL;
    EVP_PKEY *pkey = NULL;
    EVP_PKEY_CTX *ctx = NULL;
    int ret;

    // Convert public key to EC_KEY
    ec_key = EC_KEY_new_by_curve_name(NID_X9_62_prime256v1);
    // Add public key conversion code here...

    // Verify signature
    pkey = EVP_PKEY_new();
    EVP_PKEY_assign_EC_KEY(pkey, ec_key);
    ctx = EVP_PKEY_CTX_new(pkey, NULL);
    if (!ctx) {
```

```
            printf("Failed to create context\n");
            return;
        }

        ret = EVP_PKEY_verify(ctx, signature, sizeof(signature),
    message, sizeof(message));
        if (ret == 1) {
            printf("Signature verified successfully\n");
        } else {
            printf("Signature verification failed\n");
        }

        // Clean up
        EVP_PKEY_CTX_free(ctx);
        EVP_PKEY_free(pkey);
    }
```

Comparison of software-based and hardware-accelerated cryptographic workflows:

Aspect	Software-Based	Hardware-Accelerated
Key Security	Keys are stored in memory and vulnerable to attacks	Keys are securely isolated inside the hardware
Performance	CPU-intensive, slower for large workloads	Optimized and faster for cryptographic operations
Tamper Resistance	No physical security	Resistant to tampering and physical attacks
Compliance	Requires additional measures to meet security standards	Pre-certified for security standards (for example, FIPS)
Scalability	Requires scaling of CPU resources	Dedicated hardware accelerates operations

Table 7.1: *Software-based versus hardware-accelerated workflows*

Real-World Application: Secure TLS with Atmel Hardware

This section demonstrates how to integrate Atmel hardware, specifically the ATECC608B secure element, with OpenSSL to secure TLS connections. The ATECC608B acts as a hardware root of trust, enabling private key isolation and cryptographic acceleration for TLS handshakes. The setup enhances security by ensuring private keys never leave the secure hardware, mitigating the risk of key compromise.

Configuring OpenSSL to Use Atmel Hardware for TLS

Key Steps for Configuration:

1. **Install and Build `CryptoAuthLib`**:

   a. Build **`CryptoAuthLib`** with support for OpenSSL Engine or Provider framework.

   b. Ensure the ATECC608B hardware is connected and initialized correctly.

2. **Configure OpenSSL with the `CryptoAuthLib` Engine**:

   a. Modify the OpenSSL configuration file (**`openssl.cnf`**) to use the **`CryptoAuthLib`** engine for private key operations.

   b. Example configuration snippet:

   ```
   [openssl_init]
   engines = engine_section
   [engine_section]
   ATECC608B = ATECC608B_section
   [ATECC608B_section]
   dynamic_path = /usr/lib/cryptoauthlib_engine.so
   init = 1
   ```

3. **Link the TLS Server to the Hardware Key**:

   a. Use OpenSSL commands or APIs to associate the private key operations in the TLS handshake with the ATECC608B.

Example: Using ATECC608B for TLS Handshakes

Server-Side Key and Certificate Operations: The ATECC608B is used to generate a key pair and store the private key securely. The public key is used to generate an X.509 certificate.

Key Pair and Certificate Generation Example:

1. Generate a private key and store it in the ATECC608B:

   ```
   #include "cryptoauthlib.h"

   void generate_key_on_ATECC608B() {
       ATCA_STATUS status;
       uint8_t public_key[64]; // Buffer for ECC public key

       status = atcab_genkey(0, public_key); // Generate key pair in
   slot 0
   ```

```
        if (status == ATCA_SUCCESS) {
            printf("Public key generated:\n");
            for (int i = 0; i < 64; i++) {
                printf("%02X", public_key[i]);
            }
            printf("\n");
        } else {
            printf("Key generation failed: %d\n", status);
        }
    }
```

You can also use command line for using OpenSSL engine to generate a key in slot 0.

```
openssl genpkey -engine ateccx08 -algorithm EC -out public_key.
pem -pkeyopt ec_paramgen_curve:P-256 -pkeyopt key_slot:0
```

2. Generate a certificate signing request (CSR) using the hardware-stored private key. The CSR can be signed by a Certificate Authority (CA).

```
#include <openssl/evp.h>
#include <openssl/x509.h>
#include <openssl/engine.h>

#define KEY_SLOT 0  // ATECC608B key slot

void generate_csr() {
    ENGINE *e = NULL;
    EVP_PKEY *pkey = NULL;
    X509_REQ *req = NULL;
    BIO *bio_out = NULL;

    OpenSSL_add_all_algorithms();
    ENGINE_load_builtin_engines();

    // Load the ATECC608B OpenSSL engine
    e = ENGINE_by_id("ateccx08");
    if (!e || !ENGINE_init(e)) {
        fprintf(stderr, "Failed to load ATECC608B engine\n");
        return;
    }

    // Get the private key from ATECC608B slot
    pkey = ENGINE_load_private_key(e, "0", NULL, NULL);
    if (!pkey) {
        fprintf(stderr, "Failed to load private key from
ATECC608B slot\n");
        ENGINE_free(e);
```

```
        return;
    }

    // Create a new X.509 certificate request (CSR)
    req = X509_REQ_new();
    X509_REQ_set_version(req, 1);
    X509_NAME *name = X509_REQ_get_subject_name(req);
    X509_NAME_add_entry_by_txt(name, "CN", MBSTRING_ASC,
(unsigned char *)"My Device", -1, -1, 0);

    // Attach the public key to the CSR
    X509_REQ_set_pubkey(req, pkey);

    // Sign the CSR using the private key stored in ATECC608B
    if (!X509_REQ_sign(req, pkey, EVP_sha256())) {
        fprintf(stderr, "CSR signing failed\n");
        X509_REQ_free(req);
        EVP_PKEY_free(pkey);
        ENGINE_free(e);
        return;
    }

    // Output CSR to file or console
    bio_out = BIO_new_fp(stdout, BIO_NOCLOSE);
    PEM_write_bio_X509_REQ(bio_out, req);

    // Cleanup
    BIO_free(bio_out);
    X509_REQ_free(req);
    EVP_PKEY_free(pkey);
    ENGINE_free(e);
}
```

Command for same

```
openssl req -new -key engine:ATECC608B:0 -subj "/CN=MyDevice"
-out device.csr
```

3. Use OpenSSL to load the hardware-stored private key:

```
openssl s_server -cert server.crt -key engine:ATECC608B:0 -port
4433
```

TLS Handshake Process with ATECC608B

During the TLS handshake:

1. The server provides its certificate to the client.

2. The server's private key operations (for example, signing) are offloaded to the ATECC608B, ensuring the private key never leaves the hardware.
3. The client validates the server's certificate and proceeds with the handshake.

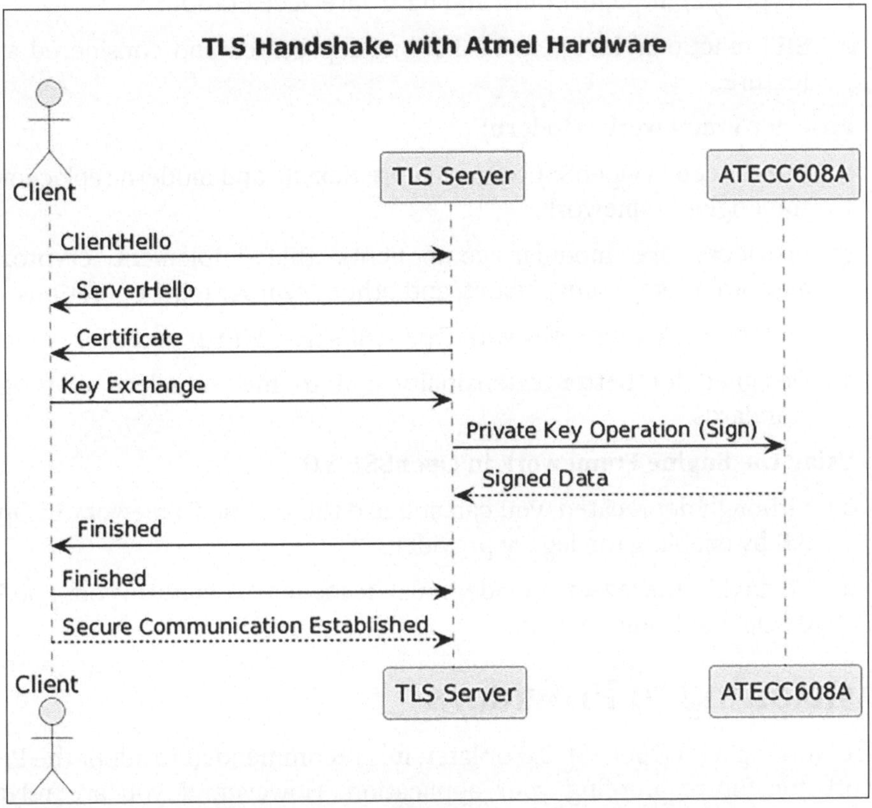

Figure 7.5: *TLS handshake with Atmel hardware*

Provider Framework for Security Hardware Integration

OpenSSL 3.0 introduced a new Provider Framework, which is intended to replace the older Engine Framework. However, OpenSSL 3.0 still maintains support for the Engine framework for backward compatibility.

Key Differences Between Engine and Provider Framework

- **Engine Framework (Legacy)**
  - Used in OpenSSL versions prior to 3.0.

  - Provides a way to interface with external cryptographic hardware or software.
  - Includes support for hardware security modules (HSMs), custom cryptographic algorithms, and hardware acceleration.
  - Still functional in OpenSSL 3.0, but deprecated and considered a legacy feature.
- **Provider Framework (Modern)**
  - Introduced in OpenSSL 3.0 as a more flexible and modern replacement for the Engine framework.
  - Providers are modular components that implement cryptographic algorithms, key management, and other cryptographic operations.
  - Built to work seamlessly with OpenSSL's new FIPS module for compliance.
  - Designed for better extensibility and to meet modern cryptographic standards.
- **Using the Engine Framework in OpenSSL 3.0**
  - Although deprecated, you can still use the Engine framework in OpenSSL 3.0 by enabling the legacy provider.
  - To do this, the legacy provider must be loaded explicitly in your application or OpenSSL configuration.

Transitioning to Providers

If you are working with OpenSSL 3.0 or later, it is recommended to adopt the Provider framework for future-proofing your application. However, if you are relying on hardware or libraries such as `CryptoAuthLib` that use the Engine API, you can continue using it until those libraries transition to the Provider framework.

There are Hardware Security Modules (HSMs) that integrate with OpenSSL 3.0 using the Provider Framework. Here are some examples:

- Securosys Primus HSM
- Entrust nShield HSM
- Red Hat PKCS#11 Provider

These integrations demonstrate the flexibility of OpenSSL 3.0's Provider Framework in supporting hardware-based security solutions.

We will discuss more on only one of the aforementioned example that is **Red Hat PKCS#11 Provider Framework**.

Red Hat PKCS#11 Provider

The PKCS#11 Provider Framework in OpenSSL 3.0 represents a significant advancement in integrating cryptographic hardware, such as Hardware Security Modules (HSMs) and smart cards, into applications. This framework supersedes the legacy Engine API, offering a more modular and flexible approach to cryptographic operations.

Key Features of the PKCS#11 Provider Framework:

- **Modularity**: Providers are dynamically loadable modules that implement specific cryptographic algorithms and operations, allowing for seamless integration of hardware tokens.
- **Enhanced Security**: By interfacing directly with hardware tokens, the framework ensures that private keys remain within the secure confines of the hardware, reducing exposure to potential software vulnerabilities.
- **Flexibility**: The framework supports a wide range of cryptographic mechanisms, including those introduced in PKCS#11 v3.0, such as advanced key derivation functions and modern algorithms such as ChaCha20-Poly1305.

Red Hat's Implementation

In Red Hat Enterprise Linux (RHEL) 10, the transition from the Engine API to the Provider Framework is emphasized, with the introduction of a new PKCS#11 provider. This shift enhances the integration of cryptographic hardware, aligning with OpenSSL 3.0's architecture.

Benefits of Red Hat's PKCS#11 Provider:

- **Seamless Integration**: Applications can utilize hardware tokens without significant code modifications, streamlining the adoption of hardware-based security.
- **Future-Proofing**: By adopting the Provider Framework, Red Hat ensures compatibility with future OpenSSL developments and cryptographic standards.

Practical Application: Developers aiming to leverage this framework can configure OpenSSL to interact with PKCS#11 modules by specifying the appropriate provider in their OpenSSL configuration files. This setup enables the delegation of cryptographic operations to hardware tokens, enhancing security and performance.

Following is an example of how to use the PKCS#11 Provider Framework in OpenSSL 3.0 for basic cryptographic operations, such as initializing the PKCS#11 provider, generating a key, and performing encryption and decryption:

Step 1: Configuration for PKCS#11 Provider

Create an OpenSSL configuration file (**openssl.cnf**) to load the PKCS#11 provider.

```
# openssl.cnf
openssl_conf = openssl_init
[openssl_init]
providers = provider_section
[provider_section]
default = default_sect
pkcs11 = pkcs11_sect
[default_sect]
activate = 1
[pkcs11_sect]
module = /usr/lib64/pkcs11/libsofthsm2.so  # Path to the PKCS#11
module
```

Step 2: Initialize OpenSSL with the PKCS#11 Provider

```
#include <openssl/evp.h>
#include <openssl/provider.h>
#include <stdio.h>
#include <string.h>

int main() {
    // Load OpenSSL configuration
    if (OPENSSL_init_crypto(OPENSSL_INIT_LOAD_CONFIG, NULL) == 0)
{
        fprintf(stderr, "Failed to initialize OpenSSL
configuration\n");
        return 1;
    }

    // Load PKCS#11 provider
    OSSL_PROVIDER *pkcs11_provider = OSSL_PROVIDER_load(NULL,
"pkcs11");
    if (!pkcs11_provider) {
        fprintf(stderr, "Failed to load PKCS#11 provider\n");
        return 1;
    }

    printf("PKCS#11 provider successfully loaded.\n");

    // Use the provider for further cryptographic operations
    OSSL_PROVIDER_unload(pkcs11_provider);
    return 0;
}
```

Step 3: Key Generation Using PKCS#11

Generate an AES key for encryption.

```
#include <openssl/evp.h>
#include <openssl/rand.h>

int generate_aes_key() {
    unsigned char key[32]; // 256-bit AES key

    // Generate random key
    if (RAND_bytes(key, sizeof(key)) != 1) {
        fprintf(stderr, "Failed to generate random key\n");
        return 1;
    }

    printf("Generated AES key: ");
    for (int i = 0; i < sizeof(key); i++) {
        printf("%02x", key[i]);
    }
    printf("\n");

    return 0;
}
```

Step 4: Encrypting and Decrypting Data

Perform AES-GCM encryption and decryption.

```
int encrypt_decrypt_aes(const unsigned char *plaintext, int
plaintext_len,
                        const unsigned char *key, const unsigned
char *iv) {
    EVP_CIPHER_CTX *ctx = NULL;
    unsigned char ciphertext[128], decryptedtext[128];
    int len, ciphertext_len, decrypted_len;
    // Initialize context
    ctx = EVP_CIPHER_CTX_new();
    if (!ctx) {
        fprintf(stderr, "Failed to create context\n");
        return 1;
    }
    // Encryption
    if (EVP_EncryptInit_ex(ctx, EVP_aes_256_gcm(), NULL, key, iv)
!= 1) {
        fprintf(stderr, "Encryption init failed\n");
        return 1;
    }
```

```
    if (EVP_EncryptUpdate(ctx, ciphertext, &len, plaintext,
plaintext_len) != 1) {
        fprintf(stderr, "Encryption failed\n");
        return 1;
    }
    ciphertext_len = len;

    if (EVP_EncryptFinal_ex(ctx, ciphertext + len, &len) != 1) {
        fprintf(stderr, "Encryption finalization failed\n");
        return 1;
    }
    ciphertext_len += len;

    printf("Ciphertext: ");
    for (int i = 0; i < ciphertext_len; i++) {
        printf("%02x", ciphertext[i]);
    }
    printf("\n");

    // Decryption
    if (EVP_DecryptInit_ex(ctx, EVP_aes_256_gcm(), NULL, key, iv)
!= 1) {
        fprintf(stderr, "Decryption init failed\n");
        return 1;
    }

    if (EVP_DecryptUpdate(ctx, decryptedtext, &len, ciphertext,
ciphertext_len) != 1) {
        fprintf(stderr, "Decryption failed\n");
        return 1;
    }
    decrypted_len = len;

    if (EVP_DecryptFinal_ex(ctx, decryptedtext + len, &len) != 1)
{
        fprintf(stderr, "Decryption finalization failed\n");
        return 1;
    }
    decrypted_len += len;

    decryptedtext[decrypted_len] = '\0'; // Null-terminate
    printf("Decrypted text: %s\n", decryptedtext);

    EVP_CIPHER_CTX_free(ctx);
    return 0;
}
```

Step 5: Running the Example

Compile and run the example code:

```
gcc -o pkcs11_example pkcs11_example.c -lcrypto -ldl
./pkcs11_example
```

Make sure the PKCS#11 module (for example, SoftHSM2) is installed and properly configured.

Conclusion

In this chapter, we explored the integration of OpenSSL with security hardware using the Atmel **`CryptoAuthLib`** and ATECC608B as an example. We discussed key concepts such as secure key management, hardware-based acceleration of cryptographic operations, and practical implementation for securing TLS connections. The use of hardware security modules (HSMs) such as ATECC608B significantly enhances the security of private keys and improves the performance of cryptographic operations by offloading computation to dedicated hardware. Through step-by-step examples and diagrams, we demonstrated how OpenSSL's engine or provider framework can simplify the integration of security hardware.

This chapter also highlighted the real-world applications of using secure hardware in modern cryptographic workflows, particularly in resource-constrained environments such as IoT devices and highly secure web servers.

In the next chapter, we will delve into managing digital certificates, a critical aspect of cryptographic operations. You will learn how to generate, parse, and validate X.509 certificates using OpenSSL, as well as understand their role in establishing trust in public key infrastructures (PKIs). This knowledge will further expand your toolkit for building secure and robust cryptographic systems.

CHAPTER 8
OpenSSL in IoT Security

Introduction

The Internet of Things (IoT) connects everything in the modern world and is rapidly transforming various industries, including healthcare, manufacturing, transportation, agriculture, retail, and smart cities. IoT has emerged as one of the most revolutionary technologies in recent years, enabling the location, transmission, and analysis of data through a network of interconnected components. In IoT, "*things*" include sensors, RFID tags, industrial machines, heart rate monitors, GPS devices, and other smart gadgets that gather and share data. With new devices being integrated into IoT networks daily, the number of connected devices has grown exponentially. For example, there were approximately 20.4 billion connected devices in 2022, up from 8.4 billion in 2020.

The expansion of IoT networks introduces significant challenges across industries, including device management, data management, computational efficiency, security, and privacy. These issues are particularly critical as IoT adoption continues to rise, making it essential to address these concerns for the technology to deliver its full potential.

In this chapter, we will focus exclusively on the security aspects of IoT, aligning with the primary focus of this book, and explore how OpenSSL can help secure IoT devices and communications.

Structure

In this chapter, we will cover the following topics:

- Importance of Cryptography in IOT Security
- Challenges in IOT Security
- Lightweight Cryptography with OpenSSL
- Examples of IOT Security with x509 Certificates

Importance of Cryptography in IOT Security

Cryptography plays a pivotal role in securing IoT ecosystems by ensuring the confidentiality, integrity, and authenticity of data and devices. It is widely used to secure communication channels within IoT deployments, with protocols such as Transport Layer Security (TLS) enabling secure communication between devices and preventing unauthorized interception or tampering of data.

Data encryption and decryption are essential for protecting sensitive information within IoT environments. Symmetric-key algorithms, such as the Advanced Encryption Standard (AES), provide efficient encryption for data at rest and in transit, while public-key infrastructure (PKI) and asymmetric-key algorithms, such as Rivest-Shamir-Adleman (RSA) or Digital Signature Algorithm (DSA), enable secure authentication, key exchanges, and non-repudiation.

The primary goal of cryptography in IoT is to ensure that access to devices and data is restricted to authorized entities only. By encrypting data, organizations can prevent unauthorized access, even if the data is intercepted. Cryptography also ensures that communications and transactions within the IoT ecosystem are protected from eavesdropping, tampering, or impersonation attacks. This makes it an indispensable component of IoT security, providing the foundation for trust in a highly interconnected environment.

Challenges of IoT Security

In this section, we will cover challenges specifically for securing IOT devices.

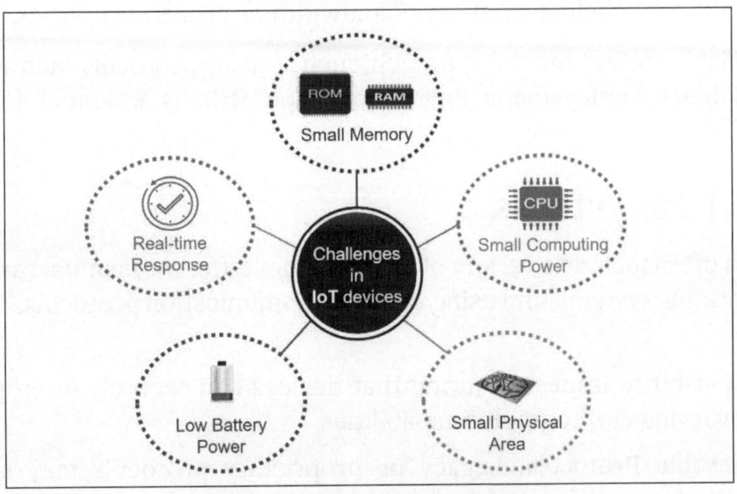

***Figure 8.1**: IOT security challenges*

Resource Constraints

IoT devices are often small, lightweight, and designed for specific, low-power tasks. This creates significant constraints in terms of:

- **Computational Power**: Many IoT devices have limited processing capabilities, making it difficult to implement robust encryption algorithms or resource-intensive security protocols.
- **Memory**: Limited RAM and storage restrict the ability to store large cryptographic libraries, key material, or logs.
- **Energy Efficiency**: Battery-operated devices prioritize energy efficiency, which can conflict with the computational demands of strong encryption and frequent communication.

  To address these constraints, lightweight cryptographic algorithms such as ChaCha20 and Elliptic Curve Cryptography (ECC) are often employed.

Scalability

IoT ecosystems can range from a handful of devices to millions connected in a single network, such as in industrial IoT (IIoT) environments or smart cities. Scalability introduces challenges such as:

- **Key Management**: Generating, distributing, and revoking cryptographic keys across a large number of devices.
- **Certificate Management**: Provisioning and renewing X.509 certificates for authentication at scale.
- **Secure Communication**: Ensuring that all devices communicate securely without overwhelming network bandwidth or processing power.

  A scalable and automated approach, such as using protocols such as Automated Certificate Management Environment (ACME), is essential for managing certificates efficiently.

Diverse Ecosystems

IoT networks often include a variety of devices from different manufacturers, running different operating systems, and using various communication protocols. This diversity creates:

- **Compatibility Issues**: Ensuring that devices can securely interoperate, even with varying cryptographic capabilities.
- **Vulnerable Protocols**: Legacy or proprietary protocols may lack modern security features, leaving devices exposed to attacks.

- **Heterogeneous Security Levels**: Devices with weaker security implementations may become entry points for attackers to compromise the network.

  Standardization and adherence to secure IoT protocols, such as MQTT with TLS, are vital in addressing these challenges.

Lifecycle Management

IoT devices often have long lifecycles, sometimes exceeding a decade, but ensuring their security throughout this period is challenging:

- **Firmware Updates**: Regular updates are essential to patch vulnerabilities, but many devices lack secure update mechanisms or are deployed in remote locations with limited connectivity.
- **Key and Certificate Expiry**: Cryptographic keys and certificates require periodic renewal, which can be difficult to manage for offline or low-power devices.
- **End-of-Life Devices**: Devices that are no longer supported by manufacturers may remain in use, creating unpatchable security risks.

  Solutions such as over-the-air (OTA) updates and lightweight certificate renewal mechanisms are necessary to ensure secure lifecycle management.

Threat Landscape

IoT devices are exposed to a wide range of attacks due to their pervasive nature and weak security measures:

- **Device Spoofing**: Attackers impersonate legitimate devices to gain unauthorized access to the network.
- **Data Interception (Man-in-the-Middle Attacks)**: Unencrypted communication channels allow attackers to intercept sensitive data.
- **Distributed Denial-of-Service (DDoS) Attacks**: Compromised IoT devices are often used in botnets to launch large-scale DDoS attacks (for example, Mirai botnet).
- **Physical Tampering**: Devices deployed in public or remote locations are vulnerable to physical attacks, such as extracting firmware or keys.
- **Ransomware and Malware**: Attackers exploit weak security to deploy ransomware, demanding payment to restore functionality.

  Robust encryption, secure boot mechanisms, and regular vulnerability assessments are critical in mitigating these risks.

By addressing these challenges with tailored security solutions, IoT networks can achieve a higher level of security and reliability, ensuring safe and efficient operation across industries.

Lightweight Cryptography with OpenSSL

Lightweight cryptography is critical for securing IoT devices that operate under resource constraints such as limited CPU power, memory, storage, and energy availability. OpenSSL, a widely used cryptographic library, can be adapted to meet the unique requirements of IoT environments. Following are the key aspects and approaches to leveraging lightweight cryptography with OpenSSL.

Adapting OpenSSL for IoT Devices

IoT devices often require streamlined versions of cryptographic libraries to reduce binary size and minimize dependencies. OpenSSL can be customized by:

- **Selective Compilation**: Disabling unnecessary features during compilation (for example, unused ciphers or algorithms) using OpenSSL's configuration options (no-xyz flags).
- **Static Linking**: Building a static version of OpenSSL to reduce runtime overhead and improve deployment efficiency.
- **Minimal Footprint Builds**: Excluding features such as ASN.1 parsing, certificate handling, or debugging symbols if they are not required for the IoT application.

Lightweight Algorithms

Some cryptographic algorithms are more suitable for IoT devices due to their low computational and memory overhead. Examples include:

- **ChaCha20**: A modern stream cipher that is faster than AES on devices without hardware acceleration.
- **AES-128**: A widely used symmetric-key encryption algorithm, offering a good balance of security and performance for constrained environments.
- **HMAC-SHA256**: Used for lightweight message authentication to ensure data integrity.
- **Elliptic Curve Cryptography (ECC)**: A highly efficient asymmetric cryptographic method for key exchange and digital signatures.

By focusing on these lightweight algorithms, OpenSSL can secure IoT communications while keeping resource usage minimal.

Algorithm	Type	Key Features	Support in OpenSSL	Use Cases in IoT
ChaCha20	Stream Cipher	• High speed in software • Resistant to timing attacks	Supported (for example, `EVP_chacha20_poly1305`)	Encrypting data in energy-constrained devices
Poly1305	Message Authentication Code (MAC)	• High performance • Designed to pair with ChaCha20	Supported	Message authentication for lightweight communication protocols
AES-128	Symmetric Block Cipher	• Smaller key size for constrained environments • Hardware acceleration support	Supported (e.g., `EVP_aes_128_cbc`)	Encrypting communication channels in IoT devices
HMAC-SHA256	Message Authentication Code (MAC)	• Strong integrity and authentication guarantees • Low computational overhead	Supported	Authenticating data or commands between IoT devices and servers
ECC (e.g., ECDSA)	Asymmetric Encryption	• Smaller key sizes compared to RSA • Efficient for signing and verification	Supported (for example, EC_KEY APIs)	Securing firmware updates, device authentication, and key exchange
RSA (small key sizes)	Asymmetric Encryption	Widely used but less efficient for resource-constrained devices	Supported	Secure key exchange for IoT devices with moderate resources
Blowfish	Symmetric Block Cipher	Lightweight encryption with variable key sizes	Supported	Legacy IoT systems or small-scale applications requiring low resource usage
Camellia	Symmetric Block Cipher	Alternative to AES with similar security and performance	Supported	Data encryption in devices requiring AES alternatives

SHA-256 (Truncated)	Hash Function	Optimized by truncating the output Secure against collision attacks	Supported	Lightweight hashing for secure token generation
X25519	Elliptic Curve Key Exchange	High-speed key exchange Small public key sizes	Supported (for example, `EVP_PKEY_X25519`)	Lightweight key exchange for IoT devices
SipHash	Hash Function	Efficient and secure hash function for short inputs	Supported	Hashing and securing data in constrained IoT devices

***Table 8.1**: Lightweight cryptography algorithms and their support in OpenSSL*

Recommendations for IoT Development:

- **Energy-Constrained Devices**: Use ChaCha20, Poly1305, and AES-128 for efficient encryption.
- **Small Key Sizes**: Adopt ECC (for example, X25519) for key exchange and digital signatures.
- **Data Integrity**: Use HMAC-SHA256 or Poly1305 for lightweight message authentication.
- **Device Compatibility**: Prefer AES-128 and HMAC-SHA256 for maximum hardware and software support.

Performance Optimization

IoT devices often require cryptographic operations to be both fast and energy-efficient. OpenSSL provides tools and techniques for optimizing performance:

- **Hardware Acceleration**: OpenSSL can utilize hardware-based cryptographic accelerators (for example, AES-NI for AES encryption or ARM Crypto Extensions) to offload computations from the CPU.
- **OpenSSL Engine Framework**: The engine framework in OpenSSL allows integration with custom hardware modules or libraries, enabling efficient use of specialized hardware for cryptographic tasks.
- **Session Reuse**: Leveraging session caching and ticket-based resumption in TLS connections to reduce handshake overhead in repeated connections.

Examples of Lightweight Encryption and Authentication

IoT applications span various industries, including smart homes, healthcare, industrial automation, automotive, smart grids, agriculture, and smart city infrastructure. Each of these domains requires robust security mechanisms to protect sensitive data, ensure device authenticity, and secure communications while operating under resource constraints.

IoT devices often have limited processing power, memory, and energy availability, making traditional cryptographic solutions impractical. Security challenges include preventing unauthorized access, ensuring encrypted communication, securing firmware updates, protecting sensitive data (such as health or industrial sensor data), and defending against cyber threats such as replay attacks, eavesdropping, and tampering. Additionally, many IoT applications require secure over-the-air (OTA) updates, mutual authentication, and data integrity verification while maintaining real-time performance.

To address these challenges efficiently, lightweight cryptography techniques using OpenSSL APIs are implemented. Symmetric encryption, such as **AES-128 in GCM or CCM mode**, ensures secure communication with minimal computational overhead. **Elliptic Curve Cryptography (ECC)**, including ECDSA and Curve25519, provides strong authentication while consuming less power than traditional RSA-based methods. OpenSSL's **TLS 1.3 and DTLS (Datagram TLS)** offer lightweight, secure communication channels for IoT devices operating over constrained networks. Secure hashing algorithms such as **SHA-256** are used for integrity checks, ensuring that firmware updates and data transmissions remain untampered. Additionally, OpenSSL's optimized cryptographic libraries allow efficient implementation of security protocols while maintaining performance in resource-constrained environments.

Using OpenSSL APIs, developers can implement lightweight cryptography in IoT applications.

- **Encrypting Data with ChaCha20 and Poly1305:**

  ```
  EVP_CIPHER_CTX *ctx = EVP_CIPHER_CTX_new();
  EVP_EncryptInit_ex(ctx, EVP_chacha20_poly1305(), NULL, key,
  nonce);
  // Encryption process...
  EVP_CIPHER_CTX_free(ctx);
  ```

  This combination provides both encryption and authentication with minimal overhead.

- **Performing ECC Key Exchange**:

  ```
  EC_KEY *key = EC_KEY_new_by_curve_name(NID_X9_62_prime256v1);
  EC_KEY_generate_key(key);
  ```

```
// Perform key exchange...
EC_KEY_free(key);
```

ECC is ideal for resource-constrained devices due to its small key sizes and high efficiency.

- **Authenticated Communication with HMAC-SHA256**:

```
unsigned char hmac[EVP_MAX_MD_SIZE];
unsigned int len;
HMAC(EVP_sha256(), key, key_len, message, message_len, hmac,
&len);
```

HMAC ensures data integrity and authenticity with minimal computational requirements.

By customizing OpenSSL, leveraging lightweight cryptographic algorithms, and optimizing performance through hardware acceleration, IoT devices can achieve robust security without compromising on efficiency or functionality. This ensures the safe operation of IoT ecosystems even under stringent resource constraints.

Examples of using X509 certificate for IOT security

In this section, we will cover a few examples of using X.509 certificates for IOT security.

Using X.509 Certificates for Secure MQTT Communication

Message Queuing Telemetry Transport (MQTT) is a lightweight messaging protocol commonly used in IoT applications for efficient device-to-cloud or device-to-device communication. Ensuring secure communication between MQTT clients and brokers is crucial, and X.509 certificates provide a robust way to achieve this by enabling mutual authentication and encrypted communication.

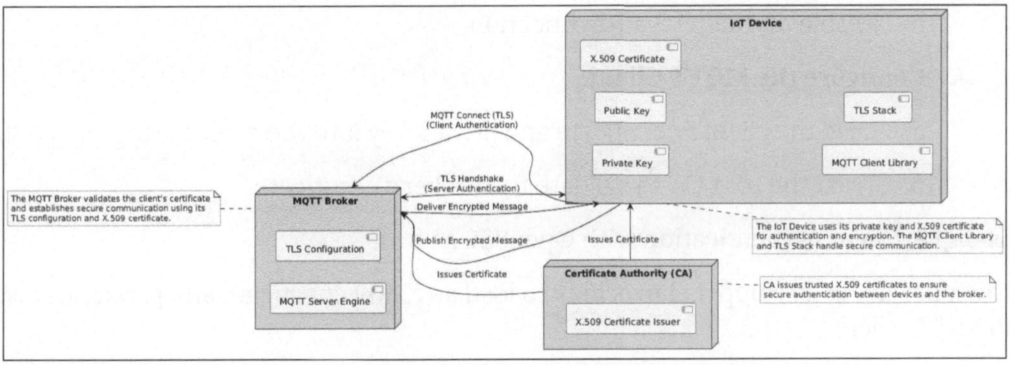

Figure 8.2: X.509 *for* MQTT

Setting Up X.509 Certificates for MQTT

X.509 certificates can be used in MQTT for:

- **Client Authentication**: Ensuring that only authorized devices can connect to the broker.
- **Server Authentication**: Verifying the identity of the MQTT broker to prevent man-in-the-middle (MITM) attacks.
- **Data Encryption**: Establishing a secure TLS channel for encrypted communication.

Steps to Secure MQTT Communication with OpenSSL:

1. **Generate a Root Certificate Authority (CA)**:

```
openssl genrsa -out rootCA.key 2048
openssl req -x509 -new -nodes -key rootCA.key -sha256 -days 1024
-out rootCA.pem
```

This creates a root CA to issue device and broker certificates.

2. **Create Server and Client Certificates**:

   a. Generate private keys and certificate signing requests (CSR) for the MQTT broker and clients.

   b. Sign the CSRs with the root CA.

```
openssl x509 -req -in server.csr -CA rootCA.pem -CAkey rootCA.key
-CAcreateserial -out server.crt -days 500 -sha256
```

3. **Configure the MQTT Broker**:

   a. Load the broker's certificate (server.crt) and private key into the MQTT broker configuration.

   b. Enable mutual TLS authentication.

4. **Configure the MQTT Client**:

   a. Load the client's certificate and private key into the device using OpenSSL.

   b. Trust the root CA to validate the broker's certificate.

Example: Client Authentication with OpenSSL API

The following code snippet shows how to load an X.509 certificate and private key for an MQTT client:

```
SSL_CTX *ctx = SSL_CTX_new(TLS_client_method());
SSL_CTX_use_certificate_file(ctx, "client.crt", SSL_FILETYPE_PEM);
SSL_CTX_use_PrivateKey_file(ctx, "client.key", SSL_FILETYPE_PEM);
SSL_CTX_load_verify_locations(ctx, "rootCA.pem", NULL);

SSL *ssl = SSL_new(ctx);
SSL_set_fd(ssl, socket_fd); // Attach the socket to SSL
SSL_connect(ssl); // Establish a TLS session
```

This ensures secure authentication and encryption for the MQTT session.

Secure Firmware Update Processes with Certificate Validation

Firmware updates are critical for patching vulnerabilities and enhancing functionality in IoT devices. Secure firmware updates ensure that only authorized updates are applied to devices, preventing tampering or malicious software installation.

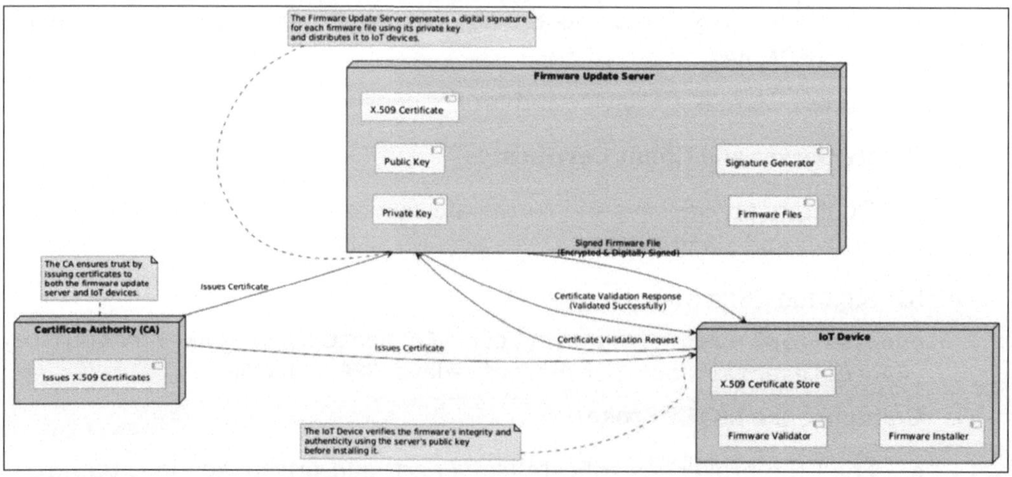

Figure 8.3: *IOT devices firmware upgrade*

1. **Using X.509 Certificates for Firmware Validation**

   IoT devices can validate the authenticity of firmware updates using X.509 certificates. This process involves:

- **Signing the Firmware:** The firmware file is signed by the vendor using their private key.

```
openssl dgst -sha256 -sign vendor_private.key -out ava_firmware.
sig ava_firmware.bin
```

- **Distributing the Public Certificate:** The vendor's X.509 certificate containing their public key is preloaded onto the device or distributed securely.
- **Validating the Firmware:** The IoT device uses the vendor's public key to verify the signature before installing the firmware.

```
openssl dgst -sha256 -verify vendor_public.pem -signature ava_
firmware.sig ava_firmware.bin
```

2. **Example of Firmware Validation Using OpenSSL APIs**

   Following is an example of how an IoT device can validate a firmware signature before applying an update:

```
#include <openssl/pem.h>
#include <openssl/err.h>

int validate_firmware(const char *cert_file, const char *firmware_
file, const char *signature_file) {
    FILE *cert_fp = fopen(cert_file, "r");
    X509 *cert = PEM_read_X509(cert_fp, NULL, NULL, NULL);
    fclose(cert_fp);

    EVP_PKEY *pub_key = X509_get_pubkey(cert);
    FILE *sig_fp = fopen(signature_file, "rb");
    fseek(sig_fp, 0, SEEK_END);
    long sig_len = ftell(sig_fp);
    rewind(sig_fp);

    unsigned char *sig = malloc(sig_len);
    fread(sig, 1, sig_len, sig_fp);
    fclose(sig_fp);

    FILE *fw_fp = fopen(firmware_file, "rb");
    fseek(fw_fp, 0, SEEK_END);
    long fw_len = ftell(fw_fp);
    rewind(fw_fp);

    unsigned char *fw_data = malloc(fw_len);
```

```
    fread(fw_data, 1, fw_len, fw_fp);
    fclose(fw_fp);

    EVP_MD_CTX *md_ctx = EVP_MD_CTX_new();
    EVP_DigestVerifyInit(md_ctx, NULL, EVP_sha256(), NULL,
pub_key);
    EVP_DigestVerifyUpdate(md_ctx, fw_data, fw_len);

    int result = EVP_DigestVerifyFinal(md_ctx, sig, sig_len);

    EVP_MD_CTX_free(md_ctx);
    EVP_PKEY_free(pub_key);
    X509_free(cert);
    free(sig);
    free(fw_data);

    return (result == 1) ? 0 : -1; // 0 = valid, -1 = invalid
}
```

This process ensures the firmware's integrity and authenticity, protecting the device from unauthorized or malicious updates.

Conclusion

The integration of OpenSSL into IoT security presents a robust solution for addressing the unique challenges posed by resource-constrained devices, diverse ecosystems, and evolving threat landscapes. By leveraging OpenSSL's support for lightweight cryptographic algorithms such as ChaCha20, AES-128, and ECC, developers can ensure secure communication, data integrity, and device authentication without compromising performance. The use of X.509 certificates further enhances trust in IoT networks by enabling secure MQTT communication and validating firmware updates.

As IoT continues to expand across various industries, the importance of scalable, efficient, and secure cryptographic solutions cannot be overstated. OpenSSL, with its flexibility and rich feature set, provides a reliable foundation for building IoT systems that are both secure and future-ready. By customizing OpenSSL for lightweight applications, optimizing performance, and adopting modern cryptographic practices, IoT developers can safeguard sensitive data and protect devices from cyber threats, ensuring the success of IoT deployments in an increasingly connected world.

In the next and final chapter, we will step back and consolidate key takeaways from the entire book, covering best practices, optimization strategies, and other OpenSSL alternatives comparisons. These insights will help developers apply OpenSSL securely and efficiently in various real-world scenarios, ensuring strong cryptographic implementations across different domains.

CHAPTER 9
Best Practices, Tips, and Tricks

Introduction

This final chapter serves as a practical guide, distilling years of real-world experience and hard-earned lessons into actionable insights. While the preceding chapters have delved deeply into the technical foundations and advanced use cases of OpenSSL, this chapter shifts focus to best practices, essential tips, and common pitfalls to avoid when working with OpenSSL in production environments. From optimizing performance and enhancing security to troubleshooting and integrating OpenSSL with modern applications, the topics covered here are designed to empower you to confidently apply OpenSSL in your projects. Whether you are a seasoned developer, system administrator, or security professional, these practical guidelines will help you navigate the challenges of implementing secure, robust, and efficient cryptographic solutions. This chapter is not just a summary but a toolkit to ensure your journey with OpenSSL continues successfully beyond these pages.

Structure

In this chapter, the following topics will be covered:

- Security Best Practices
- Code Optimization and Latency Improvement
- X.509 Certificate Conversion Tips
- Common Mistakes to Avoid
- Libraries Built on Top of OpenSSL
- OpenSSL Alternatives Comparison

Security Best practices

This section provides actionable steps and examples to ensure your OpenSSL implementation adheres to the highest security standards.

Disabling Insecure Protocols

Older protocols such as SSLv3, TLS 1.0, and TLS 1.1 are deprecated due to known vulnerabilities (for example, POODLE, BEAST). OpenSSL allows you to disable these insecure protocols using both configuration and code.

Steps to Disable Deprecated Protocols

Step 1. Using OpenSSL Configuration File (**openssl.cnf**), add the following line to your configuration file:

```
[default_tls_conf]
MinProtocol = TLSv1.2
CipherString = DEFAULT@SECLEVEL=2
```

Step 2. This ensures only TLS 1.2 and higher are enabled.

In Code (C API): Use **SSL_CTX_set_min_proto_version()** to set the minimum protocol version.

```
#include <openssl/ssl.h>

SSL_CTX *ctx = SSL_CTX_new(TLS_method());
if (!SSL_CTX_set_min_proto_version(ctx, TLS1_2_VERSION)) {
    fprintf(stderr, "Failed to set minimum TLS version\n");
}
```

Step 3. **Command-Line Example**: To test disabling protocols:

```
openssl s_server -tls1_2 -key server.key -cert server.crt
```

Figure 9.1: *Command-line example*

On another terminal:

```
openssl s_client -connect localhost:4433 -tls1_1
```

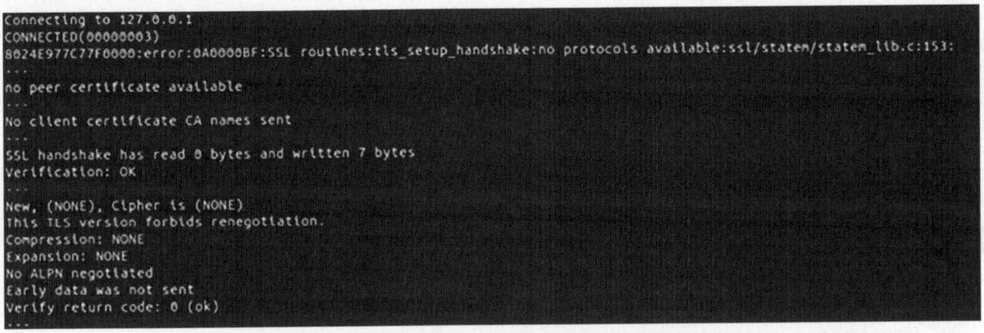

Figure 9.2: *Client connection failed*

The preceding figure shows client connection failed.

Secure Cipher Selection

Cipher suites determine the algorithms used for key exchange, encryption, and authentication. Weak ciphers, such as RC4 and 3DES, should be avoided. OpenSSL provides options to specify strong ciphers.

Best Practices for Cipher Selection

1. **Using `CipherString` in Configuration**:

   ```
   CipherString = HIGH:!aNULL:!MD5:!RC4:!3DES
   ```

   a. **`HIGH`**: Includes only strong ciphers.

   b. **`!aNULL`**: Excludes anonymous ciphers (no authentication).

   c. **`!MD5`**: Excludes MD5 due to its cryptographic weaknesses.

   d. **`!RC4`**, **`!3DES`**: Excludes deprecated ciphers.

2. **In Code (C API)**: Use **`SSL_CTX_set_cipher_list()`** to set allowed cipher suites.

   ```
   if (!SSL_CTX_set_cipher_list(ctx, "ECDHE-ECDSA-AES256-GCM-
   SHA384:ECDHE-RSA-AES256-GCM-SHA384")) {
       fprintf(stderr, "Failed to set cipher list\n");
   }
   ```

3. **Command-Line Example**: Test a connection with specific ciphers.

   ```
   openssl s_client -connect example.com:443 -cipher ECDHE-RSA-
   AES256-GCM-SHA384
   ```

Partial output:

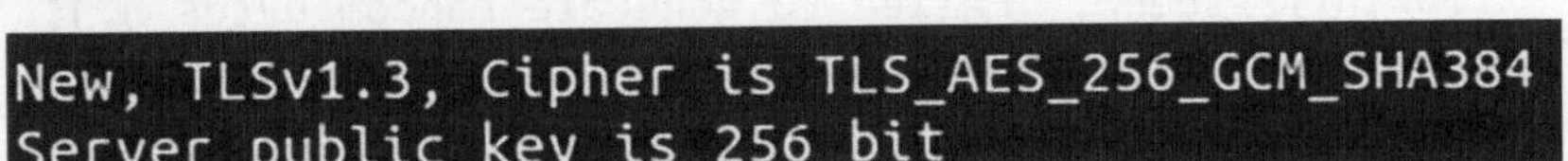

Figure 9.3: *s_client Command Output*

Certificate Validation

Improper certificate validation can lead to man-in-the-middle attacks. OpenSSL offers tools and APIs to verify certificates properly. We have covered more details on it in the previous chapters, but are just briefing here for it completeness of the topic.

Best Practices for Certificate Validation

1. **Verify Hostname**: OpenSSL 1.1.0+ provides **`X509_check_host()`** to validate the hostname in certificates.

```
if (!X509_check_host(cert, "example.com", 0, 0, NULL)) {
    fprintf(stderr, "Hostname verification failed\n");
}
```

2. **Check Expiry Dates**: Verify if the certificate is expired using **`X509_get_notBefore()`** and **`X509_get_notAfter()`**.

```
ASN1_TIME *not_after = X509_get_notAfter(cert);
if (X509_cmp_current_time(not_after) < 0) {
    fprintf(stderr, "Certificate is expired\n");
}
```

3. **Enable Certificate Chain Verification**: Use **`SSL_CTX_set_verify()`** to verify the chain of trust.

```
SSL_CTX_set_verify(ctx, SSL_VERIFY_PEER, NULL);
if (!SSL_CTX_load_verify_locations(ctx, "ca.pem", NULL)) {
    fprintf(stderr, "Failed to load CA file\n");
}
```

Secure Random Number Generation

Strong random numbers are essential for cryptographic operations, such as key generation and nonce creation. OpenSSL provides **`RAND_bytes()`** for this purpose.

Best Practices for Random Number Generation

1. **Use `RAND_bytes()`**: Always check the return value to ensure the randomness source is properly seeded.

```
unsigned char buf[32];
if (RAND_bytes(buf, sizeof(buf)) != 1) {
    fprintf(stderr, "Failed to generate random bytes\n");
}
```

2. **Seed the Random Number Generator**: While OpenSSL auto-seeds the generator, you can manually seed it for additional entropy (for example, on embedded systems):

```
unsigned char seed[32];
RAND_seed(seed, sizeof(seed));
```

3. **Avoid Predictable Seeding**: Do not use predictable values (for example, timestamps or process IDs) for seeding.

4. **Test the Randomness**: Use tools such as **dieharder** or **rngtest** to evaluate the quality of generated randomness.

Code Optimization and Latency Improvement

In performance-critical environments, optimizing OpenSSL's code and configuration can significantly reduce binary size, latency, and resource consumption. Following are practical techniques, along with examples, to achieve these optimizations.

Reducing Binary Size

When working with embedded systems or resource-constrained environments, reducing the OpenSSL binary size is essential. You can achieve this by disabling unnecessary features and modules during compilation.

Tips to Reduce Binary Size:

- **Disable Legacy Algorithms**: OpenSSL includes legacy cryptographic algorithms that may not be needed. You can disable these during configuration.

  ```
  ./configure no-legacy
  ```

  The no-legacy option removes older, less secure algorithms such as MD2, MD4, and RC4.

- **Disable Unused Protocols**: If your application does not require older TLS protocols, disable them:

  ```
  ./configure no-ssl3 no-tls1 no-tls1_1
  ```

  This ensures that only modern protocols (TLS 1.2 and TLS 1.3) are included.

- **Remove Unused Modules**: For embedded systems, disable modules such as shared library support or certain cryptographic engines:

  ```
  ./configure no-shared no-engine
  ```

- **Use the `--optimize` Flag**: Compile OpenSSL with the **`-Os`** compiler flag to optimize for size:

```
./configure linux-x86_64 -Os
```

Here is an example of a custom configuration script for a minimal OpenSSL build:

```
./configure no-legacy no-ssl3 no-comp no-idea no-shared -Os
linux-x86_64
make clean && make
```

This reduces the binary size significantly by excluding unnecessary algorithms, protocols, and features.

Minimizing Latency

Minimizing SSL/TLS handshake latency is critical for performance in applications such as web servers, IoT devices, and high-frequency trading systems. OpenSSL provides several features to reduce handshake latency.

Techniques to Reduce SSL/TLS Handshake Latency:

1. **Enable Session Resumption**: Reusing SSL/TLS sessions avoids the need for a full handshake, significantly reducing latency.

   a. **Session Caching**: Store and reuse session data on the server.

   ```
   SSL_CTX_set_session_cache_mode(ctx, SSL_SESS_CACHE_SERV-
   ER);
   ```

   b. **Session Tickets**: Use session tickets to allow the client to resume sessions without storing state on the server.

   ```
   SSL_CTX_set_options(ctx, SSL_OP_NO_TICKET); // Disable session
   tickets if not needed
   ```

2. **Enable False Start (TLS 1.3)**: False Start allows data to be sent before the handshake is fully completed in specific scenarios.

   ```
   SSL_CTX_set_mode(ctx, SSL_MODE_ENABLE_PARTIAL_WRITE);
   ```

3. **Reduce Certificate Chain Length**: Shorter certificate chains result in fewer round trips during the handshake.

   a. Use intermediate CA certificates sparingly.

   b. Combine the server certificate and intermediates into one file to send as a bundle.

4. **Preload Keys and Certificates**: Avoid runtime file reads by preloading keys and certificates in memory during initialization.

   ```
   SSL_CTX_use_certificate_file(ctx, "server.crt", SSL_FILETYPE_PEM);
   SSL_CTX_use_PrivateKey_file(ctx, "server.key", SSL_FILETYPE_PEM);
   ```

5. **Optimize Cryptographic Algorithms**: Use faster algorithms such as ECDHE over DHE for key exchange.

   ```
   SSL_CTX_set_cipher_list(ctx, "ECDHE-ECDSA-AES256-GCM-SHA384:ECD-
   HE-RSA-AES256-GCM-SHA384");
   ```

6. **Enable Hardware Acceleration**: Use hardware features such as AES-NI for cryptographic acceleration.

   For Intel processors:

   ```
   ./configure enable-asm
   ```

We have already covered hardware acceleration using OpenSSL engine in one of the earlier chapters.

X.509 Certificate Conversions Tips

One of the most frequent tasks in network security is converting X.509 certificates between different formats.

Common Conversion Scenarios:

1. **PEM to DER**:

   ```
   openssl x509 -in certificate.pem -outform der -out certificate.der
   ```

2. **DER to PEM**:

   ```
   openssl x509 -in certificate.der -inform der -out certificate.pem
   ```

3. **Extracting Public Key from a Certificate**:

   ```
   openssl x509 -in certificate.pem -pubkey -noout > publickey.pem
   ```

4. **Converting PKCS#12 to PEM**:

   ```
   openssl pkcs12 -in certificate.pfx -out certificate.pem -nodes
   ```

Here are some examples of how to perform X.509 certificate conversions programmatically using OpenSSL:

1. **Convert PEM to DER**:

   ```
   #include <openssl/x509.h>
   #include <openssl/pem.h>
   #include <openssl/bio.h>
   #include <stdio.h>

   int convert_pem_to_der(const char *pem_file, const char *der_file)
   ```

```
{
    // Open the PEM file in read mode
    FILE *pem_fp = fopen(pem_file, "r");
    if (!pem_fp) {
        perror("Error opening PEM file"); // Print error if file 
can't be opened
        return -1;
    }

    // Read the PEM-encoded certificate and convert it into an 
X509 structure
    X509 *cert = PEM_read_X509(pem_fp, NULL, NULL, NULL);
    fclose(pem_fp); // Close the input file as it's no longer 
needed

    // Check if the conversion was successful
    if (!cert) {
        fprintf(stderr, "Error reading PEM certificate\n");
        return -1;
    }

    // Open the output DER file in binary write mode
    FILE *der_fp = fopen(der_file, "wb");
    if (!der_fp) {
        perror("Error opening DER file"); // Print error if file 
can't be opened
        X509_free(cert); // Free the X509 structure before 
returning
        return -1;
    }

    // Write the X509 certificate in DER format
    if (i2d_X509_fp(der_fp, cert) <= 0) {
        fprintf(stderr, "Error converting to DER format\n");
        fclose(der_fp);
        X509_free(cert); // Free memory before returning
        return -1;
    }

    // Clean up: Close the DER file and free the X509 structure
    fclose(der_fp);
    X509_free(cert);

    return 0; // Return success
}
```

2. **Convert DER to PEM**:

```
int convert_der_to_pem(const char *der_file, const char *pem_file)
{
    // Open the DER file in binary mode
    FILE *der_fp = fopen(der_file, "rb");
    if (!der_fp) {
        perror("Error opening DER file");
        return -1;
    }

    // Read the DER-encoded certificate and convert it to an X509
structure
    X509 *cert = d2i_X509_fp(der_fp, NULL);
    fclose(der_fp); // Close the input file as it's no longer
needed

    // Check if the conversion was successful
    if (!cert) {
        fprintf(stderr, "Error reading DER certificate\n");
        return -1;
    }

    // Open the output PEM file in write mode
    FILE *pem_fp = fopen(pem_file, "w");
    if (!pem_fp) {
        perror("Error opening PEM file");
        X509_free(cert); // Free the X509 structure before
returning
        return -1;
    }

    // Write the X509 certificate in PEM format
    if (PEM_write_X509(pem_fp, cert) <= 0) {
        fprintf(stderr, "Error converting to PEM format\n");
        fclose(pem_fp);
        X509_free(cert);
        return -1;
    }

    // Clean up: Close the PEM file and free the X509 structure
    fclose(pem_fp);
    X509_free(cert);

    return 0; // Return success
}
```

3. **Extracting Public Key from a Certificate**:

```
#include <openssl/x509.h>
#include <openssl/pem.h>
#include <openssl/evp.h>
#include <stdio.h>

int extract_public_key(const char *pem_file, const char *pubkey_
file) {
    // Open the PEM file containing the certificate in read mode
    FILE *pem_fp = fopen(pem_file, "r");
    if (!pem_fp) {
        perror("Error opening PEM file"); // Print an error if the
file can't be opened
        return -1;
    }

    // Read the certificate from the PEM file and store it in an
X509 structure
    X509 *cert = PEM_read_X509(pem_fp, NULL, NULL, NULL);
    fclose(pem_fp); // Close the PEM file as it is no longer needed

    // Check if certificate was successfully read
    if (!cert) {
        fprintf(stderr, "Error reading PEM certificate\n");
        return -1;
    }

    // Extract the public key from the certificate
    EVP_PKEY *pkey = X509_get_pubkey(cert);
    if (!pkey) {
        fprintf(stderr, "Error extracting public key\n");
        X509_free(cert); // Free the certificate structure before
returning
        return -1;
    }

    // Open the output file to save the extracted public key
    FILE *pubkey_fp = fopen(pubkey_file, "w");
    if (!pubkey_fp) {
        perror("Error opening public key file"); // Print an error
if the file cannot be opened
        EVP_PKEY_free(pkey);
        X509_free(cert);
        return -1;
    }
```

```
    // Write the extracted public key to the file in PEM format
    if (PEM_write_PUBKEY(pubkey_fp, pkey) <= 0) {
        fprintf(stderr, "Error writing public key\n");
        fclose(pubkey_fp);
        EVP_PKEY_free(pkey);
        X509_free(cert);
        return -1;
    }

    // Clean up: Close file handles and free allocated structures
    fclose(pubkey_fp);
    EVP_PKEY_free(pkey);
    X509_free(cert);

    return 0; // Return success
}
```

4. Convert PKCS#12 to PEM (Extract PEM certificate and key from pfx file)

```
#include <stdio.h>
#include <stdlib.h>
#include <openssl/pkcs12.h>
#include <openssl/pem.h>
#include <openssl/err.h>

/* Function to extract certificate and private key from a PFX file
*/
int extract_pfx(const char *pfx_file, const char *password, const
char *cert_file, const char *key_file) {
    FILE *fp_pfx, *fp_cert, *fp_key;
    PKCS12 *p12 = NULL;
    EVP_PKEY *pkey = NULL;
    X509 *cert = NULL;
    STACK_OF(X509) *ca = NULL;

    /* Initialize OpenSSL */
    OpenSSL_add_all_algorithms();
    ERR_load_crypto_strings();

    /* Open the PFX file */
    if ((fp_pfx = fopen(pfx_file, "rb")) == NULL) {
        fprintf(stderr, "Error opening PFX file: %s\n", pfx_file);
        return 1;
    }

    /* Read the PFX file */
    p12 = d2i_PKCS12_fp(fp_pfx, NULL);
```

```
    fclose(fp_pfx);
    if (!p12) {
        fprintf(stderr, "Error reading PFX file\n");
        ERR_print_errors_fp(stderr);
        return 1;
    }

    /* Extract private key and certificate (without encryption) */
    if (!PKCS12_parse(p12, password, &pkey, &cert, &ca)) {
        fprintf(stderr, "Error parsing PFX file\n");
        ERR_print_errors_fp(stderr);
        PKCS12_free(p12);
        return 1;
    }

    PKCS12_free(p12);

    /* Save certificate to a file */
    if ((fp_cert = fopen(cert_file, "w")) == NULL) {
        fprintf(stderr, "Error opening output certificate file\n");
        return 1;
    }
    if (!PEM_write_X509(fp_cert, cert)) {
        fprintf(stderr, "Error writing certificate to file\n");
        ERR_print_errors_fp(stderr);
    }
    fclose(fp_cert);

    /* Save private key to a file */
    if ((fp_key = fopen(key_file, "w")) == NULL) {
        fprintf(stderr, "Error opening output private key
file\n");
        return 1;
    }
    if (!PEM_write_PrivateKey(fp_key, pkey, NULL, NULL, 0, NULL,
NULL)) {
        fprintf(stderr, "Error writing private key to file\n");
        ERR_print_errors_fp(stderr);
    }
    fclose(fp_key);

    /* Cleanup */
    EVP_PKEY_free(pkey);
    X509_free(cert);
    if (ca) sk_X509_pop_free(ca, X509_free);
```

```
    printf("Successfully extracted certificate and private
key.\n");
    return 0;
}
```

Common Mistakes to Avoid

Based on industry experience, these are the mistakes to avoid when working with OpenSSL:

- **Failing to Initialize Structures**: Always initialize structures such as `EVP_CIPHER_CTX` before use to avoid segmentation faults.
- **Ignoring Error Codes**: Always check the return values of OpenSSL functions and log errors for debugging.
- **Storing Private Keys Unencrypted**: Always encrypt private keys when storing them on disk.
- **Using Insecure Protocols or Algorithms**: Avoid deprecated algorithms such as MD5 and SHA1.
- **Hardcoding Secrets**: Never hardcode passwords or keys in source code.

Libraries Built on Top of OpenSSL

Examples of open-source, high-level C API libraries that are built on top of OpenSSL's low-level APIs. These libraries provide simplified interfaces for common cryptographic operations and SSL/TLS functionalities:

- **libcurl**
    - **Description**: **libcurl** is a widely used library for transferring data over various protocols (HTTP, HTTPS, FTP, and so on). It leverages OpenSSL for its SSL/TLS functionalities, providing a higher-level API to developers.
    - **Key Features**:
        - Abstracts SSL/TLS implementation details for secure communications.
        - Automatic handling of certificates and key management.
    - **Website**: https://curl.se/libcurl/
- **wolfSSL** (formerly **CyaSSL**)
    - **Description**: **wolfSSL** is a lightweight SSL/TLS library designed for embedded systems. It can act as a high-level wrapper over OpenSSL's APIs while offering its own optimizations.
    - **Key Features**:
        - Supports OpenSSL compatibility APIs for easy integration.

    - Highly optimized for performance on resource-constrained devices.
  - **Website**: https://www.wolfssl.com/
- **GnuTLS**
  - **Description**: Although primarily independent, **GnuTLS** provides some compatibility with OpenSSL APIs. It serves as a high-level library for SSL/TLS protocols.
  - **Key Features**:
    - Includes tools for certificate management and cryptographic operations.
    - Simplified interfaces for secure communication setups.
  - **Website**: https://www.gnutls.org/
- **Mongoose Embedded Web Server**
  - **Description**: Mongoose is a lightweight, embeddable web server and networking library. It integrates with OpenSSL to provide secure communication.
  - **Key Features**:
    - Abstracts SSL/TLS complexities for web servers and IoT applications.
    - Includes APIs for HTTPS, WebSockets, and more.
  - **Website**: https://cesanta.com/
- **OpenSSH**
  - **Description**: OpenSSH uses OpenSSL's cryptographic library for encryption and secure communications in SSH and SFTP protocols.
  - **Key Features**:
    - Provides a simplified interface for secure shell operations.
    - Leverages OpenSSL for secure key exchange, encryption, and authentication.
  - **Website**: https://www.openssh.com/
- **libgit2**
  - **Description**: `libgit2` is a portable library for working with Git repositories. It uses OpenSSL for secure network communication over HTTPS.
  - **Key Features**:
    - Provides APIs for repository operations, including cloning, fetching, and pushing.
    - Simplifies secure communication for Git over HTTPS using OpenSSL.
  - **Website**: https://libgit2.org/

- **mbedTLS** (formerly PolarSSL)
  - **Description**: Although not directly built on OpenSSL, **mbedTLS** offers an abstraction layer for cryptographic and SSL/TLS operations. Some projects use it alongside OpenSSL for compatibility.
  - Key Features:
    - Provides a high-level API for embedded devices.
    - Compatible with OpenSSL for certain functionalities.
  - **Website**: https://github.com/Mbed-TLS/mbedtls
- **LibreSSL**
  - **Description**: A fork of OpenSSL, **LibreSSL** simplifies and secures cryptographic operations. Many applications use it as a drop-in replacement for OpenSSL.
  - **Key Features**:
    - Provides simplified APIs for SSL/TLS functionalities.
    - Focuses on codebase security and modernization.
  - **Website**: https://www.libressl.org/
- **qpid-proton**
  - **Description**: Apache Qpid Proton is a messaging library that supports AMQP. It uses OpenSSL for securing communication channels.
  - **Key Features**:
    - Abstracts SSL/TLS complexities for messaging protocols.
    - Simplifies certificate management and secure connection setup.
  - **Website**: https://qpid.apache.org/proton/
- **Botan**
  - **Description**: **Botan** is a cryptography library that can act as a wrapper around OpenSSL for certain operations.
  - **Key Features**:
    - Provides higher-level APIs for cryptography, including X.509 certificate handling.
    - Flexible and modular design for various cryptographic applications.
  - **Website**: https://botan.randombit.net/

We will not cover details on all of the aforementioned example libraries that use OpenSSL APIs.

For more understanding, we will only cover one **Libcurl** example.

Libcurl Using OpensSSL APIs

1. **Initializing OpenSSL**
    - **`libcurl` Functionality**: **`libcurl`** initializes OpenSSL libraries during startup to ensure the cryptographic engine is ready. This is done internally by **`curl_global_init()`**, which initializes all SSL backends, including OpenSSL.
    - **OpenSSL APIs Used**:
        - **`SSL_library_init()`** (for OpenSSL < 1.1.0) or automatic initialization in OpenSSL >= 1.1.0.
        - **`SSL_load_error_strings()`** to load error messages.
        - **`OpenSSL_add_all_algorithms()`** to register cryptographic algorithms.

Example:

```
curl_global_init(CURL_GLOBAL_SSL); // Initializes SSL backends
```

2. **Creating an SSL Context**
    - **`libcurl` Functionality**: **`libcurl`** uses **`CURLOPT_SSL_CTX_FUNCTION`** to allow custom configuration of the SSL/TLS context. This context is created internally using OpenSSL's **`SSL_CTX_new()`**.
    - **OpenSSL APIs Used**:
        - **`SSL_CTX_new()`** to create a new SSL/TLS context.
        - **`SSL_CTX_set_options()`** to configure options such as disabling insecure protocols (for example, SSLv3).

Example:

```
CURL *curl = curl_easy_init();
curl_easy_setopt(curl, CURLOPT_SSL_CTX_FUNCTION, ssl_ctx_call-
back);

CURLcode res = curl_easy_perform(curl);
curl_easy_cleanup(curl);
```

3. **Verifying Server Certificates**
    - **`libcurl` Functionality**: **`libcurl`** verifies server certificates during HTTPS connections using **`CURLOPT_SSL_VERIFYPEER`** and **`CURLOPT_CAINFO`**.
    - **OpenSSL APIs Used**:
        - **`SSL_CTX_load_verify_locations()`** to load trusted CA certificates.
        - **`SSL_get_peer_certificate()`** to retrieve the server's certificate.
        - **`X509_verify_cert()`** to validate the certificate.

Example:

```
curl_easy_setopt(curl, CURLOPT_SSL_VERIFYPEER, 1L);
curl_easy_setopt(curl, CURLOPT_CAINFO, "/path/to/ca-bundle.crt");
```

4. **Managing Encryption**
   - **`libcurl` Functionality**: Data encryption and decryption are performed during HTTPS communication using **`libcurl`**'s **`curl_easy_perform()`** API.
   - **OpenSSL APIs Used**:
     - **`SSL_write()`** to encrypt and send data.
     - **`SSL_read()`** to decrypt and receive data.

Example:

```
CURLcode res = curl_easy_perform(curl); // Internally uses SSL_
read() and SSL_write()
```

5. **Setting Cipher Suites**
   - **`libcurl` Functionality**: Allows users to specify the cipher suites using **`CURLOPT_SSL_CIPHER_LIST`**.
   - **OpenSSL APIs Used**:
     - **`SSL_CTX_set_cipher_list()`** to set the list of allowed ciphers.

Example:

```
curl_easy_setopt(curl, CURLOPT_SSL_CIPHER_LIST,
"HIGH:!aNULL:!MD5");
```

6. **Session Reuse**
   - **`libcurl` Functionality**: Reuses SSL/TLS sessions across multiple connections using **`libcurl`**'s session ID caching, which is enabled by default.
   - **OpenSSL APIs Used**:
     - **`SSL_CTX_set_session_cache_mode()`** to enable session caching.
     - **`SSL_set_session()`** to reuse an existing session.

Example:

```
curl_easy_setopt(curl, CURLOPT_FORBID_REUSE, 0L); // Enable
session reuse
```

7. **Error Handling**
   - **`libcurl` Functionality**: **`libcurl`** provides error details through **`curl_easy_strerror()`** and uses OpenSSL error-handling APIs internally.
   - **OpenSSL APIs Used**:

   - **ERR_get_error()** to retrieve the error code.
   - **ERR_error_string_n()** to convert error codes to readable strings.

Example:

```
CURLcode res = curl_easy_perform(curl);
if (res != CURLE_OK) {
    fprintf(stderr, "libcurl error: %s\n", curl_easy_
strerror(res));
}
```

8. **Certificate Pinning**

   - **libcurl Functionality**: Supports certificate pinning with **CURLOPT_PINNEDPUBLICKEY**.
   - **OpenSSL APIs Used**:
     - **X509_digest()** to compute the hash of the server's certificate for pinning.

Example:

```
curl_easy_setopt(curl, CURLOPT_PINNEDPUBLICKEY,
"sha256//base64hash==");
```

9. **Configuring TLS Extensions**

   - **libcurl Functionality**: Configures Server Name Indication (SNI) using **CURLOPT_SSL_OPTIONS** with **CURLSSLOPT_NO_REVOKE**.
   - **OpenSSL APIs Used**:
     - **SSL_set_tlsext_host_name()** to set the server's name for SNI.

Example:

```
curl_easy_setopt(curl, CURLOPT_SSL_OPTIONS, CURLSSLOPT_NO_
REVOKE);
```

10. **Cleanup**

   - **libcurl Functionality**: Cleans up SSL-related resources during **curl_global_cleanup()**.
   - **OpenSSL APIs Used**:
     - **EVP_cleanup()**, **ERR_free_strings()**, and **CRYPTO_cleanup_all_ex_data()** to clean up loaded algorithms and free allocated resources.

Example:

```
curl_easy_cleanup(curl);        // Clean up individual handle
curl_global_cleanup();          // Internally calls OpenSSL cleanup
functions
```

You can check curl open source code for more details. This will also be helpful as a guideline if you want to implement your own libraries on top of OpenSSL.

OpenSSL Alternatives Comparison

Though OpenSSL is the most commonly used SSL library, there are many alternatives to OpenSSL that are used in different use cases based on the specific requirements. This comparison table will give you an idea of what should be chosen accordingly.

Features	**OpenSSL**	**LibreSSL**	**BoringSSL**	**wolfSSL**	**mbedTLS**	**GnuTLS**
Purpose	General-purpose SSL/TLS and cryptographic library	Simplified, modernized OpenSSL fork	Google's fork of OpenSSL for internal use	Lightweight SSL/TLS for embedded systems	SSL/TLS library optimized for embedded devices	SSL/TLS library with a focus on security and ease of use
Perfor mance	High, but may require optimization	Slightly improved compared to OpenSSL	Optimized for Google's infrastructure	Highly optimized for embedded use	Optimized for constrained environments	Moderate
Ease of Use	Moderate (low-level APIs)	Improved API clarity	Simplified for Google projects	Easy to use for embedded systems	Very easy for embedded systems	Moderate
Supported Platforms	Cross-platform (Windows, Linux, macOS, and Unix)	Cross-platform	Focused on Linux and Unix-like systems	Embedded and cross-platform	Embedded and cross-platform	Cross-platform
License	Apache License 2.0	ISC License	Apache License 2.0	GPLv2 (with linking exceptions)	Apache License 2.0	LGPLv2.1 or later
Community and Support	Large, active community	Smaller community, but active	Internal use by Google, limited public focus	Active in embedded space	Active, widely used in IoT	Active, widely used
Key Features	Comprehensive crypto support	Codebase simplificat ions	Custom features for Google services	Small footprint	Small size, high performance	Built-in cryptographic support
	Hardware acceleration support	Removed legacy features	Removes legacy features	FIPS 140-2 support	Very lightweight	Certificate verification
	Widely adopted in industry	Improved portability	Simplified APIs	Easy hardware integration	Focus on IoT security	Simplified APIs

Use Cases	Web servers, general-purpose cryptography, enterprise-grade security	Web servers, replacements for OpenSSL	Internal use by Google projects	IoT, embedded systems, lightweight devices	IoT, resource-constrained systems	Web servers, open-source projects
Hardware Acceleration	Yes	Yes	Yes	Yes	Yes	Yes
FIPS Support	Yes (via separate module)	No	No	Yes	No	No
Documentation Quality	Extensive, but complex	Improved	Moderate	Clear, focused on embedded	Clear, focused on embedded	Extensive
Backward Compatibility	High (legacy support included)	Reduced legacy support	Minimal legacy support	Moderate	Minimal	Moderate

Table 9.1: *OpenSSL alternatives comparison*

Conclusion

As we close this final chapter, we reflect on the journey of understanding and mastering one of the most powerful cryptographic libraries available today. From the foundational concepts of cryptography to advanced OpenSSL features and best practices, this book has aimed to provide a comprehensive guide for professionals and enthusiasts alike.

In this chapter, we tied everything together by focusing on practical tips, optimization techniques, and security best practices. By implementing these strategies—whether it is reducing binary size for resource-constrained systems, minimizing handshake latency for high-performance applications, or enforcing robust security configurations—you can ensure your OpenSSL deployments are efficient, secure, and aligned with modern standards.

The world of network security is dynamic, with new challenges and innovations emerging constantly. As OpenSSL continues to evolve, the skills and insights you have gained from this book will equip you to adapt and build resilient, secure systems. Whether you are designing IoT solutions, optimizing enterprise applications, or securing personal projects, OpenSSL remains a versatile tool to help you achieve your security goals.

Thank you for embarking on this journey. The knowledge you have acquired here is a stepping stone toward building a safer digital future. Stay curious, stay vigilant, and continue exploring the ever-evolving world of network security.

Index

A

C

P

R

S